Understanding Chinese politics

Manchester University Press

Understanding Chinese politics

An introduction to government in the People's Republic of China

Neil Collins and Andrew Cottey

Manchester University Press

Published by Manchester University Press
Oxford Road, Manchester M13 9PL
www.manchesteruniversitypress.co.uk

British Library Cataloguing-in-Publication Data
A catalogue record for this book is available from the British Library

ISBN   978 0 7190 8427 0 hardback
ISBN   978 0 7190 8428 7 paperback

First published 2012

Typeset
by Action Publishing Technology Ltd, Gloucester

Contents

List of tables and boxes

Tables

Boxes

Acknowledgements

We are pleased to acknowledge the generous help of academic colleagues, obliging diplomats and journalists as well as slightly dragooned students from Italy in the preparation of this book. Though the authors' research interest in China goes back many years, the establishment of the Institute for Chinese studies at University College Cork facilitated the book by providing engaged scholars, such as Jörn Gottwald, David O'Brien, Niall Duggan and Chris Connolly who read and commented on the manuscript. UCC also gave us the opportunity to visit China several times to meet with scholars there. We express special thanks to Sebastian Green, the professor of management at UCC, whose detailed annotations on an early draft were particularly helpful. Though the diplomats may wish to maintain their anonymity, Clifford Coonan, the Beijing correspondent of the *Irish Times*, harbours no such inhibitions and gave us feedback on several occasions. Yu-Wen Chen, National Taiwan University, and Jane Duckett, University of Glasgow also provided very useful feedback. Francecsa Cantalupo, Marianna Bruzzese, Marcello Banfi and Caterina Paladini, all postgraduate students from Italy, were perhaps surprised at being drawn into the project but all engaged enthusiastically in honing the manuscript. We also thank Tony Mason of Manchester University Press for his patience and encouragement.

Above all, we acknowledge the familial opportunity costs that the writing of this book involved. As well as the usual time lost for more collective family activities, we also called on family members to engage in both English and Chinese!

Neil Collins
Andrew Cottey
August 2011

List of abbreviations[1]

APEC	Asia Pacific Economic Cooperation
ARF	ASEAN Regional Forum
ASEAN	Association of South-East Asian Nations
CCP	Communist Party of China
CMC	Central Military Commission
CPPCC	Chinese People's Political Consultative Conference
CRS	Cadre Responsibility System
CSO	civil society organisations
EEZ	Exclusive Economic Zone
ETIM	East Turkestan Islamic Movement
FDI	Direct Foreign Investment
G20	Group of 20
GATT	General Agreement on Tariffs and Trade
GHGs	greenhouse gases
IMF	International Monetary Fund
KMT	Kuomintang (Nationalist Party)
MOHRSS	Ministry of Human Resources and Social Security
MOHURD	Ministry of Housing and Urban and Rural Development
NDRC	National Development and Reform Commission
NEB	National Energy Bureau
NGO	non-governmental organisation
NPC	National People's Representatives Congress
NPM	New Public Management
NPT	Nuclear Non-Proliferation Treaty
NRA	National Revolutionary Army
OECD	Organisation for Economic Cooperation and Development
PLA	People's Liberation Army
PPC	Provincial People's Congress
PRC	People's Republic of China
Rmb	Renminbi (the Chinese national currency)

SAR	Special Administrative Regions
SCO	Shanghai Cooperation Organisation
SEZ	Special Economic Zone
TVE	township and village enterprise
UN	United Nations
UNCLOS	UN Convention on the Law of the Sea
US	United States
WTO	World Trade Organisation
XPCC	Xinjiang Production and Construction Corps

Note

1 Two systems for transcribing Chinese language characters into the Roman alphabet are currently in general use. Sometimes this creates confusion as different English language versions of the names of major cities, provinces and political leaders can be found in the literature on China. This book uses the system of transcription, known as pinyin, introduced by the Chinese government in 1958. It notes other versions of names as appropriate.

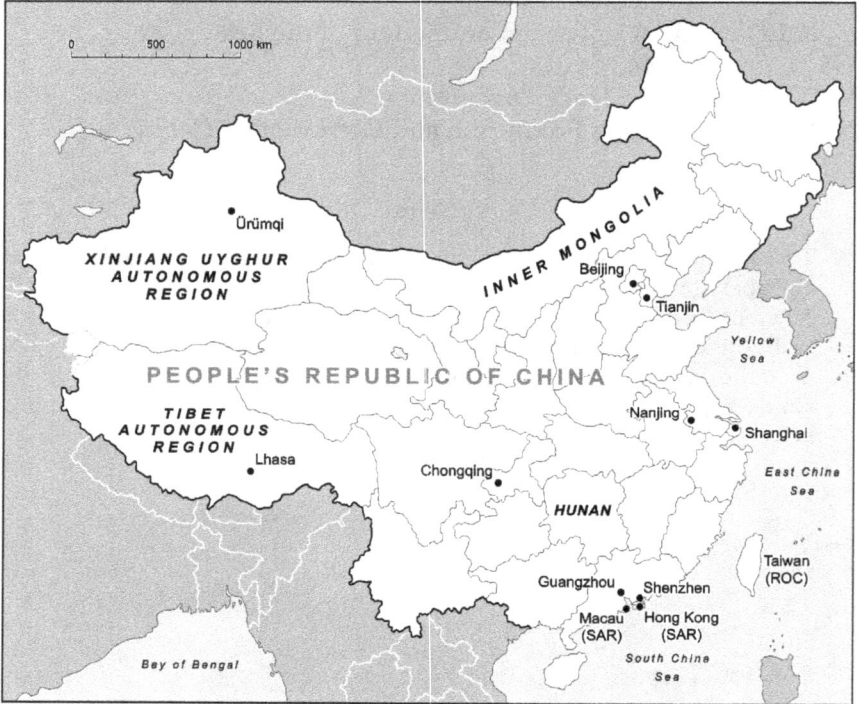

Map 1: China

Map 2: China and its neighbourhood

Introduction

The Chinese political system is the subject of much media and popular comment in part because China supports an economy with an apparently inexorable dynamic and impressive record of achievement. More fundamentally, however, the People's Republic of China (PRC) also represents an unanticipated challenge to the logic of history. At least in the West, sustained economic success and regime stability were thought to be the by-products of political systems that featured the rule of law, popular choice, an independent judiciary and the like. Indeed, democracy, as it developed in Europe and America, was assumed to be the *sine qua non* of long-term public support for the institutions of the state and for the encouragement of the entrepreneurship and innovation associated with capitalism. It might well still be that liberal democracy is the eventual destination of the majority of political systems but, for the moment, China represents a major alternative model. It is one that needs to be understood less as a historical anomaly than as a real challenger to what has been considered the norm. This book, therefore, explores the resilience and challenges of the Chinese political system without supposing either an inevitable implosion or an assured longevity.

The visit of the leader of the PRC to Washington, DC, in January 2011 was full of symbolism for both the Chinese and their American hosts. The Americans' hospitality included private meetings and meals with the leaders of both the executive and the legislature, a division of powers central to the US political system. On public occasions, troops in historic uniforms paraded to music from the American war of independence, a symbolic reminder of the importance of this era to America's self-image. For the Chinese, the importance of President Hu Jintao's trip was more in the recognition it afforded to the PRC's status in the world as equal to that of the US. President Obama was careful to echo his counterpart's use of phrases such as the 'harmonious society' and to temper his remarks on human rights and other

contentious and potentially divisive issues. The economic interdependence of the countries was a thread through all the media commentary
but, in China, in particular, the press emphasised the apparently more
effective response of Beijing to the current economic crisis. President
Hu himself stressed the validity of China's chosen 'scientific' development path to a socialist market economy, implicitly rejecting the idea of
progress as measured by Western market economic criteria alone.[1] This
book will outline the major features of the Chinese model and highlight
its claims and challenges.

A number of themes run through the analysis presented here. One is
that an effective political system needs to generate an overall level of
compliance or, at the very least, acquiescence to its authority.
Repression is an option but an expensive and dangerous one. In China,
the government does not shirk from imposing its will but its preference
is to avoid popular discontent. The limits of the system's tolerance and
the methodologies adopted to secure legitimacy and support are a
recurring theme. Because much of the political commentary on China
focuses on the authorities' proclivity for censorship and stifling open
debate, analysis of the politics of the PRC often ignores the ways in
which the system gathers information on and responds to its citizens'
views. Ironically, authoritarian states have in some ways to be more
proactively attentive to their publics because they lack the articulating
and aggregating capacities of more liberal political systems. The
Chinese authorities have paid particular attention to the fate of
European communist regimes. They adopted a very cautious approach
to allowing domestic reportage of events in Egypt in early 2011
stressing the need for social stability. The lessons of regime collapse
elsewhere are carefully assessed. This volume also addresses the
question of China's possible development towards democracy but
avoids the assumption that its path will be the same as that of Western
countries.

A second theme is that a comparative approach is productive and,
distinctive though it is, much is to be gained by considering the
Chinese system through the lens of other systems with which it shares
characteristics. Where this approach illustrates the dilemmas and
options faced by the PRC reference will be made to similar choices
elsewhere though it has to be acknowledged that the scale and diversity
of China frequently limit direct comparison.

A form of analysis that is also used regularly in scholarship on China
and a third theme here is to draw parallels with previous historical
periods. The search for insights into systemic continuities is popular
with both Chinese and outside observers despite the obvious

procrustean danger. In part, it reflects the continuity of China as a political entity for such a long period but the use of history also suggests that today's state is returning to a position of global importance lost briefly to a 'century of humiliation'. The legacy of history is examined in Chapter 1 but the theme recurs throughout.

The efficiency of the machinery of government has a major impact on the lives of Chinese citizens and, by extension, on their assessment of the political system. The process of policy-making and the relations between the central and local governments are examined to explain how some localities, classes and businesses fare better than others. The book addresses as its fourth theme the impact of institutions and their patterns of development because the people's support for the Chinese political system is in large part dependent on its outputs – material and ideological. All political systems need to handle competing claims for privilege and resources so the analysis presented here addresses the role of policy advocates and special interests in the PRC. The book also stresses the impact on China of global trends in public management.

No political system directly commands all resources and, by the same token, none eschews public ownership completely. Nevertheless, China is a noteworthy case in which the underlying balance between the public and private has changed remarkably in recent decades. As an overarching theme, the political economy of China is discussed in this book in terms of the broad choices available to the government of the PRC for regulating economic activity. The success of the Chinese economy is in many ways extraordinary but the balance between the social upheavals associated with growth and the goal of a politically harmonious society is a serious issue for the regime. The book briefly discusses how the decreased role of the state in micro-managing the economy, the increased role of market incentives and the political imperatives of the ruling party are aligned though, in the PRC overall, politics trumps economics if a choice has to be made.

In practice, the Communist Party of China (CCP) and the state are effectively merged. All state institutions are in practice subordinate to and penetrated by the CCP, which exercises a determining influence over all policies and decisions. CCP rule is analysed to identify the sources of the Party's ideological flexibility and organisational responsiveness but, most importantly, the durability of its grip on power. The CCP's use of Chinese nationalism as a policy tool resonates strongly with the vast majority of the citizens of the PRC. The book also examines, as a fifth theme, the ethnic sources of tension within the state and the rival interpretations of the dominant discourse on the PRC's unity.

President Hu Jintao's 2011 visit to Washington recorded the eighth meeting between himself and President Barack Obama in just two years. This is some measure of China's new global role – a topic covered in Chapter 6. China's re-emergence as a major power is the single most important geo-political trend of the early twenty-first century. The analysis presented here will address the question of what kind of role the PRC will play in global politics as a whole, the implications for the West and the rebalancing of relations between China and its neighbours.

Note

1 For a summary of the *Washington Post* coverage, for example, see www.washingtonpost.com/wp-srv/special/artsandliving/chinavisit/index.html.

1

Chinese politics
The legacy of history

What political scientists refer to as political culture – the deeply embedded distinctive patterns of political, economic and social behaviour that fundamentally shape politics – is best viewed as the accumulated legacies of a country's history. History, however, is not destiny: while a country's past shapes its politics it does not determine it. Change is ever present though the pace at which it occurs varies: sometimes glacial (with the political system appearing unchanging), sometimes evolutionary and sometimes revolutionary. In China's case, the collapse of the imperial system in 1911, the subsequent decades of turmoil and war and the coming to power of the Chinese Communist Party (CCP, 中国共产党) in 1949 constitutes a truly revolutionary period in Chinese political history. The foundation of the Communist People's Republic of China (PRC, 中华人民共和国) inaugurated a fundamentally new political, economic and social order and many of the core features of Chinese politics today remain those that were put in place by the Communists after 1949. Yet Chinese politics has also evolved since then. In particular, after the death in 1976 of Mao Zedong (毛泽东) – the foundational leader of the communist revolution – China has experienced not only dramatic economic growth but also a significant liberalisation in terms of people's daily lives. This political change, while not challenging the fundamental principle of one-party communist rule, makes current Chinese politics very different to that of the Mao era. At the same time, although 1949 marked a revolutionary break, contemporary Chinese politics is also moulded in a variety of ways by legacies from before 1949. These stretch back from the imperial system through to the period of weakness, internal disorder and foreign interference from the mid-nineteenth century until 1949.

Against this background, this chapter provides an overview of Chinese history. The first section highlights key features of the imperial system. The second examines the stage from the mid-nineteenth century until 1949, a particularly turbulent period in Chinese history, which the Chinese have come to refer to as 'the century of (national) humiliation'. This period saw the gradual collapse of the imperial system. It was marked by foreign intervention symbolised, in particular, by the Opium Wars that lasted through the 1840s and 1850s. The revolution of 1911 finally brought down the imperial system, but was followed by a period of authoritarian rule under the nationalist Kuomintang (KMT, 国民党) and the so-called 'warlord era' of the 1920s when power fell into the hands of a series of regional military leaders. This was followed by the occupation of much of the country and prolonged war with Japan from 1937 to 1945, and intermittent conflict between the KMT and the Communists. Eventually, after this prolonged period of national disunity, the civil war of 1946–49 brought the Communists to power. This chapter also examines Mao's rule from 1949 until the late 1970s, which saw the entrenchment of the core features of the communist system and the re-establishment of a functioning Chinese state. The Mao era also produced the extreme cult of personality around the Great Helmsman, as Mao was frequently called, as well as periods of widespread disorder. In particular, the Great Leap Forward (大跃进, 1958–61), a flawed attempt to modernise the country, resulted in the deaths of tens of millions through coercion, forced labour and famine. Later, the Cultural Revolution (文化大革命, 1966–76),[1] a frightening period of violence and chaos, involved mass mobilisation of young people against perceived reactionary, bourgeois and bureaucratic forces within society (including many within the CCP). The leaders of China, the so-called 'fifth generation', who will assume office in 2012 after the 18th National Congress of the CCP, were heavily influenced by the turmoil of the Cultural Revolution (see Table 1).

> [They] belong to the so-called lost generation [who] . . . lost the opportunity to receive primary and high school education. Instead, many became 'sent-down youths' who were rusticated, usually as teenagers, from cities to the often remote countryside to do manual labor for years or even a decade . . . These extraordinary life experiences resulting from the Cultural Revolution had a lasting impact on each of these leaders and a unique collective impact on the fifth generation as a whole. (Li 2010: 13)

It would be hard to exaggerate the impact of this period on current Chinese politics.

Table 1 Major CCP leaders

	Date	Comments
Mao Zedong ('First generation')	1949–76	Paramount leader
'Gang of Four' Jiang Qing, Zhang Chunqiao, Yao Wenyuan, Wang Hongwen	1966–76	Powerful political influence during final years of Mao's life played key role in Cultural Revolution
Hua Guofeng	1976–78	'Interregnum' Chairman of the CCP (1976–81); Chairman of Central Military Commission (CMC) 1976–81
Deng Xiaoping ('Second generation')	1978–92	Paramount Leader but not CCP Secretary-general. Chairman of CMC 1981–89
Hu Yaobang	1982–87	CCP Secretary-general in charge of Deng's policies of reform and opening up. General Secretary of CCP from 1982–87
Zhao Ziyang	1987–89	CCP Secretary-general after Hu Yaobang's dismissal in 1987; Premier 1980–87
Jiang Zemin ('Third generation')	1992–02	CCP Secretary-general. After the death of Deng Xiaoping in 1997, 'Core of third generation' (with Premier Li Peng and Zhu Rongji). Chairman of CMC 1989 to 2004
Hu Jintao ('Fourth generation')	2004	CCP Secretary-general incumbent (retires 2012); Chairman of CMC 2004–

Source: http://english.gov.cn/2007–10/22/content_923081.htm

The final section of this chapter examines the period since the late 1970s, an era characterised by market oriented economic reforms which have produced sustained high levels of economic growth and moved the country far from the economic and social model developed after 1949. Despite these radical economic and social changes, at the political level the basic principle of one-party Communist rule has remained intact. While the Tiananmen massacre of 1989 illustrated the potential for mass popular dissent, it also highlighted the continued willingness of the CCP to use military force to maintain its rule. Nevertheless, in a variety of more subtle ways, the period since the late 1970s has produced changes within the communist political system. The chapter concludes by highlighting the way in which legacies from these various historical periods shape contemporary Chinese politics.

The imperial era

Although the PRC's official history emphasises unity and continuity, the exact footprint that China makes on the globe has varied enormously over time. Today's Chinese frontiers may be relatively recent but for its citizens much of history is measured not by territory but by the reign of successive imperial dynasties (see Map 1 and Box 1).

Box 1 Major dynasties of China[a]		
Qin	秦	221–206 BC
Han	汉	206 BC–220 AD
Sui	隋	581–618
Tang	唐	618–907
Song	宋	960–1279
Yuan	元	1271–1368
Ming	明	1368–1644
Qing	清	1644–1911

Note: [a] From the Qin which first unified China.

Some scholars have seen in the imperial track record the characteristics of the PRC, especially under Mao: the imposition of an official ideology; the concentration of power in the hands of a few; the exercise of state power over all aspects of social life, including the economy; the use of the law as a tool of governance wielded by the ruler, without legal constraints; and, the constriction of private individuals as subjects and possessions of the state (Fu 1996). Given the time span involved, it is clear that such generalisations can be challenged as overdrawn and, in particular cases, inaccurate (Andrew and Rapp 2000). Nevertheless, there are indeed continuities in the autocratic tradition of Chinese politics. Similarly, the idea, contained in the dynastic concept of the Mandate of Heaven that Chinese political leaders derive legitimacy by being just, still resonates today. Coercion alone does not justify a regime's hold on power and the victorious can cite the Mandate to justify the removal of the incompetent and tyrannical. Unlike its European equivalent, the divine right of kings, the Mandate of Heaven does not privilege those of noble birth.

> No country boasts a more enduring or more colourful history of rebellion and revolution than China … [Its] impressive record … is due not simply to the country's extraordinary size and longevity, but also to the fact that central elements in Chinese political culture have directly encouraged such protests. The … concept of a 'Mandate of Heaven' bestowed instant legitimacy upon successful rebel leaders. (Perry 2001: 163)

The first imperial dynasty was founded by Qin Shi Huang (秦始皇) who unified China in 221 BC and who, crucially for today's nationalists, standardised the written language. Qin Shi Huang was a monumental figure in many ways bringing major economic and political reforms to China, starting with the Great Wall project (Pingfang 2001) and leaving the iconic Terracotta Army.[2] Former US Secretary of State Henry Kissinger lists him, along with Julius Caesar and Peter the Great, as among the seven most powerful people in history (quoted in *Forbes Magazine*, 30 November 2009). His rule was brutal (Crowe 2009) but it laid the groundwork for dynastic hegemony in the region. Militarily, he annexed territory, defeated rival states and suppressed internal opposition (Kiser and Cai 2003). Administratively, he standardised the legal code, measurements and coinage. As the first emperor Qin Shi Huang is particularly important to the Chinese worldview: his central legacy is the idea of Chinese unity and the physical and administrative infrastructure associated with the Chinese empire-state. The more chaotic period before Qin Shi Huang, known tellingly as the Warring States era, witnessed an intellectual diversity but Qin imposed a new conformity based on the idea of legalism and, literally, the destruction of its rivals – books were burnt and scholars buried alive. Legalism posited that successful leadership and political order must be based on a clearly defined and decisively enforced system of law. Leaders themselves, however, should not be constrained by moral or legal precepts, but must rather pursue whatever tactics are necessary to achieve and enforce a system of law (Winston 2009).

The tenets of legalism derived from attempts to counter poor standards and corruption in government by specifying very precise methods and standards of performance. They resonate with modern reforms in addressing the principal-agent problem, i.e. how the ruler constructs a system that ensures his interests are put above those of public servants. The bureaucrat should be given very tightly drawn criteria then rewarded for meeting them and severely punished for any deviation. The ruler judged the performance of ministers and they judged others in turn. In this way, royal mistakes were never acknowledged but the agents of the state were always liable to blame.

For the subject, legalism pitched loyalty to the state above that to the family. This was a significant departure from the system of philosophical and ethical maxims developed by Confucius (孔子) from ancient Chinese traditions and thereafter known as Confucianism. For adherents to Confucianism, virtue in the personality of the leader would have a ripple effect among the ruled. A fair and just ruler would facilitate efficient government and provide the context for individual fulfillment by his subjects. The Confucian worldview is laid out in voluminous texts that cover almost all aspects of life, often in minute detail. It draws on ancient Chinese religions but its precepts are providential and, unlike other revered texts that influence today's global politics, Confucianism makes no claims of divine revelation. The cultivation of virtue is a *sine qua non* and a Confucian approach, while clear on the ends, allows considerable pragmatism on the means. The individual is assumed to be inherently virtuous but corrupted by ignorance. The example of virtuous authority figures and familiarity with the wisdom of sacred texts and other ancient classics are keys to a good life based on sincerity, benevolence, filial piety and propriety. Confucianism and legalism have been part of a very long-standing Chinese debate on the underpinnings of political and social order, with Confucianism stressing the way in which a just and wise ruler's policies will underpin a successful system and legalism emphasising the necessity of an all-powerful ruler to underpin a legally based system. For much of the imperial era Confucianism was the predominant theoretical doctrine, but the influence of legalism never entirely abated. Despite the Communists' desire to do away with old doctrines, especially Confucianism, observers suggest that both doctrines continue to affect the political praxis of the current Chinese state (Fu 1996; Winston 2005).

Qin Shi Huang's immediate successors were unable to exercise the same authority and the next major regime to impose a centralised grip on China was the Han Dynasty, the founder of which, Emperor Gāo, generally referred to as Gaozu (高祖), took power in 206 BC (Twitchett and Loewe 1986).

The Han Dynasty built on its predecessors' organisational achievements, expanded its territory further and introduced Confucianism as the unifying ideology. As Nylan shows, the Han spin on Confucianism conflated 'the public and private aspects of two virtues, *xiao* (孝), [filial piety] and *rang* (让) ['abdication' or 'renunciation']'. With the adoption of Confucianism as a state ideology in 136 BC, the 'stage was set for the government's widespread propagation of both political virtues' (Nylan 1996: 8). Loyalty to the state complemented that to the family rather than compromising it. Han rule was less authoritarian than that of Qin. Its reign of over 400 years left an indelible mark on modern China and the majority of the PRC's population identify themselves as 'Han Chinese'. The pride taken by today's Han is based, in part at least, on the technological and cultural achievements of this dynasty and on its system of rule, which included a central examination system, the basis for merit recruitment to the state bureaucracy. As will be discussed in Chapter 5, the sense of pride in Han innovation and sophistication governs the majority's opinion on other ethnic and national identities in the PRC. Reinforcing the importance of the Han Dynasty's pivotal position in modern Chinese historiography is the nearly four centuries of war and disunity that followed its eventual collapse in 220 AD.

Though the interim period was also one of invention and cultural expansion, the next dynastic period of note lasted from 618 to 907, known as the Tang Dynasty. Again, though there was a marked Buddhist influence, Confucian scholarship was celebrated and provided a means of upward social mobility and social integration in what, even then, was the world's largest state. During the Tang's ascendancy, China's public administration was further developed and land reforms, graduated taxation and periodic military service were introduced. Advances in printing also increased the pace of literary and musical development (Benn 2004). The Tang Dynasty, however, eventually declined as a result of military setbacks and internal disunity.

In popular Chinese culture today, such as in television dramatisations, the Tang Dynasty is portrayed as a golden age (Kutolowsky 2007). The continuities in Chinese history from the major dynasties also remain the focus of much scholarship on China. Among these are the developments of a state bureaucracy capable of controlling China's vast territory, together with unified legal codes, taxation systems and money. One of the other features of the country's advancement relative to other parts of the world was in the production of food. The resultant population increase, however, challenged the capacity of the state. The Song Dynasty (960 to 1279) experienced a doubling in the number of Chinese during the tenth and eleventh centuries (Mote 1999: 353). Though the Song did not start the trend, under them the 'fashion for "food as medicine" found its most widespread expression'. The Chinese medical tradition of foods 'for everyday consumption with medicinal ingredients' received a particular boost (Jinsheng 2006: 41).

A population of approaching 200 million required new institutions of governance especially in relation to economic matters such as the production of food. What emerged was a more graduated public service with greater reliance on market forces and local administration. In government, legal and military affairs, the Song period was one of greater autonomy for local entities and a reaffirmation of merit recruitment and promotion. Ironically, this was accompanied by more autocracy at central government level with a rebalancing of the relationship between the military and civil powers in favour of the latter. The emperor was less vulnerable to his generals than ever. 'Neo-Confucianism', as it is referred to in some texts, was influenced by Buddhist thought as well as older Chinese traditions. 'The Song revival of the Confucian way is universally recognized as the second great wave in the history of Confucianism and is the wave that washed beyond the shores of China into Korea, Vietnam, and Japan' (Berthrong 2003: 26).

The Song Dynasty fell as a result of military failures that first cost it the northern part of its territory and, after 150 years of partition, the south. Reunification eventually came as a result of Mongol invasion and the setting up of the Mongol Yuan Dynasty. Despite being foreign, the new regime adopted Chinese ruling mores and political institutions. The cultural differences between the Mongol Yuan Dynasty and the majority of the populace were nevertheless real and find echoes in current Chinese nationalist rhetoric relating to the impositions of foreigners.

Like many occupying forces, the Mongols themselves retained the most important state positions and the natives were relegated to a second-class citizenship. Indeed, the official class system further divided Chinese into northern and southern categories liable to different taxes and privileges. In 1368, the rule of Yuan Dynasty was overthrown by a popular rebellion. The nature of the regime change was reflected in the newly established Ming Dynasty – a return to Han Chinese rule. The new rulers were very suspicious of educated bureaucrats and their leader, Zhu Yuanzhang (朱元璋), who rose from poverty to the top in just 16 years, set a style of harsh, secretive and authoritarian rule. Andrew and Rapp, drawing parallels with Mao, explain 'Zhu's attempts to open channels of communication between the throne and the village community and to circumvent the bureaucracy once and for all' (Andrew and Rapp 2000: 61). The Ming Dynasty held power until 1644.

The Ming Dynasty was replaced by another foreign Dynasty, the Manchurian Qing, who ruled for the final 268 years of imperial China. For most of the Qing Dynasty, the incumbent emperor governed in an autocratic and absolutist manner. Despite initially imposing Manchurian styles and manners on the Chinese, the Dynasty eventually relented allowing Han Chinese traditions to be re-established. Only the compulsory queue, a braid of hair worn at the back, remained as a constant sign of Manchu dominance. Nevertheless, the Han remained conscious of their earlier harsher treatment.

The Manchurian policy of expansionism was evident in the Qing period, when China's territory grew to its largest under any dynasty. In the mid-eighteenth century, the Qing ruled over 13 million square kilometres, including a garrison in Lhasa, capital of Tibet. The major erosion of Qing power occurred in the nineteenth century as a result of population induced food shortages, internal dissent and natural disasters. The regime also faced fiscal crises, foreign interference and faltering leadership. By this point, Han opposition to Manchu rule was growing:

> In the last years of the dynasty ardent young men were sometimes moved to demonstrate patriotic feelings by cutting off their queues, hated symbols of submission to Manchu rule, even though such an act was punishable by execution ... [M]any ... raised their voices to blame China's weakness on the Manchus ... Han Chinese resentment against alien rule was not a new phenomenon ... a similar note was sounded by Chinese insurgents denouncing the Mongol Yuan dynasty. (Farmer 1995: 1–2)

By the mid-nineteenth century, anti-Manchu sentiment was a rallying point for rebellions, motivated primarily by religious and economic interests, which weakened the regime. Domestic problems hampered the Qing's response to European imperial encroachments, but they also failed to recognise the significance of European technological, economic and military breakthroughs.

The opium trade became a focus of Sino-European conflict and in 1840 Chinese attempts to combat the impact of the drug led to the first Opium War. 'The clash between the two empires in the Nineteenth Century was a total mismatch. Britain was at the zenith of *Pax Britannia*, and China was at the nadir of its long history. Britain had advanced modern weapons, while China was still fighting with bows and arrows' (King 2008: 17). Militarily, China, for all its impressive numbers and access to gunpowder weapons like cannons and muskets, was ill-equipped to combat the British and other forces. As a consequence, it was obliged to make concessions to the Western powers that further weakened the internal security of the Qing rulers. Various unequal treaties and agreements which the Chinese were forced to accept, most notably the 1842 Treaty of Nanking[3] which made Hong Kong Island a British colony, are now seen as grievous slights. The Treaty of Tianjin 1858–59,[4] which ended the Second Opium War, legalised the import of opium, further opened up Chinese ports to Western traders, military vessels and missionaries as well as demanding substantial reparations.

From imperial collapse to People's Republic

The Chinese political establishment entered the nineteenth century secure in its view that China was an empire at the 'centre of heaven': all outsiders were uncultured barbarians. Many Chinese technological and cultural achievements supported this outlook. But the insularity and the arrogant grandiosity it encouraged led to significant political miscalculations. As Crow suggests: 'the Manchu government . . . always assumed the attitude that commerce was beneath the dignity of court . . . [and it] did not deign to notice it' (Crow 1933: 69). Recently, historians have nuanced this view of the Qing and it is certainly true that not all Chinese were so oblivious: 'the treaty ports were . . . the cradle of modern Chinese nationalism . . . Residents of the treaty ports knew that the new barbarians would never rally to the Chinese ideology or fall in line with Chinese culture. In other words, the strategy – indeed the very idea – [of] Sino centrism was pointless' (Bergère 1998: 21).

The current received wisdom portrays China as the duped victim. As Callahan argues: 'it would not be an exaggeration to argue that the master narrative of modern Chinese history is the discourse of the century of national humiliation' (Callahan 2004: 204). The focus on humiliation in Chinese accounts of the modern period allows the foundation of the PRC to be seen as a moment of national liberation. The CCP also can separate itself and occupy the high moral ground while it paints previous regimes, especially the Qing Dynasty, as corrupt and incompetent. In contemporary Chinese accounts, occasions of resistance and victory are downplayed or ignored. The Taiping Rebellion from 1850 to 1864, for instance, which was once seen as heroic resistance to Qing rule, is now portrayed as futile, misguided and wasteful of Chinese lives: '[T]hat pivotal event is not included in such [school text] books because it does not fit in with the moral narrative of national humiliation: foreign imperialism encouraged by domestic corruption' (Callahan 2004: 205).

Of course, at the end of nineteenth century, following defeat in the First Sino-Japanese War (1894–95), China did indeed experience intensifying internal disorder and increasing foreign penetration. There were risings in various provinces. British warships were sent in to restore order several times in coastal areas. The public finances, already burdened by war reparations, were in chaos and inflation was rising. The situation and the sense of impending doom were exacerbated by a wave of natural disasters, including floods, droughts, plagues and famines. Some regarded these as a sign of a Heavenly rebuke. The foreign powers began to carve up China: Japan established outposts (known as 'treaty ports') in China where it was permitted to set up factories; Germany expanded into Shandong and the port of Qingdao[5] (青岛); Britain gained leases on territory north of Kowloon, opposite Hong Kong Island; France established footholds close to its possessions in Indochina; and, Russia expanded its influence into northern China. Under the Treaty of Shimonoseki of 1895, Taiwan became part of the Empire of Japan as its first overseas colony. The American government, also in expansionist mode, sought consensus among the foreign powers on an 'open door' policy to China. Though Japan and Russia resisted the policy, some scholars credit such approaches with preventing full-scale colonisation as the foreigners could achieve all their goals through 'unequal' treaties without the expense of full control.

By the end of the nineteenth century, '[T]he scale of China's defeat brought a wave of national questioning and a growing desire to make a fresh start' (Fenby 2009a: 61). There were increasing calls for reform, with arguments that China's rulers should be held accountable, but equally that the country's entire institutional, economic, technological and social basis needed radical modernisation. Reformers demanded the establishment of a modern army, a state banking system, a railway network and a merchant fleet. Study societies, modern schools and publishing houses were set up to encourage debate and reform, in what became known as the 'Young China' movement.

The Guangxu Emperor (光绪帝) (1875–1908) supported reform:

> [Although he] had previously left all governmental affairs to his aunt, the Empress Dowager, and former concubine ... [In 1898, he] unexpectedly took over affairs of government himself. To the surprise of everyone he entered on a series of reforms as ambitious as they were visionary. He gathered about him some of the most progressive and radical reformers in the country and for 100 days issued an edict which threw down the established institutions and set up new ones. (Crow 1933: 77)

The Hundred Days' Reform initiatives, however, threatened the power of the nobles on whom the imperial system rested and they resisted. The Empress Dowager Cixi[6] (慈禧太后) was ambiguous about reform and more engaged in traditional court politics:

> her objection to the political reform ... strangled the Hundred Days' Reform and hindered all-around progress of the Chinese society ... [S]he was an extremely contradictory and complicated historical figure. (Zhang 2010: 154)

In September 1898, Cixi mounted a successful court *coup d'état* against the emperor, forcing him to retreat to the Summer Palace outside Beijing where he was detained for the rest of his life. Other leading reformers were banished, arrested, killed or fled. The proposals had been overly radical, lacked a sufficient support base and were regarded by many as too 'foreign'. Conservative rule was re-established under Cixi but the imperial system had been further weakened with her tenure depending on court politics and support from those in the tiers below her.

The twin problems of internal disorder and foreign intervention were dramatically symbolised at the turn of the century by the Boxer Rebellion. Christian missionaries were a major component of Western encroachment into China and became a focus of Chinese resentment of the foreign powers, with periodic anti-Christian violence in the late nineteenth century. The Boxer movement – so-called because they were also known as the Righteous Harmony Society, 'Righteous Fists of Harmony' or 'Society of Righteous and Harmonious Fists' – first emerged in 1898 in protest at the building of a Catholic church in Shandong. The movement reflected a combination of the marginalisation of the peasants, anti-foreigner sentiment and traditional spiritual beliefs and rituals (Preston 2000b). The Boxers adopted the traditional red and yellow garb of earlier risings and were widely believed to have supernatural powers. 'The leaders declared themselves immune from harm by foreign bullets and gave each member a talisman which would ensure a similar protection for him' (Crow 1933: 78). Although usually described as a Rebellion, the Boxers supported the imperial dynasty, as reflected in their battle cry 'Support the Qing [the Manchus], destroy the Foreign' (Preston 2000a: 30). The imperial regime was divided over the Boxers, viewing them as both a threat and a force that might be directed against the foreign powers, but eventually adopted the second strategy.

The Boxer movement grew in 1899 and 1900 and moved north and west towards Beijing. In 1900, a large group of Boxers massacred

Christian converts and burned a cathedral in Beijing. The foreign powers began to mobilise military forces for intervention. In June China declared war, the Boxers were brought into the imperial militia and a 55–day siege of the Western legations in Beijing began. Violence escalated in other parts of China too, with thousands of people, including Chinese Christians and foreigners, killed and many atrocities committed. Eight foreign nations (Japan, Britain, France, Russia, the US, Germany, Italy and Austria) assembled a force of 54,000 troops. The superior military technology of the foreign powers enabled them easily to defeat the Boxers and the imperial troops. A force of 20,000 troops, led by the British, marched on Beijing and Cixi and the Court fled. Foreign forces took revenge, killing and injuring many Chinese at the sites of alleged Boxer atrocities (Esherick 1987). In 1901, negotiations were opened with the foreign powers: under the so-called 'Boxer Protocols', forts protecting Beijing and Tianjin were to be destroyed, foreign forces would be stationed on the approaches to the capital and guards posted at legations, China would pay a very large indemnity to the foreign powers and the treaty port system was extended to 25 locations (Preston 2000a).

The shame of defeat in the Boxer war and the subsequent protocols drove the imperial regime to institute a number of reforms which it hoped would make China a modern state capable of standing up for itself against the major Western powers. In 1901, the education system was changed from its traditional focus on Confucianism and the Chinese classics to Western mathematics, science, engineering and geography. The state administration was modernised, with new central government ministries established. The military was re-organised based on Western and Japanese models, with a professional officer corps. Industry and commerce were promoted. A putative central bank, initially known as the Bank of the Board of Revenue (大清户部银行), was established in 1905 and private banks also expanded. The central bank was upgraded into the Great Qing Bank (大清銀行) in 1908.

The reforms inadvertently exacerbated the socio-economic circumstances of the Chinese people and the weakness of the imperial regime. Yet they were also insufficient to quell growing demands for change. Old economic and social systems broke down further, without anything to replace them. The commitment of the Chinese gentry to public duty and service, which had been a central pillar of the imperial system (Goetzmann and Ukhov 2001: 25), declined. Further, irrigation systems, which had been the basis of Chinese agriculture, fell into disrepair (Sun 2009). Inflation soared, increasing the prices of basic goods. The government increased taxes, giving rise to violent protests. Strikes and machine-breaking occurred at factories in the cities. Military opposition groups emerged and, though easily defeated by imperial forces, their frequency and latent political support ensured that, when it came, 'the 1911 Revolution would not be just another dynastic change' (Rankin, Fairbank and Feuerwerker 1986: 8). Resentment became directed against the foreign powers, the benefits conceded to them in the Boxer protocols and against the Manchu Qing regime for its failure to reverse the concessions. These demands were given voice by a so-called 'rights recovery movement'.

Alongside discontent amongst the peasantry, demands for socio-economic and political reform, including an elected parliament, began to surface amongst the gentry and intellectuals. Sun Yat-sen (孙中山) emerged as a key figure in these revolutionary movements. Born in 1866, Sun was educated in Honolulu and influenced by ideas of democracy and socialism. He imagined three revolutions in one: a nationalist revolution to overthrow the foreign Manchu dynasty and the foreign powers; a democratic revolution to establish a Chinese republic; and, a social revolution to equalise land rights and wealth. These were distilled into his 'Three Principles of the People: national-ism, democracy and welfare' (Bergère 1998: 352). In 1895, Sun led an unsuccessful coup attempt against the Qing regime, the defeat of which forced him into exile in Europe, the USA, Canada and Japan for the next 16 years. In 1905, in Japan, Sun established the Tongmeng Hui (United League, 同盟会), bringing together various revolutionary groups into a single movement. Sun envisaged three stages to the revo-lution: a military government for three years, six years of 'political tutelage', followed by a constitutional democracy.

The death of the Guangxu Emperor (光绪帝) in November 1908 precipitated a political crisis. Cixi identified her two year old grandson Puyi (溥仪) as the new emperor, giving him the reign name Xuantong (宣统皇帝). Cixi would retain ultimate authority as Empress Grand Dowager, but Cixi herself died immediately after anointing Puyi, leaving the country on a precipice. Demands for political reform inten-sified and could no longer be resisted by the imperial regime. An 'Outline of Constitution' published in 1908 put off the establishment of a parliament for nine years, only provoking demands for reform to be accelerated. In 1909 provincial assemblies were established in all provinces and in 1910 a national democratically elected Consultative Assembly was created. The Qing, however, still sought to retain real power. Events in 1911 finally brought an end to the imperial regime, but, as Jonathan Fenby argues, the revolution of 1911 was 'a ragged affair that caught fire province by province. That it unseated the system which had survived so many challenges over the millennia was a reflection of the fragility of the central power, the strength of regional interests and the depth of the feeling that China had to change its ways' (Fenby 2009a: 117).

In the summer of 1911, decisions by the regime to assert national control over railway building and hand much of the work over to foreign companies triggered protests by the gentry and led them to join forces with revolutionaries. Protests in Sichuan province in south-west China[7] caused fighting with imperial troops. In October 1911, a bomb in the office of a revolutionary group in Wuchang signalled the beginning of further unrest. The revolt quickly spread to other regions: in October–November provinces declared their independence from the Qing and, by end of November, two-thirds of China had seceded from the empire. Once the revolution began, Sun Yat-sen returned from exile as its leader. Splits emerged within the imperial regime and its senior military figure Yuan Shikai[8] (袁世凯) concluded that there was no alternative but to negotiate with the revolutionaries. A provisional assembly was called in Nanjing[9] and, at end of 1911, it voted for Sun to become President, a post he took up on 1 January 1912. The young Emperor Puyi's resignation was formally announced in February. 'The takeover of power was generally quick and relatively bloodless, a sign that the Qing dynasty has outlived its support' (Phillips 1996: 11).

Divisions quickly emerged within the new government. Yuan, who still controlled the imperial armed forces, forced Sun to resign as president and had himself elected to the post by the assembly. Yuan allocated the key ministries (in particular, war, interior, navy and foreign affairs) to his cronies, giving the revolutionaries the least important cabinet posts.

In summer 1912, Sun's Tongmeng Hui absorbed four other revolutionary parties to form the KMT (Phillips 1996). Elections were held at the turn of the year and, by early 1913, the KMT was the largest party in the bicameral National Assembly. The Senate was indirectly elected mainly by provincial assemblies with some presidential nominees. In the lower house, the KMT initially won 392 of the 870 seats. Nevertheless, the political scene was very unclear with some politicians being members of more than one party and corruption, intimidation and intrigue rife. The KMT, which promised to rein in Yuan, eventually secured 438 seats and their opponents began to consolidate into the Progressive Party (进步党). The KMT set about forming a government with its leader Song Jiaoren (宋教仁) to be prime minister. Yuan responded by organising the assassination of

Song in March 1913. Yuan's increasing authoritarianism triggered the so-called 'Second Revolution' in July 1913, as provinces began to secede from the new republic. Yuan dissolved the parliament, extended his powers as president, abolished the limit on his term as president and made use of martial law, secret police and terror. Revolutionaries and anti-Yuan soldiers fled, while opponents engaged in attacks from bases in the provinces. Yuan also began to re-establish imperial practices and, in December 1915, had himself declared emperor. A National Protection Army, also known as the Anti-Monarchy Army, emerged in Yunnan in the southwest and was quickly joined by other provinces. Yuan was forced to issue an edict ending his monarchy, which had lasted barely three months. Weaker than ever, Yuan died of blood poisoning in summer 1916.

Since defeat to Japan in the 1890s, China had been in a gradual process of internal disintegration, with regional military and political leaders gaining growing power at the expense of the centre. With Yuan's death in 1916, fighting broke out between the forces of various regionally based military leaders and China entered what became known as the 'warlord era'. Fenby summarises the period:

> China could be seen as a continent, split into rival states, with the warlords as the equivalent of kings in early medieval Europe ... the central government was like the papacy at its weakest, with whichever general controlled Beijing acting as pope-maker. No single militarist was strong enough to take charge of all China at the head of the national government ... [B]elow the main players stretched an array of petty militarists, such as the fifty in Sichuan. (Fenby 2009a: 145)

Not surprisingly, the warlord era produced further economic decline. Poor harvests resulted in food shortages, with an estimated four to six million deaths due to famine in 1921–22. Banditry and kidnapping became commonplace in some areas.

While the warlords were the dominant force in the north, the two forces that were to shape modern Chinese politics – the Nationalist Party of Kuomintang (KMT) and the Communists – were consolidating in the south. Guangzhou in Guangdong province in southern China[10], in particular was a political hothouse, with a wide range of radical and revolutionary forces developing there. There were repeated protests and strikes and periodic violence between different political factions. In 1923, Sun returned to Guangdong – his home region – and established a parallel KMT government (Van de Ven 2003).

From its beginnings, the KMT regime was characterised by a number of features. With advice from the Soviet Union, the KMT established a highly centralised system under which the Party held ultimate control over the government. The military – again modelled on the Soviet Red Army with its political commissars – was also a central aspect of the regime. At the same time, the KMT was riddled with corruption, criminality and incompetence, with its troops engaging in robbery, piracy and kidnapping and running protection rackets, gambling, prostitution and the drug trade (Coble 1980).

In March 1925, Sun died: although he had failed in achieving his objective of a strong, united and modern China, in death he achieved the unique status of being revered as the Father of the Revolution (or the Father of the Republic) by both the nationalist KMT and the Communists. His political philosophy and achievements were sufficiently ambiguous to be claimed by both sides. Chiang Kai-shek (蔣介石) succeeded Sun as leader of the KMT. Chiang adopted Sun's Three Principles of the People, but used his control of the KMT military and party apparatus to establish a dictatorial and highly personalised regime (Fairbank and Goldman 2006).

Since the late nineteenth century, a variety of radical ideas calling for social, economic and political change gradually permeated China and these provided the context from which the CCP was formed. In the mid-1910s and 1920s, the New Culture Movement emerged, calling for radical changes to China's conservative and hierarchical society. The 1919 Versailles Peace Conference provided a further impetus for radical forces within China. At Versailles, the Western Allies granted Japan the former German concessions in China. This provision triggered protests that have subsequently assumed a symbolic role in Chinese history (Mitter 2004). On 4 May 1919, 3,000 students protested at foreign legations in Beijing and similar demonstrations broke out in other cities. The protests – which became known as the May Fourth movement – blamed China's woes on Confucian traditions, calling for the old system to be destroyed. The New Culture and May Fourth movements were diverse including liberals, moderate conservatives and anarchists, but Marxists played a prominent role – amongst them, though not to the fore, was a young Mao Zedong. In the wake of the May Fourth protests, the CCP was established in June 1921 (Lynch 2005).

At this point, the KMT and the CCP faced the question of how far it was desirable or possible to form an alliance against the northern warlords. Both groups were revolutionaries and nationalists who had opposed the old imperial regime. The Communists, however, advocated radical economic and social reform, whereas the KMT was more conservative and included middle classes and business people.

Each was itself fragmented between moderates and radicals who were divided over whether to cooperate with the other party. The Soviet Union played an important role in this period, sending advisers to support the development of both the CCP and the KMT and pressing the CCP, in particular, to accept a united front. This was eventually formed in 1923. The united front – which was re-established but broke down from various points up to the 1940s – was always an alliance of convenience and characterised by deep mistrust on both sides.

The mounting of an offensive against the northern warlords emerged as a central issue. From a nationalist perspective, the warlords had to be defeated if a united and strong China was to be re-established. So long as the warlords remained in power, they would prevent this goal. In 1925, the northern government sent forces to attack the KMT in its southern bases, but these forces were defeated in what became known as the Eastern Expedition – the precursor to a larger offensive against the northern warlords. In July 1926, the KMT announced its Northern Expedition. The warlords' forces were numerically superior, but the KMT's National Revolutionary Army (NRA, 国民革命军) was well organised, politically motivated and could gain support from significant parts of the population. Additionally, the KMT also built alliances with some warlords and together their forces numbered 260,000. The KMT made rapid progress, taking Hunan and the city of Wuchang and moving its forces towards Nanjing and Shanghai.

As Chiang's forces advanced northwards tensions with the communists escalated, with Chiang executing communists and closing down leftist organisations. In Shanghai communists and trade unions were attempting to establish a Soviet and called a general strike that was joined by 100,000 workers (Perry 1993). Rather than advancing to Shanghai to support the strike, Chiang chose to wait, allowing local forces to execute many strikers. In March 1927 KMT forces entered Shanghai and Nanjing. Chiang had already built alliances with local crime bosses in Shanghai to tackle the leftists and on 12 April 1927 the KMT's local allies used machine gun fire and bayonets to slaughter between 5,000 and 10,000 demonstrators, including women and children. Chiang's 'White Terror' then spread out from Shanghai to other regions under KMT control. In December 1927 a communist uprising in Guangzhou produced a brutal response from the KMT, with an estimated 5,700 people killed. Soon, being taken for a communist was enough to risk summary execution or imprisonment (Van de Ven 2003: 117). The Communists were greatly weakened and their forces fled to the countryside and the mountains. The 'White Terror' that 'Chiang and his gangster allies unleashed against the labor movement in April 1927 irrevocably colored the character of the emerging Nationalist state' (Perry 1993: 3) and created an unbridgeable legacy of mistrust between the Communists and the Nationalists.

In 1928, Chiang formed alliances with two warlords to enable the KMT to defeat the northern government in Beijing. The KMT now controlled most of China and ostensibly governed the country from 1928 to 1949.[11] Chiang set about building a new political system and introducing economic and social reforms: the government was moved from Beijing to Nanjing; provincial currencies and taxes were standardised; power plants and radio stations were built and the railway system was expanded; the working day was set at eight hours and child labour was officially banned. At a Party Congress in March 1929, it was agreed that the KMT would practice 'political tutelage' on behalf of the people until 1935. The features of the KMT, which had emerged in the 1920s, became stronger. The regime became more authoritarian, with Chiang having himself declared *Generalissimo* and increasingly reliant on a brutal secret police that used torture, execution and arbitrary arrest to stamp out dissent. Corruption, criminality and violence became defining parts of the KMT's *modus operandi*. Under the so-called 'New Life Movement', Chiang sought to reassert traditional Confucian values – with himself as the national father figure – as a way of restoring order and respect to a society increasingly engulfed by chaos and violence.

The KMT regime, however, was weaker than it appeared. Many provinces remained under the control of warlords and the KMT lacked the military power to assert control over the entire country. A new anti-Nanjing coalition was set up in Beijing and fighting broke out between the KMT and its opponents in 1929. The KMT remained the government of China, but it faced continual challenges from regional forces, while the long conflict gradually eroded its position.

The late 1920s and early 1930s was also a formative period for the Communists. The Chinese Communists were divided between those, backed by the Soviet Union, who supported the traditional Marxist argument that any revolution had to be based around the industrial proletariat and those, led by Mao, who argued that China's primarily rural society meant that revolution could only succeed by mobilising the peasants. After the breakdown of the united front in 1927 and the KMT's 'White Terror', the Communists were forced to retreat to the countryside – providing the context in which Mao's strategy won out and Mao came to dominate the CCP. The Communists began a series of rural risings, seizing land and redistributing it to the peasants and setting up Soviet governments in areas under their control.

Under Mao's leadership, the Communists perfected a strategy of peasant uprisings and guerrilla warfare under the centralised control of the Party – often exercised by violence and terror. The base areas under Communist control grew to some thousands of square kilometres and the Communists used them to launch attacks on KMT controlled towns and cities. Mao did not actually come to dominate the Party until 1935 and his main rival, Wang Ming (王明), was much closer to the Soviet ideological line. Nevertheless, when in November 1931, the First All-China Congress of the Soviets was called, Mao was elected Chairman of the Central Executive Committee of the All-China Soviet Government and made Chief Political Commissar of the People's Liberation Army (PLA, 人民解放军). It is possible his rival thought this position would rein Mao in and, notably, he was unable to gain admission into the politburo, which remained in the hands of his CCP opponents.

In 1931, the KMT launched a military campaign against the Communists: KMT forces encircled Communist controlled areas and a brutal conflict broke out. The larger numbers of the KMT allowed it to prevail. As KMT forces advanced, they engaged in scorched-earth tactics and massacres of those accused of being Communists. By mid-1934, the Communists were on the verge of defeat. The Communists decided to flee as a single group in what was to become known as the 'Long March' (长征). When the Communists left their main base in Jiangxi in October 1934, they had approximately 90,000 men (Lynch 2005: 86). The Communists retreated first westwards then northwards, marching for just over a year, and eventually arriving at one of the few areas that remained under their control in Yan'an (延安)[12] in Shaanxi province in northern China in October 1935. The marchers travelled thousands of kilometres, estimates vary up to 12.5 in the official version, through extremely difficult territory and suffering appalling hardship. After death and desertion, only 10 per cent of the marchers reached Yan'an. The Long March is a central founding event for the PRC. Like all such events, the version with the most currency is that of the winners and, in it, Mao cuts a heroic figure. In fact, the March saw further bitter political infighting within the Communist movement, but Mao emerged pre-eminent (Shuyun 2007).

By the mid-1930s, the KMT faced a greater foe than the Communists – the Japanese. Since the late nineteenth century, Japan had had expansionist ambitions towards China (Lim 2003). After the 1894–95 war, Japan had tried to gain control of the Liaodong

Peninsula in the south of Manchuria and, after defeating Russia in 1905, Japan had gained control of the Kwantung Leased Territory in eastern Manchuria, which effectively became a separate state with its own army. Manchuria[13] was viewed by the Japanese as a highly important agricultural and industrial area, which might be central to Japan's economic and imperial development (Sugihara 1997). Japan's imperial ambitions intensified in the 1930s as the country's politics became increasingly militaristic and nationalist. In September 1931, the Japanese Kwantung Army staged an explosion on a train near a Japanese barracks in Mukden[14] in Kwantung. The Mukden Incident, as it became called, was used as a pretext by the Japanese to take over the city and then advance rapidly across Manchuria. By the beginning of 1932, Japan controlled Manchuria and proceeded to establish the puppet state of Manchukuo. In early 1932, the Japanese organised an assault on Japanese Buddhists visiting Shanghai, which was again used as a pretext to begin an attack; a cease-fire was brokered, however, with Japan withdrawing its forces from Chinese areas and the Chinese accepting the de-militarisation of Shanghai. In 1933–34, the Japanese took further territory in northern China, bringing them close to Beijing, but they were wary at this stage of being drawn into a full-scale war in China (Mitter 2000).

In 1937, the conflict escalated to all-out war between the two countries. In July, Japan invoked a provision of the Boxer Protocols that allowed it (and the other foreign powers) to station troops east of Beijing: it held military exercises and, claiming that a soldier had gone missing, initiated military action against the Chinese. In August, Japan occupied Beijing. In late 1937, the Japanese took Shanghai: naval gunships and aircraft engaged in massive attacks on the city and KMT losses were estimated at anywhere between 180,000 and 300,000 (Van de Van 2003: 211–17). At the end of 1937, the Japanese also captured Nanjing, the capital of Jiangsu province, inland from China's eastern coast. The taking of the city, previously known in English as Nanking but now referred to as Nanjing, was followed by a six-week orgy of violence and inhumanity that subsequently became known as the 'Nanjing massacre' or the 'rape of Nanking' – an event now widely recognised as one of the worst war crimes in modern history (Chang 1998).

The Nationalists and the Communists formed a new united front against the Japanese at the end of 1936, but tensions between the two groups soon re-emerged and, in 1941, the united front broke down completely with fighting between the two. After this, the Nationalists and the Communists continued largely separate wars against the

Japanese. Chiang employed traditional military tactics while Mao's forces engaged in guerrilla warfare.

After taking Nanjing in 1937, the Japanese gradually became bogged down in central and Western China and a protracted war emerged. The Japanese won battles, but could not consolidate or extend their control: 'the Japanese spent the next few months expanding the area under their control, but without achieving their goal of pacifying China or gaining acceptance of their ambitions' (Phillips 1996: 127). By 1941, the war had reached a stalemate and, in 1942–43, there were fewer major battles. The scale of the war and the death and suffering it caused were huge. Battles often involved some hundreds of thousands of troops and somewhere between 10 and 20 million people were killed, with most estimates at the higher end of this range (Dover 1986; Gruhl 2007).

The end of the Second World War and the Japanese withdrawal started a scramble between the Nationalists and the Communists to control post-war China. With much of Japanese occupied China in the north of the country where the Communists were strongest and likely, therefore, to fall into Communist hands, the US sent 53,000 Marines to occupy Beijing and other key cities and hold them until the Nationalists arrived (Fairbank and Goldman: 2006). Both the Soviets and the US pressed the Nationalists and the Communists to form a united front but negotiations to this end collapsed in 1946 and fighting once more broke out between the two sides. Initially, the KMT appeared to be in the stronger position: they were the internationally recognised government of China and had the larger armed forces. They had, however, been greatly weakened in economic and military terms by the long war, while the regime remained plagued by corruption, inefficiency and internal disagreements. The Communists, in contrast, having faced near extinction twice (during the White Terror of 1927 and the Long March), had re-built themselves from their base in Yan'an during what is sometimes referred to as the 'Yan'an Period' (1935–47) (Sheldon 1971).

By the end of the Second World War, the Communists had consolidated their hold over areas under their control, CCP membership had been expanded significantly and the PLA built up. The strategy of mobilising the peasants and re-distributing land proved successful in building popular support. As they took territory from the Japanese, the Communists also gained armaments and military recruits, as well as receiving equipment from the Soviets (who had invaded Manchuria at the end of the Second World War). The PLA was transformed from a guerrilla force into a mechanised army. By 1948, the civil war had shifted decisively in favour of the Communists, with a series of military victories in 1947 and frequent defections of Nationalist forces and military commanders to the Communists: '[the] Nationalist Government lost public support and seemed to be the instigator of the civil war [...] [it] had become so militarized that it could think only of a military solution to the civil war without regard for its function as a government to serve the public' (Fairbank and Goldman 2006: 332–4).

By 1948–49, the civil war was turning into a rout, with the Nationalists suffering a series of massive defeats and the Communist military now heavily outnumbering that of the KMT. The Communists took Beijing in January 1949 and Shanghai in May. On 1 October 1949 Chairman Mao declared the establishment of the communist People's Republic of China. In December, Chiang and the KMT fled to the offshore island of Taiwan. To this day, Taiwan remains the one part of China not under PRC control and a source of considerable tension. Taiwan is discussed further in Chapter 6.

The Mao era

The newly victorious Communist government imported much of the political structure, as well as the economic system, of the Soviet Union. Paradoxically, this new political order could draw on many of the traditions of the *ancien régime* ... [It] was bureaucratic and authoritarian ... What distinguished the new Communist political system from its predecessors was that modern transportation and communications now made possible the creation of a genuinely totalitarian state. (Harding 1987: 25–6)

The Mao-led China was indeed influenced by the Soviet Union, though Harding's characterisation of it as 'totalitarian' probably exaggerates the state's capacity for control. China's system 'while closely modeled on the Soviet Union under Stalin, fell short of realization in fact' (Lai 2006: 56). The creation of the PRC represented a very abrupt turning point in China's history but it also drew on elements of the imperial tradition. Andrew and Rapp cast Mao himself as 'a rebel founding emperor in Zhu Yuanzhang's mould' (2000: 5). A new political order was enforced by centralised power, brute force and massive disruption. The new ideological orthodoxy, a Sinocised Marxism, stressed the need to force the pace of history by the use of dictatorial powers. The major operational mantra was 'democratic centralism' which, in theory at least, means that the Party adopts its positions democratically, and then demands unquestioning support even from those who voiced counter views. In practice, it equated to the concentration of power in the hands of a small élite.

The élite itself was dominated by Mao who became the centre of a 'cult of personality' that facilitated purges of opponents and abrupt policy changes of monumental consequence. Mao's regime nationalised industries, banks and property and portrayed any resistance as reactionary and counter-revolutionary. It redistributed land and moved the once-marginalised peasantry into a central role both in its ideological worldview and as foot soldiers of the revolution. Campaigns of rectification, as in 1950–51, were aimed at those deemed class enemies or spies. Mao's edicts that launched such campaigns of mass arrests, denunciation, terror and executions were often couched in slogans. In two separate campaigns there were the 'three antis' (corruption, waste and bureaucracy) in 1951 and a year later the 'five antis' (bribery, theft of state property, tax evasion, cheating on government contracts and stealing state economic information). Millions of people were caught up in chaos, uncertainty and danger. As Friedman notes: 'one hallmark of Maoism was that popular vigilantism, rather than a bureaucratically centralised secret police, was the preferred state instrument for controlling, crushing and doing away with purported class enemies, the real political targets' (Friedman 2008: 390).

Mao's regime sought to control the maelstrom by registering and monitoring all city dwellers in 1951 and restricting peasant migration to the cities in 1952. In effect, free movement was ended (Phillips 1996). For much of his *modus operandi*, Mao had a blueprint in the methods used in the Soviet Union to impose socialist ideas. Stalin and later Khrushchev supported Mao with both *matériel* and personnel. Although China and the Soviet Union were bound together by ideological solidarity, more traditional geo-political tensions between the two states also remained. Stalin's own priorities included retaining the independence of Mongolia from China and regaining positions in Manchuria formerly held by tsarist Russia (Shen 2000).

The 1950 Sino-Soviet Treaty of Friendship, Alliance and Mutual Assistance seemed to cement the tutelage arrangement. Mao's model of revolution was, however, different from that of the Soviet Union. It included the 'leading role' of the CCP but centred the focus of power in the peasantry not the urban population. Mao codified his thoughts in a template for the Asian model of revolution that was eventually, particularly after Stalin's death, seen as a rival to the Soviet one. Initially, however, the Chinese regime followed the classic Russian Marxist prescription of centralised economic development with a privileging of heavy industry. The work unit or *danwei* (单位) system was set up to implement change. Under this, state-owned enterprises were organised hierarchically with close CCP control. The individual worker was bound to the unit for life but, in exchange, enjoyed certainty of employment and social security. This system may have been inflexible, controlling and lacking incentives but, though very much less important today, has influenced Chinese expectations of the state's role. The notion of what became known as the 'iron rice bowl' (铁饭碗), the guarantee of a job that the *danwei* system provided, came with very significant restrictions on social life, family formation and personal mobility. Under the uncertain conditions of Maoist China, however, the exchange of personal freedom for economic security reassured many citizens.

The emphasis on heavy industry created a major imbalance economically and the CCP came to reassess the role of agriculture as a potential source of income. Mao favoured a radical approach and in a policy called 'the Great Leap Forward' (1958–63) the collectivisation of farms became the cornerstone of a push to greatly increase agricultural output. The collective farms were also to support industrial production units. The policy was pursued with extraordinary vigour. All private ownership of land was ended and families were assigned to communes. Targets were set and draconian measures, accompanied by relentless propaganda, put in place to ensure compliance. Mao, however, was not without critics within the CCP. At the Lushan Conference (庐山会议), a meeting of the Central Committee in 1959, Peng Dehuai (彭德怀), then defence minister, made clear his opposition to aspects of the Great Leap Forward. Peng was eventually dismissed and open criticism ended as any debate was taken as a sign of disloyalty to Mao himself. The policy was a disaster and, according to Mahoney, 'as many as 50 million deaths are at least partially attributable to Great Leap policies, and among these, nearly 33 million resulted from famine' (Mahoney 2009: 319).

Mao for a while after the 'Leap' took a step back; as Gittings puts it, he 'retired to his study' (Gittings 2005: 35) and permitted more pragmatic figures to take the lead. Despite attempts to sideline him, Mao returned to the fore in 1966 in a series of campaigns called collectively the Cultural Revolution. Again, this is a cataclysmic event in the PRC centred on Mao's personal leadership. 'The Cultural Revolution ... was not simply a Stalinist purge but a much more complex affair which mobilised millions of activists to defend one man at the top and his version of the road to Communism' (Gittings 2005: 41). It involved a process of renewal of revolutionary purpose and fervour aimed at unsettling those who were suspected of backtracking on communism, as Mao understood it. Indeed, a popularised and pithy book of his thoughts became a symbol of the campaign in which a group of young people called the Red Guard sought to root out pockets of bourgeois influence. Some of the Red Guard portrayed themselves in the role of the Boxer rebels, now interpreted as patriots who had fought against a 'corrupt and decadent court as well as foreign aggression' (Preston 2000b: 35). The Cultural Revolution saw many holders of even minor authority in education, public service or social life sent to the country for re-education through manual labour. The Red Guard humiliated and forced self-criticism from many in the older generation. Perhaps one million people died in the accompanying violence. In 1969, when he declared the Cultural Revolution over, the PRC was in turmoil but Mao's control was unchallenged.

The extremism of the Mao era was reinforced by isolation from the rest of the world and a foreign policy that initially assumed the inevitability of conflict with the US and the West but later saw a *de facto* Cold War between the PRC and its former communist ally the Soviet Union. After 1949, most foreign residents abandoned China or were expelled. Those who did not leave, predominantly from the Eastern Bloc, had their movement restricted. Information was difficult to obtain from anywhere except official sources and much of the internal history of the Mao period is still being written from fragmented sources. China's foreign relations are discussed in more detail in Chapter 6, but a number of features should be noted here. The US refusal to recognise the PRC and the Korean War put China on the frontline of the Cold War. Both internationally and domestically China was on semi-permanent war footing against perceived external and internal enemies. From the 1950s the Sino-Soviet alliance gradually broke down, bringing the two countries to the verge of outright war in 1969. Although the Sino-Soviet confrontation facilitated Sino-US détente, the breakdown of relations between the two communist giants nevertheless reinforced the Chinese leadership's sense of encirclement and isolation. The ultra-radical ideological purism and the aggressive but constantly insecure approach of Mao and his allies were thus both reflected in and fuelled by China's foreign relations during this period.

Following his death in 1976, the leadership of the PRC continued to portray Mao as an icon of the Party and a national hero. As Friedman argues Deng Xiaoping (邓小平), the eventual successor: 'would abandon Maoist economics, dismantle parts of the Stalinist state, and open China up to the dynamism of the world economy. China would again become a great power. But the new rulers felt a need to embrace some of Mao's legacy to stabilise their hold on power' (Friedman 2008: 389). To this day, Mao's portrait sits affront the entrance to the historic

Forbidden City at the heart of Beijing and his image is used on bank notes, public buildings and official offices. School children were, for many years after his death, encouraged to venerate the 'Great Helmsman'. As the CCP sought to come to terms with Mao's legacy, it developed the official line that he was 70 per cent right and 30 per cent wrong. Mao, however, remains a deeply sensitive subject and open discussion of his rule is not encouraged. Today, in school texts, 'he is mentioned fleetingly' (Kahn 2006).

The era of reform

Following the death of Mao, a leadership struggle in the mid-1970s saw Deng Xiaoping emerge to lead the CCP. Deng was purged twice in the Cultural Revolution and, while his credentials from the Long March and the foundations of the PRC were impeccable, his leadership represented a marked change from Mao. Not least, he discouraged the cult of personality and introduced constitutional changes, examined in Chapter 4, to limit the length of any office holders' tenure. Deng's central objective was to modernise China's economy without relinquishing the CCP's grip on power (Shirk 1993).

Economic reform
As was noted earlier, the Mao period had seen the establishment of a centrally planned economy with almost all economic activity directed and controlled by the state. Table 2 summarises the main differences between a centrally planned economy and a free market one. The devastating economic consequences of the Great Leap Forward and the Cultural Revolution had presumably made Deng Xiaoping acutely aware of the failings of a rigid centrally planned model and willing to consider alternatives. Deng was a pragmatist and his central objective was to make China a functioning modern economy. Despite its radical impact, Deng's presentation of the new approach emphasised continuity of the CCP's socialist ambitions. Gabriel reports him as saying:

> There is no fundamental contradiction between socialism and a market economy ... the overriding task in China today is to throw ourselves heart and soul into the modernization drive. While giving play to the advantages inherent in socialism, we are also employing some capitalist methods – only as methods of accelerating the growth of the productive forces ... China has no alternative but to follow this road. (Gabriel 2006: 4).

In the 1980s Deng launched economic reforms that allowed certain sectors and enterprises to operate outside the central plan, responding

Table 2 Main features of centrally planned and free market economies

Centrally planned economies	Free market economies
• Command economy • Economic activity the result of state planning and imposition • Control by state of production, prices, education, jobs and resources • Focus on production, neglect of private consumption • Job security • Restrictions on personal career mobility • Orientation towards heavy industries • Mandatory five-year-planning • Limited foreign trade – closed economy	• Freedom of movement, expression, association etc • Economic activity result of individual choices • Most production in private hands – well-defined secure property rights • Limited role of state (safety, rule of law, public goods) • Consumption oriented • Market creation by innovation • Prices set by supply and demand • Open economy – low barriers to foreign trade

to market forces rather than government directives. As these steps succeeded in making more goods available for both export and domestic consumption, such measures were extended to much – though not all – of the economy in the 1990s. The characteristics of China's move towards a new economic order are summarised in Table 3 and, more figuratively, by the slogan accredited to Deng: 'Crossing the river by feeling for stones'.

Table 3 Characteristics of China's transition to a new economic order

1. Step by step, trial and error
2. Growing out of the Plan
3. Simple things first
4. Central role of Foreign Direct Investment (FDI)

The transformation of China's economic order has been a process of trial and error or, as Yang suggests, its progress has been 'gradual, evolutionary, and path dependent' (Yang 1996: 439). Indeed, as Tsai describes it, the process was hastened almost despite the CCP as 'ordinary people were finding ways around midlevel rules and regulations that were anachronistic and impractical' (Tsai 2007: ix). Letting the economy grow out of the plan, as Naughton famously put it, the leadership partly followed bottom-up examples of spontaneous change by the population and partly initiated and implemented reform policies top-down (Naughton 1996). In the 1980s, central officials stepped back from trying to plan everything and, especially in rural areas, tolerated the emergence of market forces. These processes resulted in a diffuse and incoherent co-existence of traditional norms and modes of behaviour stemming from Maoist and centrally planned traditions together with different forms of market-oriented institutions. Tensions between formal and informal institutions proved a strong stimulus for continuous change.

The Chinese government, like most others, could not resist the promotion of national champions, i.e. making special rules for sectors it assumed would have strategic or high market potential. These are not necessarily state-owned companies but firms that may develop globally.

> The advantages conferred on these 'national champions' vary, but the rationale for their promotion by parts of the Chinese government is straightforward. Chinese government officials, largely for reasons of national pride, favor the existence of Chinese national companies that operate on a world stage with a stature comparable to US, Japanese and European multinationals. (Freeman 2010: 7)

Today, help for such firms generally takes the form of selective application of commercial laws and regulations and declaring substantial parts of the Chinese economy to be of strategic importance and thus not open for foreign investments beyond a minority stake. In green technology, for example, the PRC sees a competitive international commercial battleground that it could dominate, given the scale of its domestic market for wind and solar power.

Nevertheless, openness to direct foreign investment has also been a defining characteristic of the transition:

> FDI has contributed importantly to its exceptional growth performance ... China's success [rests on] ... market size, labor costs, quality of infrastructure, and government policies. FDI has contributed to higher investment and productivity growth, and has created jobs and a dynamic export sector. (Tseng and Zebregs 2002: 6)

Though for many countries, FDI has been an important feature of economic development strategies, the Chinese leadership had to overcome resistance based on the association of such involvement in the country with the Opium Wars discussed above. The opening up was, therefore, tentative at first and featured experiments limited to a few locations. In the 1990s, the Chinese authorities gradually relaxed their restrictions and bureaucratic hurdles to FDI.

In the late 1970s, FDI had been virtually nil and today China is the world's leading destination for such investment. Hong Kong and Taiwan are the longest standing sources of FDI but multinationals from the EU, Japan and the USA have become major players in China, especially in labour intensive manufacturing sectors. Much of the FDI has been concentrated on the eastern provinces where Special Economic Zones (SEZ) were created. In the early reform period, China allowed only joint ventures between foreign and domestic firms, except in the SEZs, but has since allowed wholly foreign-owned enterprises (Tseng and Zebregs 2002: 6).

In the decades since Deng's 'Reform and Opening Up', the way the Chinese economy functions has altered fundamentally. The reforms have allowed private firms, food rationing has ended and foreign investment has been vast. Tens of millions of people have escaped poverty and, especially along the eastern seaboard, new enterprises have flourished. The transition has not been to a fully free market but to a hybrid described as 'a socialist market economy', which is seen by other developing countries as an instructive example. The CCP definitely thinks so:

> This most recent global economic crisis has left many Chinese feeling triumphant ... There is a palpable sense among many Chinese that China's economic and political system has distinct advantages ... Despite a long-time view that the US model of development – based on the so-called 'Washington Consensus' – had much to be admired, many Chinese now perceive that there is a distinct Chinese model of growth. (Freeman 2010: 2)

Capitalism without democracy

China's transition to a substantially free market economy raised questions about how far economic reform might trigger political change, in particular because some theorists argue that a market economy is both a pre-requisite and likely cause of democracy. Economic reforms in the 1980s were accompanied by some cautious easing of political restrictions but these were abruptly revised following the massive political protests in Tiananmen Square, the symbolic national gathering point, in Beijing and in other major cities in 1989. The immediate cause of the demonstrations was the death of reformist CCP official, Hu Yaobang (胡耀邦), but this quickly became the occasion for the expression of general discontent with the political system. The protestors were not without supporters in the regime but, for the CCP leadership as a whole, they represented an unacceptable challenge. The number of people in Tiananmen Square reached 100,000 and the protest went on for weeks. Those in the Party who advocated a tough response finally won out and the PLA was ordered to clear the Square. Many protesters were killed, many more arrested and several prominent student leaders escaped to various Western countries. In the following year, the CCP was purged of supposed sympathisers of the protest. The Tiananmen events stand as a reminder of the limits on political freedom in the PRC and discussion of them in China is actively discouraged. For a short time, relations with the West were disrupted but, though the incident still resonates with public opinion, governmental contacts were restored relatively quickly. In particular: 'China's economic reforms and 'opening up' to the world had encouraged international business to forget Tiananmen Square and vie for new opportunities on the mainland' (Gittings 2005: 292).

Although there was considerable loss of momentum, the economic reforms continued after 1989 but political opening up was halted. Any development that could represent a challenge to the CCP is met by uncompromising official action. Politically, as will be discussed in Chapter 2, the CCP has sought to incorporate the newly affluent entrepreneurial class and to undergo internal reforms. Nevertheless, competition to the Party is still not being tolerated and the regime is alert to any attempt to subvert its leading role. Further, as discussed in Chapter 4, the political freedoms thought by many to be a *sine qua non* of the market system, are especially constrained.

The association of capitalism and democracy has been central to two important schools of thought. Both modernisation and structural theorists have anticipated that economic growth would have as a corollary political liberalisation. This was the pattern, after all, in the historically most successful capitalist countries, notably Britain and the US. Tsai and others argue, however, that 'China's conditions . . . differ from those of earlier industrialising countries' (Tsai 2007: 201). In particular, Tsai notes that, though there numbers have expanded rapidly, 'private entrepreneurs remain politically passive and the PRC remains authoritarian. We have, in short, a case of (emerging) capitalism without democracy'.

The political and economic order of the PRC exhibits an unusual combination of institutions – some regulating the market economy, while others bolster a Leninist one-party political establishment. While nobody would doubt the tremendous degree of change within the Chinese one-party-state, progress towards a democratic multi-party system representing differing interests within the society, the rule of law and other liberal democratic freedoms is still absent, especially when the CCP discerns any danger to its position. China's socialist market economy can, therefore, be understood as a dynamic, diffuse and post-Leninist order with a limited degree of political and social pluralism.

Conclusion

This chapter has sought to explore the ways in which China's history shapes its politics in the early twenty-first century by looking at the main legacies from the past. Many of the core features of China's political system today are still those that were put in place after 1949 and had been developed earlier in areas under Communist control during the 1920s, 1930s and 1940s. Foremost among these are: the centrality – the 'leading role' in Marxist terms – of the CCP in all major political and economic decisions; the fusion of the Party and the state, so that state institutions, not only at the high level but throughout the system, are ultimately under the control of the Party; the prohibition of alternative centres of political power, most obviously other political parties but also other social or economic organisations or movements that are perceived as potential threats to Party rule; and, the maintenance and use of a coercive state apparatus to enforce Party rule.

While these core features of the Chinese Communist system remain, the system has also evolved significantly since the reform era began at the end of the 1970s. The extreme control and regimentation of all aspects of peoples' lives that existed during the Mao era has been greatly reduced. Market economic reforms and more general social liberalisation have allowed the emergence of at least partially independent economic and social actors, although in many cases the Party retains an important stake in, and arguably a veto over, notionally independent entities. The Maoist model of a single dominant leader underpinned by a cult of personality has moved closer to a model of collective leadership. Although the top leaders still wield great power, Hu Jintao (胡锦涛) (General Secretary of the CCP, 2002–), the fourth generation leadership of the CCP, is distinctly more collegial than either Mao or his immediate predecessors in the top position such as Deng Xiaoping (Paramount Leader of the PRC1978–92, despite not holding the formal post of CCP Secretary-General) or Jiang Zemin (江泽民) (General Secretary of the CCP, 1989–2002). The fifth generation of leaders, due to assume the top jobs in 2012, seem set to continue this consensual approach to policy-making though, as Li asserts, 'the political survival of the Chinese Communist Party is the most important consideration for this new generation of leaders' (Li 2008: 55). Chapters 2, 3 and 4 will explore in more detail how key elements of this system operate and are evolving.

A second and longer-term set of legacies relate to the problem of governing a country as large as China. As this chapter has illustrated, China has a long tradition of popular protests and violent uprisings, stretching back to the imperial era, which have threatened the power of the central government. In Mandarin, 'revolution is comparable with *geming* (革命), the tradition of a violent but righteous (Heavenly) mandate to rule' after overthrowing a dynasty that has lost its heavenly mandate (Wang 1993: 73). As a consequence, China's Communist leaders are deeply sensitive to popular discontent, fearing that it could all too easily escalate to overthrow their rule. These concerns are interwoven with another element of China's historical legacy: the persistent emergence of regional power centres and regional leaders and the risk that such devolution of power will weaken the Chinese state or even lead to its *de facto* disintegration. As is explored in more detail in Chapter 3, the management of relations between the central state and the provinces is a significant issue in Chinese politics. Arguments about the necessity of maintaining political, economic and social order and ensuring the unity of the Chinese state may be used by the Communist leadership to protect their power. Nevertheless, awareness of earlier periods of disorder and disintegration is embedded in the Chinese popular consciousness – meaning that such arguments also have credibility in the eyes of the Chinese public.

Another major historical theme in Chinese politics is nationalism. China is the world's oldest continually existing political entity and the Chinese people take great pride in their country's history and achievements. Nationalism was one of Sun Yat-sen's three 'People's Principles' and the 1949 revolution was a nationalist – as well as political, economic and social – revolution, aiming to restore China as a strong and respected state. Part of the Communist Party's credibility and legitimacy, therefore, rests on its claim to be the defender of the Chinese nation-state and China's national interests, an assertion that has become all the more important with the abandonment of key elements of the Communist economic system and ideology since the late 1970s. The power of nationalism, alongside a strong historical sense of national vulnerability, helps to explain the sensitivity of two other important issues in Chinese politics. As will be explored in Chapter 5, one is the concern that China is deeply vulnerable to the threat of uprisings by its non-Chinese ethnic minorities, in particular in Tibet and Xinjiang. The other is the fear that foreign countries may take advantage of internal weakness or divisions within China, as they did during the 'century of national humiliation'.

A further issue is the extent to which legacies from the imperial era still shape contemporary Chinese politics. In many ways 1911, and even more so 1949, marked a fundamental break with the imperial era, with much of the old political, economic and social order swept away. Despite this, however, certain features of the imperial era arguably continue to shape Chinese politics. The notion of a single ruler or a single ruling regime has arguably outlived the imperial era: Mao's rule was certainly imperial in style and, even since Mao, the CCP's rule can be viewed as containing elements of an imperial system. Inter-linked with this are other legacies from the imperial era – such as the concept of the 'mandate of heaven' and the idea of a professional governing class embodied in the imperial civil service exam – which find echoes in contemporary Chinese politics. An additional legacy from the imperial era that continues to shape Chinese politics is Confucianism. Although Mao vowed to do away with it, Confucianist ideas, such as respect for authority and one's elders and the importance of hierarchy and social order, continue to have a significant sway over Chinese institutions, society and politics.

Notes

1 The exact end-point of the Cultural Revolution is a matter of debate. The main phase of violence and chaos was 1966–69, but the Cultural Revolution is often said to have extended until 1976 because only then did elements of the ideological extremism and political purges associated with the period end.
2 Qin Shi Huang's role in the Great Wall project is disputed and, though he did construct some walled fortifications, the majority of the existing wall was built during the Ming Dynasty (Waldron 1990).
3 Nanking is now known in English as Nanjing.
4 Also referred to as the Treaty of Tientsin, as the city in which the initial treaty was signed, was then known in English. The 'treaty' was, in fact, a series of treaties with the various imperial powers.
5 Formerly known as Tsingtao.
6 Also known as Empress Dowager Tz'u-His.
7 In English formerly known as Szechwan or Szechuan.
8 In English formerly known as Yüan Shih-k'ai.
9 In English formerly known as Nanking.
10 In English the city of Guangzhou was formerly known as Canton and its home province of Guangdong as Kwangtung.
11 As is discussed below, much of the country, especially the eastern coastal areas, was occupied by Japan from 1937 to 1945.
12 In English formerly known as Yen'an.
13 Manchuria is now known as Northeast China, Guandong (关东) or Dongbei (东北).
14 Now known as Shenyang (沈阳).

2

The Party-state

The CCP is at the heart of Chinese politics. In Western liberal democracies, the separation between state and political parties is a fundamental principle and political parties compete via regular elections to govern the state. In the Chinese system, the formal separation between state and Party has little meaning with the CCP and the state effectively merged. Most people, irrespective of the political system, judge politics by its outputs – material and ideological. The PRC's political system's principal offerings of stability, prosperity and national pride enjoy widespread support. Nevertheless, those who do run the country and who work the system are very exercised by its sustainability because, at its core, it depends on the acceptance of the CCP as a monopoly supplier, having exclusive control of politics.

> The key to the viability and durability of the ruling party in an authoritarian regime is its capacity to mobilize mass political support and maintain legitimacy. Despite the conventional wisdom that authoritarian regimes depend mainly on repression for survival, monopolistic ruling parties actually use a mixture of ideological appeal, redistributive economic policies, organizational penetration, and repression in governing their societies. (Pei 2006: 181)

The Party strategists assess ideas and technologies for their impact on its leading role. They fear anything they cannot control. They worry that citizens in significant numbers might come to question the political system itself. They reason that:

> economic growth ... while providing a short term fillip to party legitimacy, was ... bound to be exhausted ... Indeed, Chinese elites have worried for years about the fleeting nature of economic success ... [and that] party rule would come under growing pressure as the satisfaction of material needs would breed immaterial ones, such as demands for political participation and pluralization, and as social inequalities fuelled a sense of injustice. (Holbig and Gilley 2010: 11–12)

Internal debate among Chinese élites is often extremely coded, as open criticism of the established order is not encouraged. But the objective of strengthening the 'governing capacity' of the Party has been explicitly on the CCP's agenda since in 2004. While the Party's monopoly is non-negotiable, its working methods are being reformed.

State/Party fusion

The key organising principle of the political system of the PRC is the leadership of the CCP. The Party is at the hub of all public policies. Such single party dominance is not unique to China, as there are monopoly parties in other countries. Yet the distinctive feature of Chinese politics is the fusion of Party and state. As Zheng, Jong and Koppenjan observe from their case study of health policy-making, 'although the ideological fervour that used to characterize the CCP seems to have subsided in recent years, its institutional position remains largely the same' (Zheng *et al.* 2010: 413).

In political science, a political party is generally understood as an openly formed association that contributes to authoritative state decision-making through promoting ideas as well as seeking and holding public office. A political party claims public support on the basis of either election or ideology or manifest destiny. Most political parties compete in elections, however imperfectly conducted, because of the mantle of legitimacy associated with the ballot box. But this is not essential. What is essential is that the party be separate from the state at least formally even if the distinction is *de facto* empty. This does not occur in the PRC where the division is indeed a fiction.

> The basis of Chinese state-party constitutionalism requires a reconception of an understanding of constitution ... as understood in the West ... [and] on a different understanding of the character of the Communist Party – not as a political party or as a private actor but as an integral part of the institutional structure of government, and more importantly, as the holder of political citizenship. (Backer 2009: 101)

Nevertheless, the political science perspective prompts a comparison of the CCP with parties elsewhere and helps isolate changes in its survival strategy.

Structure and conduct
Formally, the highest authority in the CCP rests with the National Congress (中国共产党全国代表大会),[1] which meets at least once every 5 years.[2] Its two functions are to approve changes to the Party consti-

tution and to elect a Central Committee to run the CCP between National Congress meetings. Elections to the Committee are carefully orchestrated and reflect the realities of emerging CCP power dispositions. The outcomes are not in doubt but the result is a crucial signal of who is in the ascendance. The Central Committee in turn elects the Politburo of 25 members.

The Politburo is supported by the Secretariat, the principal administrative mechanism of the CCP, headed by the General Secretary. The most powerful body in practice is the Politburo Standing Committee, which currently consists of 9 members. (See further discussion in Chapter 3). The Discipline Inspection Commission, which is concerned mostly with corruption, is also high in the organisational hierarchy. In the hierarchy, it comes directly under the National Congress and sits on the same level as the Central Committee. With similar prominence is the Central Propaganda Department whose role is promoting the party's ideologies and projecting its legitimacy.

At all levels of the state structure, there are small groups of CCP members that ensure the Party's preferences and interests are reflected in policies, appointments etc. Further, in banks, universities and other agencies, which in other systems are afforded wide autonomy, party members are appointed to ensure CCP hegemony. Thus, for example, when the Politburo decided its response to the financial crisis in late 2008, central bankers and bank regulators, regardless of any professional misgivings, delivered the CCP's stimulus package without delay.

The scale of the CCP's penetration of the state machinery is remarkable and all-encompassing. According to CCP figures, 595,000 enterprises also have established Party committees of which over half are private businesses (*news.xinuanet.com* 2009).[3] Additionally, among employees, 'CCP membership is an important criterion of holding key positions in enterprise unions as a result of union affiliation to the state' (Qingjun 2010: 349).

The CCP's *nomenklatura* system of personnel management is a key element of its control. Through it, party committees have the authority to appoint, promote, demote, transfer and remove officials of even moderate importance. Notwithstanding the devolution of many economic powers, the relative liberalisation of the media and other apparent transfers of sectoral responsibility, the *nomenklatura* system remains an effective tool for maintaining discipline. Naughton and Yang credit it with holding China together in contrast to other communist regimes in which subordinates often gain power and a modicum of autonomy at the expense of the centre:

This nomenklatura personnel system is the most important institution reinforcing national unity ... Even when not actually utilized, this power remains latently available to central officials, making the Chinese political system far more unitary than it might otherwise appear ... Moreover, the personnel function is a monopoly of the Communist Party. (Naughton and Yang 2004: 9–10)

Nomenklatura authority over leaders extends one level down. So in local government, the Central Committee appoints provincial leaders; provincial party committees appoint prefecture leaders and so on. For the most part, each CCP committee manages its *nomenklatura* responsibilities through its organisation department that vets prospective leaders and significantly influences their selection through its reports. Naughton and Yang warn against underestimating the degree of hierarchical control *vis-à-vis* local autonomy, a topic which will be discussed further in Chapter 3. 'It is one of the most important bases – perhaps the ultimate foundation – of Communist Party power. But Party decision-making is not exposed to public scrutiny, and it is forbidden to publicly discuss personnel decisions or decision-making' (Naughton and Yang 2004: 10).

Popular support, legitimacy and compliance

One of the general functions of political parties everywhere is to recruit and socialise people into the political system. They also mobilise popular support for policy options and attempt to aggregate opinion even if rather narrowly. Most of the comparators to the CCP are in states that have ready recourse to repressive methods to ensure the *status quo*. Unless the methods are particulaly crude, it can be difficult to assess the extent of bullying and intimidation in such systems because the techniques used are insidious and secretive. Nevertheless, there is much evidence of harassment, imprisonment and the cynical misuse of the judicial system for political purposes in the PRC. (See Chapter 4 for further discussion of dissent in China.) A central assumption of this book is that, in the long run, repression is an expensive and unreliable method for preserving a monopoly party's position as compared to consent or, at least, assent, even when this is sullenly and perfunctorily given. The CCP's primary aim is to stay in power but the key to this is to achieve popular support, legitimacy and voluntary compliance.

The CCP is the world's largest party. As of mid-2011, the total membership was 80.27 million. The formal basis of its power is the role assigned to it in the Chinese constitution.[4] All Chinese state functions are under the control of the CCP. Nevertheless, it is important to recognise, China is an authoritarian rather than totalitarian state. The power of the CCP, while being pervasive, does not extend to the control of everything. Totalitarianism permits no independent, even non-political, institutions. Total control is attempted and no freedom of action is allowed in any sphere of life. So in the PRC, entrepreneurial citizens can form businesses, accumulate wealth and invest in enterprises independently of the state.

The assumed incompatibility of such an authoritarian state with the kind of quasi-capitalist market system that has emerged in China has prompted many commentators to point to an implicit instability in the country's political and social order. Extrapolating from the experience of the West that it is taken as given that liberal democracy was a corequisite of thriving capitalism. The hegemony of the Western model of democracy seemed so entrenched after the fall of 'the Wall' in 1989 that some proclaimed the 'end of history' (Fukuyama 1992). A market economy seemed to depend on the existence of democratic political institutions such as competitive parties and representative pluralist democracy. The case for the incompatibility between the market economy and the command and control politics of socialist states seemed to have been confirmed by the simultaneous restructuring of the economic and the political order in most previously socialist countries after 1989. The one astonishing exception is the People's Republic of China.

The survival of CCP rule in an increasingly pluralist social and market economic environment has been the subject of much analysis. Part of the explanation, however, must lie in the Chinese leadership's proven track record in institutional learning and innovation. An important milestone for the CCP was the Tiananmen Square challenge to its rule in 1989. Yet, contrary to its popular image in the West as a top-heavy, rigid and stagnant Leninist machine, Shambaugh demonstrates the extent to which, the CCP has adopted a self-conscious strategy with the aim of remaining ideologically flexible, organisationally responsive, relevant to its people and, crucially for its leadership, a party with a monopoly grip on power (Shambaugh 2008).

Patriotism, populism and philosophy

Seen in Western commercial terms, the Party's marketing strategy is to maintain a trusted brand with a consistent, differentiated, and relevant positioning in the marketplace of ideas and loyalties. The core products of the CCP are material and ideological and its survival depends on the delivery of both though different customers will 'demand' varying combinations. So the Party emphasises different aspects of its overall package to different audiences and at various times.

The CCP has promoted strong and stable leadership, respect for social harmony and the privileging of collective well being over individual rights by claiming that they are more grounded in local experience than the structured conflict of pluralism.

The essential claim of the CCP's marketing strategy is similar to that of its commercial counterparts. Contrary to free market competition advocates, any monopoly elements are justified in terms of maintaining the interests of the customer. In a country like this, the Party reassures doubters, competition is contra-indicated by virtue of size, diversity and history:

> China is a developing country with a territory of 9.6 million sq km, 1.3 billion people and 56 ethnic groups. To push forward modernization in such a populous country with such a vast landmass, it is imperative to have a strong core of leadership. The CCP represents the development trend of China's advanced productive forces, the orientation of China's advanced culture, and the fundamental interests of the overwhelming majority of the Chinese people. (quoted in *China.org.cn*, 15 November 2007)

The recent past (in Chinese timescales) was a dark period of Western imperialist domination, a corrupt and weak feudal ruling class and national humiliation. Bourgeois democratic institutions failed to halt the onslaught of 'domestic and foreign reactionary forces'. Without the CCP, past ignominies and weakness would be a real threat and national unity undermined.

> The strong leadership of the CCP is the fundamental guarantee for China's socialist modernization, for national unification and social harmony and stability, and for the unity of over one billion people as they work together to create a bright future. This has become a political view shared by people of all ethnic groups formed in the long years of revolution, construction and reform. (quoted in *China.org.cn*, 15 November 2007)

Harmel and Tan (2011) question the uniformity of this view but, using data from *The China Survey*,[5] find that 'feelings of satisfaction with life and with the government' explain support for China's current one-party system. Respondents were not as concerned with the dangers of 'multipartyism', a fairly abstract notion in the context of a survey of Chinese public opinion. A bare majority accepted the CCP's assertion that 'multiple parties necessarily bring chaos'. Nevertheless, 'the vast majority support the one-party regime for China, suggesting that even if Chinese citizens were to adopt more pro-democratic attitudes, rejection of the current one-party rule would not necessarily follow' (Harmel and Tan 2011: 1).

As will be discussed further in later chapters, the CCP makes increasing use of an appeal to Chinese nationalism, a chord that resonates strongly with the vast majority of the citizens of the PRC. It is important to note, however, that the dominant form of nationalism in China is not of the bottom up, ethnic and separatist type that cause dissent in European communist states. Writing about the patriotic education campaign in post-Tiananmen China, Zhao suggests that: 'Chinese nationalism was mainly reactive sentiments to foreign suppressions in modern history, and this new wave of nationalist sentiment also harboured a sense of wounded national pride and an anti-foreign (particularly the US and Japan) resentment' (Zhao 1998: 287). He goes on to suggest, however, that these feelings are leveraged by the CCP to counterbalance the declining salience of Communist ideology in post-Cold War and economically vibrant China. '[The CCP] striving to maintain authoritarian control ... warned of the existence of hostile international forces in the world perpetuating imperialist insult to Chinese pride ... Patriotism was ... used to bolster CCP power in a country that was portrayed as besieged and embattled' (Zhao 1998: 287).

Scholars of China have come to distinguish this as 'state-led nationalism' because it: 'stresses the role of the communist state as the bearer of China's historic struggle for national independence and prosperity in order to provide the legitimacy for CCP rule' (Scalapino 2007: 31).

The pride many Chinese feel in their government's model of authoritarian development is affirmed by the travails of capitalism following the post-2008 global financial crisis. Obviously, the CCP tries to avoid ethnic nationalism, even among the Han, as inappropriate for a multiethnic state but this is not easy to do. What it is more successful at, however, is presenting itself as the heir to a long tradition of Chinese achievement – this was a major theme in the 2008 Olympic Games opening ceremony in Beijing. Though the event was broadcast worldwide:

> The message is as much, if not more, for the Chinese audience – a message of a powerful authoritarian government with the will and the means to hold China together politically and territorially ... [T]he Chinese nation, whatever its exact content or territorial parameters, will persist. (Schrag 2009: 1086)

The CCP's state-led nationalism places the PRC at the centre of a 5,000-year-old Chinese civilization that exists beyond its current borders. As will be discussed further in Chapter 5, its inherent claim to Chinese or Han superiority makes it intolerant of the claims of others, notably Uyghurs or Tibetans. As Dickson affirms: 'toward the end of the Jiang [Zemin] era, the CCP followed a strongly elitist strategy ... Under the new Hu-Wen leadership, the CCP has ... emphasize[d] ... the interests of the vast majority of society ... both symbolically and substantively' (Dickson 2005: 9). The party promotes an image of ethnic harmony and downplays ethnic conflict.

The use of the media to project a sympathetic image of the current leadership will be discussed later, it is useful here, however, to note the increasing importance of populism for the CCP because it too shows the ideological adroitness of the Party in garnering popular support. The harnessing of populist sentiment also points to a danger similar to that associated with nationalism because both can generate a fervour that the political élite may struggle to control. Populism, like nationalism, appeals to a sense of unity among 'the people' though the definition of the group can be very divisive. For the CCP, the danger is that populism's 'other' can easily become the élite itself. For the Party to use populist appeals by trying to show that it is close to the ordinary citizen, it must be able to deflect blame for grievances to others. Clearly, foreigners often fit the bill but some kinds of discontent can remain troublingly local. Thus, the popular energy generated to denounce the West's criticism of the Olympics and of the PRC's policy on Tibet could be used to rail against corruption. Pei, who is not as sanguine as some commentators about the CCP's survival capacity, sees other dangers from the use of populist appeals at times of economic downturn:

> Rising social discontent may not be enough to force the party out of power, but it might be sufficient to tempt some members of the elite to exploit the situation to their own political advantage. Such political entrepreneurs could use populist appeals to weaken their rivals and, in the process, open up divisions within the party's seemingly unified upper ranks. (Pei 2009: 2)

CCP social base as strategy

It's easy to forget that the 74–million-strong Chinese Communist Party is a large and diverse organization. Elderly cadres, still influenced by Maoist antipathy to tradition, often condemn any efforts to promote ideologies outside of a rigid Marxist framework. But the younger cadres in their 40s and 50s tend to support such efforts, and time is on their side. (Bell, quoted in *New York Times*, 11 May 2009)[6]

Today, the CCP's membership is 5.5 per cent of the total population of China organised officially according to democratic centralism but with an emphasis on top-down control. Internal dissent is frowned upon and the Party aims at promoting the loyalty and compliance of local-level activists. As Zheng reflects in the context of China's 'openness' policy:

> The existing ruling class [CCP officials and bureaucrats] was strongly resistant ... To overcome the resistance ... the Deng [Xiaoping] leadership adopted a strategy of 'external reform first, and internal reform later,' ... The rationale behind this strategy is that external reforms are easier to undertake than internal ones ... deeply entrenched vested interests which had consolidated their positions in the three decades of Maoist rule. (Zheng 2008: 9)

The Party operates in very diverse conditions in terms of levels of local economic development, urbanisation and ethnic tension. The current leadership has, therefore, sought to promote an integrated ideology that addresses potential divisive economic and social concerns. The rhetoric of the CCP talks of creating a 'harmonious society' using the concept of 'scientific development' but the tone is much more nationalist than socialist. Nevertheless, as Shambaugh makes very clear, ideology is very significant (Shambaugh 2008).

For a monopoly party, the demographic character of its organisation is an important strategic consideration. Around 21 per cent of the membership is female and ethnic minorities account for 6.5 per cent compared to 8 per cent in the population. Both figures represent increases but more significant is the broadening of the social range. Traditionally the CCP was supposed to represent only five major groups, namely workers, peasants, intellectuals, the military and state officials. In fact, in recent years, the Party has widened its social base even to include the once ideologically spurned private entrepreneurs.

> CCP members now are younger and better educated ... [It] has been undergoing a drastic transformation from being peasantry and workers based to being a 'catchall' party. Party members now come from increasingly diverse social and economic backgrounds ... Embracing the new social classes will certainly enable the party to expand its social base ... In order to sustain the country's development, the new leadership continues to institutionalize the political influence of the newly rising social groups. (Zheng 2008: 24)

The success of this strategy can be gauged from Dickson's assertion that the new business recruits have become partners with the CCP in promoting economic growth while maintaining the political *status quo* (Dickson 2008). Chen and Dickson, drawing on a survey of private entrepreneurs in five coastal provinces, show that they:

> are closely tied to the state through political and financial relationships, and these ties shape their views toward democracy. While most . . . favor multi-candidate elections under the current one-party system, they do not support . . . multi-party competition and political liberties . . . The key to regime support lies in the capitalists' political beliefs and their assessment of the government's policy performance. China's capitalists tend to be conservative and status-quo oriented. (Chen and Dickson 2010: 79)

Some estimates suggest that a third of private business people are CCP members including a similar proportion of China's 500 richest citizens (Li 2009: 20).

According to Shambaugh, the Party is so conscious of the importance of its membership to its popular image that, after a recent vetting, 44,738 members were expelled as unfit or unqualified. According to media reports, 'the CCP actually rejected 80% of membership applicants'.[7] Similarly, there has been a rapid turnover in the CCP's Central Committee, Politburo and Standing Committee. The Party, despite being a monopoly, is quite openly self-conscious about the link between the perception of its members by the public and popular support. In June 2008, for instance, it published a five-year plan calling for better systems to prevent and punish official corruption, including more public consultation. 'Resolute punishment and effective prevention of corruption has a relation to whether the people support or oppose the party and whether it lives or dies' (quoted in *AFP*, 23 June 2008). By 2011, Hu Jintao, speaking to the CCP's anti-corruption commission, 'pledged to combat graft strictly and punish corrupt officials severely so as to win trust from the people' (cited in *English.xinhuanet.com*, 10 January 2011). Similarly, expressions of concern about public reaction to low ethical standards among officials continue to be a theme in the speeches of the CCP leadership.

The role of local membership in safeguarding the image of the party is well acknowledged. This was illustrated in the major earthquake in 2008 by the very rapid setting up of branches in the tented relief camps in the areas most devastated. The state press agency quotes Shoulun, head of one such tiny branch: 'although we have no party flag or office, we surely play an important role in easing people's minds, maintaining social order and leading the work of epidemic prevention' (cited in *Xinhua Economic News Service*, 28 May 2008).

The leadership of the CCP is very aware of the sudden demise of other monopoly parties and the perils of organised transitions. Though it appears unassailable now, collapses in Eastern Europe hold cautionary messages. The implosion of autocratic regimes in North Africa in 2011 was also looked at very cautiously in Beijing. Citing the behavioural logic of the commercial world, Pei suggests: 'like corporate monopolies that eventually succumb to the ills of inefficiency, political monopolies like the CCP, in the absence of competitive pressures from rival parties, will inevitably develop a full range of pathologies such as cynicism, patronage, organizational dystrophy, and unresponsiveness' (Pei 2006: 188). Other authors argue that, on the contrary, the CCP's programme of renewal and reform at the grassroots level has strengthened its capacity at higher levels to maintain an 'authoritarian resilience' (Brødsgaard and Zheng 2006).

The advantages of a dense network of party members influencing all aspects of public life may be dissipated by unpopular behaviour by the few. The CCP's strategy to resist its own demise is evident in several trends within the Party's membership profile, its use of the media and the employment of ICT.

CCP's adroit use of the media, discussed more fully later, was highlighted by the positioning of the leadership in coverage of the disastrous earthquake in Sichuan in 2008.[8] As *The Economist* noted, 'despite not having to face elections, China's Communist Party wants to be liked' (quoted in *The Economist*, 14 June 2008). Prime minister, Wen Jiabao or 'Grandpa' Wen was shown on the state television broadcasts in the earthquake zone, wearing trainers, ordering troops through a megaphone and comforting victims. The image of a Party close to the people was reinforced at impromptu news conferences amid swirling helicopters. Similar messages were contained in pictures of Wen joining stranded travellers during a major disruption to public transport over a holiday weekend in January 2008. More subtly, during a domestic media blackout of serious labour protests in Guangzhou in 2010, Wen addressed migrant workers in Beijing telling them: 'our society's wealth and tall buildings are embodiments of your toil and sweat ... Your labour is glorious and deserves respect from all society' (Mitchell 2010).

The 2008 examples of a responsive CCP have been taken by many Western commentators to signal a new openness in Chinese politics but much of the public message evokes older symbols of social solidarity. Heroic troops digging through debris to find victims, 'diligent' officials and 'grateful' victims are the long established staple of the official media in the PRC. A similar situation occurred after the 2010 earthquake in the northern part of Qinghai province. The devastation was on a comparable scale and the response was likewise portrayed to emphasise unity and cooperation. Premier Wen Jiabao, visiting the rescue effort said: 'your suffering is our suffering, your family members are our family members'.[9]

These comments in particular were aimed to assuage ethnic tensions as the suffering population was predominantly Tibetan and there had been local criticism of the central government's initial response.[10] The Party was keen to show that its efforts were unstinting. Nevertheless, the CCP felt it had to write out of the media accounts the contribution of the large number of Buddhist monks who mobilised to assist the local population. Television pictures shown on PRC based-stations featured almost exclusively rescue efforts by state personnel, many of whom wore uniforms with the word 'China' emblazoned in English on their backs. Chinese flags also flew incongruously among mounds of debris. CCP leaders on national television spoke only in Mandarin, a language little understood by the shaken population. A national day of mourning, during which all television stations showed uninterrupted official news footage, underlined the message of solidarity.[11] Business leaders and celebrities were encouraged to present large donations in front of the cameras. A natural disaster was thus 'used' as a marketing opportunity to promote loyalty to the CCP.

There is, however, a shadow side to this marketing opportunity. The challenge to the CCP is how to handle public discontent in the period after the initial wave of shock and grief associated with catastrophes has dissipated. For monopoly parties, survival strategies need to employ means of deflecting issues of 'accountability' for catastrophes and major disruptions. Major failures of public policy, even if triggered by natural disasters or extraordinary weather, can create millions of potential political malcontents. The CCP's actions are partially targeted at this group. The state can, of course, also employ more repressive instruments but these are less efficient.

In 2008, after the initial relief work, there was some very clumsy bullying of potential critics among the survivors, especially the parents of school children that died when poorly constructed public buildings collapsed (Wong, quoted in *New York Times*, 24 July 2008). It is not possible to know how high up in the organisation this kind of action was sanctioned but it undermined the initial public relations gains. The foreign press frequently reports similar and even more petty acts of repression by the police and local officials, especially the vicarious application of rules or cancellation of permits, visas etc. Any strategy drawn up at headquarters is only as good as its local implementation.

Pei warns: 'polling data suggest that local governments may have lost their legitimacy, but the central government has maintained a surprisingly high level of authority in the eyes of ordinary citizens' (Pei 2006: 203).

The CCP leadership has spent very considerable resources on continuing professional development for Party members especially in their 'mid-career' grades but the principal agent issues are very significant. The Party leadership, conscious of the unintended consequences of radical reforms in the former Soviet Union and other Eastern European countries, is keen to keep tight control of the internal reform process. Li (2008) assessing Chinese democratic development cites a survey of mid-level officials at the Central Party School showing 90 per cent of the respondents indicated that they were not enthusiastic about political reform. He quotes an editorial from *Shijie ribao* (*World Journal*): 'neglect of the need for political reforms among CCP officials is the new hidden problem for the Hu-Wen administration' (quoted in *Shijie ribao*, 25 December 2006).

Monopoly parties generally find it difficult to impose organisational rules in relation to succession and promotion though these may be essential to avoid major lurches in political philosophy or in marketing and other functions. An intensive internal debate about China's market reforms has taken place and some observers detect the evolution of interest groups within the CCP. In addition, the two major cliques within the Party – the so-called Gang of Princelings (Taizidang, 太子党), the offspring of party elders, and the Communist Youth League faction – continue to jockey for position in anticipation of the Eighteenth CCP Congress in 2012 when the current leadership yields power. Nevertheless, Hu Jintao's ideological dominance seems unrivalled (Holbig 2007; Shambaugh 2007). As Miller shows: '[despite] tensions early on between the paramount leader's personalized power (*renzhi*) and the CCP's institutional norms and rules for collective leadership ... two decades of institutional development have made Chinese leadership politics more stable, regular, and on the whole, more predictable' (Miller 2008a: 2).[12]

Miller presents a picture of 'deliberate', 'incremental' and 'dynamic' institutionalisation in élite promotion, retirement regulations, policy formulation and political succession. She sees these as signs of a newly consolidated 'leadership work system' and increasingly consensus-oriented collective leadership. The so-called Fifth Generation of leaders that emerged at the Seventeenth Party Congress in October 2007 and the Eleventh National People's Congress in March 2008 is likely to continue the organisational reforms (Miller 2011).[13] Despite speculation of a rift in the hierarchy on how to respond to the collapse of other authoritarian regimes in 2011, Miller asserts:

> China's leadership under Hu Jintao has functioned as an oligarchic collective that appears to make decisions on the basis of consensus ... As a consequence, leadership differences over power and policy ... [are] fought out behind a rigorously sustained public façade of leadership unity and discipline. (Miller 2011: 11)

Use of the media, market research and ICT

As with all political systems, feedback is vital to the policy process. Monopolies, however, do not experience the same acute market prompts as their equivalents in competitive environments. Yet, it is especially necessary for them to be responsive and alert. The CCP relies on both internal and external mechanisms to gauge popular reactions including the use of market research. For example, a survey conducted by the Beijing-based China Mainland Marketing Research Company showing that citizens rate corruption, unemployment and the widening income gap as the top three social problems was cited by the CCP at a meeting attended by Hu Jintao in 2006 (*People's Daily On line*, 17 June 2006). As Zhang outlines, the CCP uses surveys: 'to justify their reform policies by referring to "public opinion" and to mobilize the public consent ... Surveys are still heavily regulated by the government and the Party draws resources from the market to conduct polls for its public control' (Zhang 2003).

Some published survey material is surprisingly frank about the Party itself. In 2010, for example, the *People's Daily* (人民日报), which is strictly controlled by the CCP, published the results of an on-line poll that found that 91 per cent of respondents believed all rich families have political backgrounds. This was taken as a reference to the nepotism and the wealth of the 'princelings' (quoted in *Financial Times*, 29 March 2010).

The marketing of a unified image to the external world glosses over the internal machinations of the CCP making them difficult to analyse. As Murphy explains: 'the process is opaque for good reason: the popular legitimacy of a one-party authoritarian regime depends in no small part on the outward appearance of inner consensus. To most casual observers, therefore, Beijing projects an almost monolithic sensibility' (Murphy 2008: 3).

Even though details might be vague, the CCP, like all political parties, does have both formal and informal methods of articulating and aggregating intelligence. For example, the Seventeenth Party

Congress in October 2007, cited above, offered some important insights on China's future political and economic direction as proposed by the CCP.

> While recognising our achievements ... they still fall short of expecta-tions of the people ... [E]conomic growth is realised at an excessively high cost of resources and the environment. There remains an imbalance ... between urban and rural areas ... There are still many problems affecting ... employment, social security, income distribution, education, public health, housing, production safety, administration of justice and public order ... some low-income people lead a rather difficult life. (Hu Jintao, quoted in the *Shanghai Daily Online*, 15 October 2007)

Party Congress debates are staged managed but, as discussed in Chapter 4, increasingly arguments over policy direction are acknowl-edged.

At a broader level, Leonard observes how a monopoly party (not his expression) needs frank debate more than its counterparts in competi-tive systems. Thus, in China, party forums, universities, semi-independent think tanks, journals and, in a different way, the internet all contribute to the debate about policy direction.

> Paradoxically, the power of the Chinese intellectual is amplified by China's repressive political system ... [i]ntellectual debate in this world can become a surrogate for politics. (Leonard 2008: 17)

The Party is experimenting with various marketing devices on what, for China, is a small scale. So focus groups, 'deliberative polling' and random consultations are all being tried though all within a controlled environment that discourages questions about the Party's leading role. Similarly, elections are held at village level but they:

> are designed to increase mass support for the Party, and grassroots democracy is understood to be fully compatible with strong state control. In this context, the self-government programme is best seen as an effort to rejuvenate village leadership by cleaning out incompetent, corrupt and high-handed cadres, all for the purpose of consolidating the current regime. (O'Brien and Li 2000: 489)

The use of various techniques for gauging opinion in China is often first undertaken on an experimental basis and then incrementally expanded. An assessment of their usefulness as market research for the monopoly party is somewhat obscured by the emphasis in the litera-ture on whether they represent the early sprouting of Western democratic competition. The focus here, however, is on their use as part of a strategy to copperfasten the CCP's position.

The CCP has rapidly embraced the internet as a means of both market research and promotion. The prime minister, Wen Jiabao, advocated in May 2008 using the internet as a source of 'customer' feedback. He is reported to use Facebook himself. In February 2011, Wen Jiabao held a two-hour online interview with citizens in which he pledged to reduce food costs, tackle surging property prices, punish corruption and address China's growing wealth gap. The CCP is, of course, making a virtue out of necessity. Home installation of broadband, blogging, instant messaging, emailing, online chatting and internet forums have been growing exponentially especially since 2004, although still low by comparison to Europe, the US and other developed countries (quoted in *Reuters*, 15 January 2010). In 2010, there were 384 million internet users and 3.23 million web sites in China (CINIC 2009). A Pew survey conducted in May 2008 showed that: 'more than one-in-three Chinese report using the internet (38 per cent) and owning a computer (36 per cent), and one-in-four send email at least occasionally. The use of information technology is more common among the young, educated, wealthy and urban' (PGPA 2008: 6). The vast bulk of internet use has no explicit political intent and concerns shopping, entertainment and other sources of day-to-day information.

While it encourages internet use for business[14] as well as for education, the state is, of course, also wary of its use by political rivals.

> The government believes that this task demands a great control of infor-
> mation flows. It is vital to let the citizens know what it wants them to
> know ... On the other hand, both the leadership and the bureaucracy
> need to be well informed of any problems that may damage the state's
> image and control. (Zhang 2002)

It tries to block access to websites deemed subversive or showing anti-government protests such as those in Tibet in March 2008. The internet has also facilitated protests to occur almost spontaneously. This happened in June 2008 outside a police station in Weng'an County in Guizhou province after pictures and video linked to an alleged rape and murder were posted (quoted in *UK Reuters*, 28 June 2008). Thousands of protesters, convinced of a cover-up, took to the street. Even quick response by the authorities could not prevent the ensuing riot. As with similar instances of protest over the behaviour of public servants, the CCP had no way of distancing itself from the incidents other than severe public punishment of the state officials presumed to be involved where possible.

Similarly, state officials were quick to disrupt internet traffic discussing the unrest and revolts in authoritarian countries in the Middle East and North Africa in early 2011. The suggestion of a 'Jasmine Revolution', a name borrowed from the Tunisian revolt, brought a partial block on the word 'jasmine' on popular social networking sites and chat rooms. The word occurs too often in everyday Chinese culture for a blanket prohibition by the censors.[15] The task that those in authority face in controlling the new media was further illustrated in July 2011 when news of a fatal high speed train crash, which the censors had hoped to 'manage', was the subject of over four million messages on Sina Weibo, China's equivalent of Twitter, within hours. Ominously for the official version of the derailment in Wenzhou, a poll on Sina Weibo recorded 98 per cent of participants believed evidence of the causes of the derailment was being deliberately hidden.[16] Interestingly, the state-run *Global Times* commented in both its English and Chinese language versions:

> Chinese society is changing and public democracy is booming in the Internet era, but the arrogance of certain authorities has stagnated. (27 July 2011)

The government devotes considerable resources to controlling politics on the internet but the Party also seeks to use it as a positive marketing tool. Official web sites, have content that is 'on message', and are slick and full of features. The CCP is reported to pay part-time writers to participate in blogs and bulletin boards to 'steer public opinion and monitor the tone of debate online' (Yardley 2008). For the authorities, it is easier than is the case for the internet to control the print media.

Despite the size of the market and the number of titles, newspaper and magazine editors are more vulnerable to pressure.

> While the triad of state coercion – administrative punishment, imprisonment and violence – touches less than 0.2% [of journalists] . . . in China, deep-rooted uncertainty about the boundaries of the permissible magnifies the effect of these isolated incidents . . . [U]npredictable flashes of repression instill fear and amplify silence. (Hassid and Stern 2010)

Of course, there are attempts to test the boundaries but both central and local government monitors criticism in print closely. Even popular journals are not exempt from closure and other penalties. Thus, for example, in 2010, *Party* (独唱团),[17] a new magazine published by Han Han, an iconic figure for young Chinese as a racing car driver and blogger, which sold 1.5 million copies of its only edition, was closed because its indirect but edgy social comment offended the censors. It failed to secure a publisher for a second issue. In 2009, the international NGO Freedom House suggested that:

> China's media environment remained one of the world's most restrictive ...
> The Chinese authorities increased censorship and pro government
> propaganda ... during the periods surrounding high-profile events, such as
> politically sensitive anniversaries ... While central authorities tolerated, and
> possibly encouraged, investigative reporting on localized corruption, lower-
> level officials sought to repress such reports. (Freedom House 2010: 84)

The Chinese state nevertheless has to deal occasionally with 'bad' news and there are interesting parallels in the private sector. The internet has had an impact on how businesses deal with unwelcome events such as product safety compromises or accidents. Together, on-the-spot reporting, emails, text messaging and voice calls undermine the attempts, perhaps strongest in monopolies, to bury unwelcome news. The SARS incident, a serious health scare in 2003, was handled badly by the Party. The CCP monitored the widespread online criticism of officialdom but it struggled to contain it. Private reporting and public denial fed popular anxiety. Thus, the more sensitive change in the reporting style noted above in the coverage of the Sichuan earthquake.

Patriotism is an important element in the Party's offer; cyber nationalists, such as those who target Japanese issues, are often ahead of official policy. This incongruence between the official and netizens' positions illustrates a dilemma for the CCP. As Datong reports: 'Chinese politicians are increasingly aware that in the online age, trying to control the distribution of information only succeeds in damaging the government's image' (Datong 2008). The impulse to deal with the internet heavy-handedly is still sometimes evident. During the Xinjiang riots in 2009, for example, the government cut off the internet in parts of the province for six months. The disruption irked Uyghurs and Han alike. Many in the CCP, however, realise that there is little point in such blanket measures as they simply alienate large groups of citizens. The Party is trying instead to deal with the internet proactively. Yang (2009) calls the use of the internet by citizens to engage in political debate 'citizen activism online'. In his analysis, 'popular nationalism' is among the top issues but he shows that the subject matter is extremely diverse. Both the activists and the government have, in his view, tacitly agreed what is acceptable and what not. In this way, the internet has become a genuine mechanism for some bottom-up input into the policy process. So, for example, the outrage on the internet about suggestions of corruption and mismanagement in the rolling out of the high-speed train project that followed the July 2011 accident is likely to temper future infrastructural transport projects. As Xu Wu, reviewing Yang's book, puts it:

> Twenty years after ... Tiananmen Square, the majority of Chinese people and their leaders ... seem to share one ironclad consensus: evolution is better than revolution. This common mind-set explains the central government's unreserved enthusiasm toward online technology, as well as the preference of various activist groups for negotiation rather than confrontation. Certainly, omnipresent censorship and political pressures contribute to this cooperative relationship, but these factors are only secondary.[18]

In the West, much negative attention has been given to the 'Great Firewall of China', the monitoring of internet activity, and the associated censoring of political comment (Pei 2006).[19] The dispute with Google, the internet search provider, in 2010 ensured the issue got worldwide coverage. For Chinese speakers, clever use of homophones to evade the censors has become a particular feature of discourse among netizens. The content of videos in this genre posted on the internet in response to censorship, such as the government's 2009 'anti-vulgarity campaign', is often both lewd and funny. Little has been written, however, about the direct use by the CCP of the internet as a marketing tool. Nevertheless, the Party has much to gain even from the netizens' political contestation. As Xu Wu suggests in relation to the marketing perspective of digital contention in China, it can be:

> a win-win-win situation for the parties involved: the commercial online portals received surging Web traffic, the online activists received all kinds of social capital, and the government received a cost-effective pressure-reducing valve or an emergency alert system.[20]

The CCP is, as Holbig and Gilley describe it, 'an assiduous poller and a trenchant analyst of its own legitimacy' (Holbig and Gilley 2010: 11). It avails of polling data to keep track of popular reactions. For example, just ahead of the March 2008 National People's Representatives Congress (NPC, 全国人民代表大会) and People's Political Consultative Conference (CPPCC, 政协) 'two sessions' (两会), the Party carried out polling on a number of policy areas and, as it had done continually since 2006, published at least some of the rather critical responses via the state news agency.[21] Unsurprisingly, the public's concerns were reported to be rising commodity prices, housing and corruption. More notably, the public's largely critical assessment of the government's handling of the January 2008 snow-storms-induced transport chaos was also made known. As Leonard affirms: 'the regime seems to be developing increasingly sophisticated techniques to prolong its survival and pre-empt discontent' (Leonard 2008).

The 2010 version of the poll informed the NPC that the top issues were corruption followed by house prices (survey published in *Chinadaily.com.cn*, 1 June 2010). In 2011, a similar poll reported in the *People's Daily* put 'affordable housing' in the number one spot.[22] Polls are even published that reflect popular sentiment on governance *per se* but criticism is very muted and generic. The Global Poll Center, a subsidiary of the Beijing English language newspaper the *Global Times*, published figures in March 2011 showing that:

> 38.5 per cent of respondents believed the central government should be the most important force behind the [economic] restructuring, and 13.1 per cent said State-owned enterprises should be the driving force.[23]

Hardly criticism, but the respondents were being asked to comment on the balance between state and private control over the economy. Only 16.8 per cent thought the goal of restructuring should be 'to explore an economic development path with Chinese characteristics'.

In the PRC, particularly in urban areas, the mobile phone is ubiquitous. It is regularly used for voting though only by the entertainment media. In 2005, for instance, 40 million Chinese voted for their favourite singers through mobile phone text messages. Its use by the CCP was demonstrated in March 2008 at the full sessions of the NPC and the CPPCC when Wen Jiabao took text questions in an 'Ask the Premier' slot. According to the *People's Daily*, more than '250,000 short messages, a substantial portion of which were from blue-collars, farmers, and students' were received. The paper went on to 'explain': 'the Chinese government encourages grass-root citizens to "orderly participate in politics" to expand democracy ... mobile phone messages are becoming a new way for the Chinese to participate in politics, in addition to the traditional way of direct voting at grass-root level' (cited in *People's Daily*, 13 March 2008).

Mobile phone users in China do not enjoy much data protection so dissident voices may be easily monitored. Nevertheless, the volume of calls from over 300 million subscribers is so great that censorship is almost impractical on a broad scale.[24] As Li points out in commenting on the impact of new restrictions introduced in 2010: 'It's not because the government does not want to regulate the mobile Web, it's because the system and the situation makes it much harder to regulate the mobile Web than the real Web ... Technically, for the moment, the mobile Web is less regulated than the real Web' (quoted in *cnn.com*, 15 June 2010). The major use of phone records is for marketing research.

Relationship with other social actors

Among the methods for maintaining the CCP's monopoly is a new relationship with other social actors such as non-governmental organisations (NGOs).

> People living in China in 1978 would not recognize the degree of civic and political freedom in the country today. New social forces unleashed by China's economic reforms have been transforming the country's political landscape. The expansion of new social and economic groups alone has been spectacular. (Li 2008: 2)

Due to recent reforms, NGOs have increased not just in number but their scope has altered significantly. Many have been created and sponsored by the state as a way of subcontracting certain functions that it used to perform.

> CCP is ridding itself of some functions to enable it to become more efficient in carrying out others ... The Chinese party-state is restructuring its governing institutions, and it is reinventing itself ... The state is withdrawing, market forces are given greater rein, and government functions are delegated while others are contracted out or privatised. Reforms ... do not, however, necessarily lead to a reduced state involvement ... On the contrary, the state is reasserting itself. (Edin 2003: 1)

This process may be seen as similar to the Osborne and Gaebler maxim of 'steering not rowing'. The caveat remains that other social actors: 'perform their role according to the party's wishes they will be 'helping hands' rather than independent organizations' (Zheng 2008).

As will be explored further in Chapter 4, coercion remains a method for dealing with groups whose potential strength or political purpose threatens the CCP's hegemony but consensus forming and negotiation are more efficient. 'When coming to the political process, the CCP becomes the key determinant since it decides whether and how to open the process to different social forces' (Zheng 2008).

Of course, such relationships have to be reciprocal and neighbourhood groups, environmentalists and other nascent NGOs need to see results. What is less often acknowledged is the 'use' of NGOs to bolster internal party policy debates. Party officials, especially those with a role in policy for marginalised sections of Chinese society, have been known to 'seek popular support to increase their clout' (French 2008). The CCP is slow to acknowledge that such pressure produces results but officials who can point to expressions of concern from the NGOs may be more likely to be heeded. Indeed, Yadav shows that the need for accurate and regular feedback from the business community in particular means that the CCP:

> is not as dominant a figure in business lobbying strategies as most of the literature claims. Given the institutional design of the policy system that has been in practice in China since the 1982 constitution onwards, individuals with certain desirable characteristics are also lobbied with surprisingly high frequency. (Yadav 2008: 75)

The points of influence for business groups are, Yadav suggests, CCP members holding key local and provincial level offices. He also suggests that the NPC legislative process, long ignored as perfunctory in the literature, affords opportunities for lobbying:

> At each reading, the designated committee can visit various places, hold conferences with administrators and government technical experts, as well as invite outside experts, groups and individuals to comment on the bill. This stage offers one of the best and most accessible opportunities for groups and organizations to present technically relevant information. (Yadav 2008: 78)

Such NGO inputs, which do on occasion lead to policy changes, can be viewed as useful but, for a monopoly party, the temptation is to see them always as an impertinence to be rebuffed. The CCP has adopted both approaches but increasingly allows local implementation of policies as a form of market testing.

> This increasing political importance of local jurisdictions should create major incentives for groups to lobby at the local level rather than the central level. Local officials are more easily accessed and influenced and, in general, delivering politically at the local level in response to interest groups pressure is easier than at the national level. (Yadav 2008: 79)

Yadav's research, which involved comparison with the more competitive Indian political system, shows that: 'information is more valued and used in the Chinese policy system because it provides political value for both the CCP and individual policymakers at every level' (Yadav 2008: 82). As with any large enterprise, effective local knowledge allows problems to be dealt with before they get out of hand (Fewsmith 2008).

Major marketing opportunities

For all politicians, whatever the regime type, association with successful sporting and cultural events is a major marketing chance. The 2008 Olympic Games, held in Beijing, were an unprecedented opportunity for the CCP to mobilise the patriotism of the Chinese (Gottwald and Duggan 2008). The Games also facilitated the internal Party reforms by giving a sense of urgency within the organisation. The popular expectations and international attention associated with the Games were used by the CCP though both also represented potential dangers. The Party was wary that intensified world scrutiny and political demonstrations before the 1988 Olympic Games contributed to the fall of the military dictatorship in South Korea.

Even if the Chinese had not sought deliberately to leverage the Games as a marketing opportunity, the international media attention alone would have influenced the way the PRC was seen abroad. As Manzenreiter observes, the Olympics are generally taken to be an appropriate occasion for projecting a positive message:

> because of the easy association with the Games' positive images of excellence, fairness, universal friendship and mutual exchange ... However, these platforms are extremely difficult to control. Meaning is never uncontested, and free riders or interlopers are striving to seize the opportunity to perform in a global theatre of representation.[25]

In the event, the Chinese government made a very conscious effort to capture the marketing opportunity presented to them and, though foreigners were important, the internal Chinese audience was the prime target. The themes were not new and prominent among them were the CCP's role in Chinese history and social harmony.

Nationalism is an essential ingredient in the Party's justification of its monopoly. A heroic narrative, emphasised in the spectacular opening ceremony, places the CCP as the saviour of China in 1949 while airbrushing out events between then and the reforms of the late 1970s. The 2008 Games highlighted this orthodoxy as well as other messages:

> The design of the mascots and the display of the ethnic minorities at the opening ceremony both delivered a harmonious message acknowledging their differences as much as their shared happiness under Communist party rule.[26]

Of course, this version of history is particularly challenged by rival minority ethnic, religious and nationalistic interpretations. For example, as will be discussed more fully in Chapter 5, the official history of Tibet emphasises the freeing of this integral part of China from feudalism and economic backwardness. Events in 2008, when the Olympics were being exploited to present a very positive image of the CCP at home and abroad, challenged the core message.

Similarly, the provinces of Xinjiang and Yunnan witnessed violent protests at CCP rule, which was presented less as liberation with social and economic advancement than ethnic domination by the majority ethnic group, the Han who are about 92 per cent of the population.

As Li affirms: 'Hu Jintao and other top leaders have publicly placed priority on enhancing social harmony, the frequent occurrence of ethnic-related riots and other incidents in the country significantly undermines the central leadership's claims to be building a "harmonious society"' (Li 2008: 1). An important part of the CCP marketing strategy, therefore is to present itself as an all-China organisation and its potential challengers as at least misinformed or, more tellingly for the majority of its audience, under foreign influence. Thus, being 'wrapped in the flag' is very important for the monopoly party. The CCP leadership keenly promoted its 'soft power' agenda by exploiting events such as the 2010 Shanghai Expo. Major public events are, therefore, full of the symbolism of unity both culturally and rhetorically even when, to an outside audience, this might appear tokenist and clichéd.

Conclusion

The PRC shares with other political systems the central task of orderly government – ready acceptance of the restraints, benefits and obligations that it allocates to its citizens. For the most part, it is successful though, again in common with all governments, the Chinese government does employ force when its will is challenged. Indeed, because, in an authoritarian state, almost any dissent can be categorised as a challenge, the threshold for repression is much lower than in liberal democracies. The Chinese state is notably intolerant of anything that appears to be coordinated expressions of dissension. Nevertheless, the frequent use of force should be seen as a signal of a system's inefficiency and potential failure (Brady 2009).

The Chinese political system is distinguished by its *de facto* merger of the state and the ruling party. Indeed, the constitution of the PRC allocates to the CCP a leadership role not constrained by the need for competitive elections. Nevertheless, the Party realises that, to fulfil this mission and to protect its own interests, it needs to be regarded as fulfilling its side of an implicit contract to provided stability, prosperity and national pride – features often found wanting in China's recent history.

The absence of large-scale organised opposition to the CCP may be taken as evidence that the Party has broad public support within China or at least sufficient popular legitimacy to retain its hold on power. Nevertheless, the large number of protests, strikes and other incidences of public 'disorder' that take place every year in China suggest that satisfaction with the existing socio-economic – and by implication political – order is limited. Furthermore, the absence of large-scale organised opposition to the CCP rests not only on public satisfaction with the existing political system but also on continued use of repression to prevent the emergence of any such opposition. The Tiananmen Square protests of 1989 stand as a reminder that opposition to the CCP can coalesce very rapidly from smaller protests relating to 'non-political' issues into a larger political movement and the stability of the existing political order in China may be fragile.

In this chapter, the emphasis has been on the strategies and technologies employed by the CCP to assure the greater number of those within its jurisdiction that their core interests are safeguarded. The Party is attentive to popular aspirations and grievances, to the potential for rivals for the people's loyalty and to the demise of similar monopolies elsewhere. It has broadened its social base, attended to potential organisational vulnerabilities and attuned its core message to the demands of its hybrid economic system. Even so, the party/state remains vulnerable to internal division and unfulfilled popular expectation both of which can represent latent dangers to a political system with a limited understanding of loyal opposition.

In July 2011, the CCP celebrated its 90th anniversary. The event was marked by television documentaries, books, museum exhibitions and much else to make the point that the Party had re-established China to its rightful place in the world after a 'century of shame and humiliation'. It had also delivered prosperity. New histories of the CCP airbrushed past disasters, restored some reputations but reloaded the usual scapegoats with the guilt of acknowledged mistakes. The anniversary came, however, at a time of worrying upheavals in other authoritarian regimes as well as renewed ethnic tensions in Tibet, Xinjiang and Inner Mongolia. Despite being, for the most part, the flexible and learning organisation portrayed in this chapter, the CCP's reaction to this instability was to tip the policy balance in the direction of repression. The faction in the central leadership led by Prime Minister Wen Jiabao, which advocates more open politics, seemed for a time to lose the argument to others for whom political reform spells only risk and danger for the CCP's central mission – retaining its monopoly on power. This division on the future of the party-state and the correct response to uncertainties in its environment will form the context for the major leadership transition in 2012.

Notes

1 The National Congress is a CCP body as opposed to the National People's Congress, the legislature of the People's Republic of China.
2 There was 11 years between the 3 and 4 National Congress (1964 to 1975).
3 Many ostensibly private businesses have substantial state ownership so these official figures have to be treated with caution (Brødsgaard 2002).
4 Article 1 of the State Constitution describes China as a 'socialist state under the people's democratic dictatorship'.
5 Conducted with a nationwide sample in 2008.
6 See also Bell (2008).
7 http://shanghaiist.com/2010/06/29/ccp_membership_now_up_to_78_million.php.
8 Referred to as the 'Wenchuan' earthquake in China reflecting the precise main area affected.
9 John Vause's CNN report on 14 April 2010, sourced at: http://edition.cnn.com/2010/WORLD/asiapcf/04/14/china.quake/index.html.
10 Tibetan 97.25 per cent, Han 2.56 per cent and Hui 0.01 per cent according to *2005 Yushu Statistical Yearbook*, www.absoluteastronomy.com/topics/Gy%C3%AAgu_Tibetan_Autonomous_Prefecture, accessed 30 April 2010.
11 Cnn.com, 30 April 2010, sourced at http://edition.cnn.com/video/#/video/world/2010/04/21/chang.china.day.mourn.cnn?iref=allsearch.
12 See Miller (2008a).
13 See Miller (2008b) for an account of how importantly the leadership are taking organisational reforms since the Seventeenth Party Congress in October 2007.
14 See Bi (2002).
15 Since May 2011, the State Internet Information Office has had primary responsibility for regulation but other agencies at both central and provincial levels are also involved in monitoring and censoring the internet, http://chinadigitaltimes.net/2011/05/china-sets-up-state-internet-information-office/, accessed 27 June 2011).
16 *China Digital Times*, http://chinadigitaltimes.net/2011/07/poll-98-say-wenzhou-train-buried-to-destroy-evidence/, accessed 27 July 2011.
17 Also translates as 'solo group'.
18 Xu Wu (2010), 'A Revolutionary Technology for an Evolutionary Cause', *Asia Policy*, No. 10, p. 169.
19 See Minxin Pei, *China's Trapped Transition: The Limits of Developmental Autocracy*, London: Harvard University Press, 2006.
20 Wu (2010).
21 Source: BBC Monitoring research in English, 18 February 2008.
22 Online poll found at *xinhuanet.com*, the website sponsored by the Xinhua News Agency, reported on 12 February 2011.
23 *Global Times* (Beijing) 18 March 2011 reporting a poll conducted from 16 February to 6 March of 1,347 respondents aged 15 or above in 10 mainland cities.

24 Regulators have tried to tighten the rules on registering ownership of phones but the market in 'ready to go' and the huge demand has thwarted the efforts so far.
25 Manzenreiter (2010).
26 *Ibid.*

3

The state apparatus and centre-local relations

The efficiency and legitimacy of the government of the PRC are ever more bound together as the CCP increasingly justifies its monopoly of power by the material conditions of the people. Of course, social stability remains a key goal but, like many other governments of developing states, the Chinese ruling élite has to meet rising expectation from a population increasingly attuned to economic growth. The institutions of government have, therefore, been changing steadily to accommodate new demands and complexities. As Wong affirms: 'whether intended or not, by adopting the goal of building a Harmonious Society, the Hu Jintao – Wen Jiabao administration has committed itself to a program of large increases in public spending and a huge agenda of reform of government and its institutions' (Wong 2007: 1).

Indeed, organisational theorists suggest that the machinery of governments everywhere survives by adaptation to two broad forces, firstly, the demands imposed by the technical tasks of governing and, secondly, the need to meet external expectations of acceptable practice. 'These days, more and more ordinary Chinese citizens demand that officials live up to their proclaimed principles, that the government delivers what it promises, and that the authorities obey the state's laws and constitution' (Zheng 2003: 52).

Both the pressures of adaptation and expectation need to be borne in mind when analysing the governing of the PRC because, even more than in most jurisdictions, the formal rules and organisational charts of China's government are often a misleading pointer to the realities of power. Similarly, the constitution of the PRC can be only a very partial guide to political analysis, though, being relatively recent, it has fewer anachronisms than some comparable documents. Nevertheless, as Clarke warns: 'any account of the legal system of the People's Republic of China must be prefaced by a warning of the need to distinguish between the formal system and what actually happens. Such a gap is of course present in some degree in all countries, but in many areas it is particularly broad in China' (Clarke 2005). As was examined in Chapter 2, further, all state institutions are in practice subordinate to and penetrated by the CCP, which exercises a determining influence over all policies and decisions.

The current Constitution with 138 articles dates from 1982. It was revised in 1988, 1993, 1999 and 2004. The 2004 amendments concerned private property and human rights. The Constitution supersedes documents adopted in 1954, 1975 and 1978 but, of course, there are continuities including elements borrowed from the Soviet Union or deriving from traditional Chinese law. The main changes are a toning down of 'class struggle' with new emphasis on economic development. The rights and obligations of citizens also get more attention, possibly a comment on the excesses of the Cultural Revolution, but there is a counterbalancing assertion of the need for discipline and public order. For example, Article 35 states that 'citizens ... enjoy freedom of speech, of the press, of assembly, of association, of procession, and of demonstration' but the right to strike was dropped in the 1982 document. The Constitution also now expresses the 'ideal of "rule according to law" ... although the practical effect of adding these words is small' (Clarke 2005).

All constitutions are written by the winners of political struggles and signal their interests. Thus, the reforming authors were, in effect, chastising their predecessors by making less feasible the concentration of power in the hands of a few leaders or lifelong tenure in leadership positions. They also changed the tone of the Constitution in relation to foreigners deleting references to 'proletarian internationalism' and 'social imperialism'. But, lest there be any doubt on the balance of the 1982 document, its preamble states:

> Our country is in the primary stage of socialism. The basic task before the nation is the concentration of efforts of socialist modernization construction in accordance with the theory of building socialism with Chinese characteristics under the leadership of the Communist Party of China. (Preamble of the Constitution of the People's Republic of China)

In effect, the PRC is run by the CCP.

> The doctrine of a political party is the most important and dominant element in the Chinese political stream. The government machinery is almost composed of a single party, the Chinese Communist Party (CCP). There is no distribution of power among the most important state agencies of China. (Zhu 2008: 318)

Power, defined in terms of having your preferences prevail, is gained and retained by having the support of the party élites. The state and, to a decreasing extent currently, the People's Liberation Army (PLA) are the other two elements of the formal power structure. Both are junior partners. But, to be routinely effective, the central party oligarchy, in turn, needs the support or, at least the acquiescence, of party members, local and regional leaders, influential non-party members and the population at large. Thus, Lieberthal and Oksenberg (1988) present the PRC as displaying fragmented authoritarianism – policy is not the product of a random or pluralistic process but disputes among different bureaucratic and party interests do have a bearing on the outcome (Yue 1998). Reflecting on policy debates in the 1980s, Kosuth observes: 'throughout this period of growth, the ruling class fought internally about the direction of the country. With 'modernizers' in one wing and 'conservatives' in the other, they all agreed that China needed to develop. The debate was about the degree of economic control over society' (Kosuth 2009).

Recent research posits an even more diffuse power structure in which, on some policies at least, the central party oligarchy's preferences can be rebuffed or, at least, redefined (Mertha 2008). Mertha considers the keys to such policy changes are, firstly, reframing or defining the central issues by advocacy involving a broad spectrum of governmental actors and, secondly, identifying a 'champion' or 'policy entrepreneur' to drive the agenda. Interestingly, Mertha suggests that non-party organisations and public opinion play an increasing role in the process of reframing policy issues and that the policy entrepreneurs may also be from outside the CCP.[1] Zhu looking at how the PRC vagrancy laws were changed also uses the idea of policy entrepreneur:

> Defined as those who are willing to devote their time, energy, reputation, and money to make policy changes ... [E]ntrepreneurs perform similar functions [to their business counterparts] as they seek to discover unfulfilled needs and suggest innovative means to address them ... They identify the right opportunity to bring their opinions to light in order to generate maximum attention, but also determine the arguments needed to persuade others to support their policy ideas. (Zhu 2008: 317)

These observations on policy-making in a country so large and diverse and undergoing such major economic adjustments point to the issue that keeping broad support among competing interests is increasingly difficult and that the public need to be heeded. In the PRC, many old certainties are being challenged but the CCP is still at the core and dissent needs to be 'non-political', code for not posing a threat to party hegemony. Similarly, the mobilisation of public opinion has to stop well short of threatening 'social and political stability' – when it comes to 'framing' issues the CCP still has the trump cards. As Liu puts it with reference to Mertha's account of the influence of policy entrepreneurs: 'their fights are delicate, cautious, and small because the government has become too adept at framing expanding popular participation or deepening protests as sinister plots to damage the interest of the people and the state' (Liu 2009: 140).

An additional element in the framing process, however, is less under Chinese control and this is the recognition of international obligations. Among its legal agreements, the PRC adheres to the World Trade Organisation (WTO) and associated frameworks. The PRC was, for example, reluctantly forced to lift restrictions on imported books and movies as a result of a WTO ruling in August 2009. It also chose to drop proposals to force all manufacturers to install so-called 'anti-pornography software' in new computers sold in China in the face of international pressure.[2] As the *Financial Times* (London) noted in an editorial on a ruling against China in relation to mineral export restrictions in 2011: 'The country has a reasonable record of abiding by WTO rulings'.[3] Earlier Lieberthal observed: 'this is a country in the middle of a big transition in its global role ... [Its leaders] always looked in the past to what's good for China, and they still do. But for the first time, added to that is the consideration that they're in the position of being rule-takers, not just rule-makers' (quoted in *New York Times*, 14 August 2009).

In this chapter, the machinery of government will be looked at in terms of both the formal structures of government and the daily reality for Chinese citizens. Nevertheless, persistent themes will be the significant power in the state structure of the CCP, the importance of hierarchy and the multilayered nature of policy management. In very broad terms, the machinery of state has been overhauled progressively since 1979 with the effect of pushing policy discretion and financial responsibility downwards. As Davis observes of more recent reforms: 'Chinese leaders appear to realize that the China of 2010 is far too complex to be ruled entirely by fiat from Beijing and has to be governed by competent institutions enjoying the public's confidence' (Davis 2009: 201).

The delivery of public services is now further removed from central ministries and their role has been assumed by a variety of agencies of which local government is the most important. Similar trends have been seen in many states with various political systems but, in the case of the PRC, the paradox is that service fragmentation is matched by a strong tradition of political centralisation. As Zheng *et al.* observe from their case study of health policy-making:

> 'obedience' on the part of these lower tiers is substantially greater than in Western countries, and maintaining order and stability are highly valued in Chinese culture. Bottom-up network activities and initiatives ... seem to be less common, although passive resistance and unspoken refusal to implement policies and regulations imposed is far more common. (Zheng *et al.* 2010: 413)

Further, there are many policies implemented locally on which the central direction is either sparse or silent.

The democratic notion of a distinction between the state and the party is not as clear in China as it is in the West because, in Europe in particular, the modern state took shape before parties formed to compete for control. In China, the founders of the modern state, especially revolutionaries such as Sun Yat-sen, though initially believing in republican government, based on the multiparty model, came to understand that a strong state was a prerequisite to political progress. The 1911 Revolution, which overthrew the Qing dynasty, failed to deliver a viable democracy and the multiparty system proved unstable. Other models of state formation came to the fore, especially that offered by the Russian Revolution. In Russia, the party took precedence over the state. In 1924, Sun's ideas were embodied in the Kuomintang (KMT), a Leninist-style party with a tightly disciplined pyramidal structure. Though ideologically distinct and opponents in the 1945–49 Civil War, the victorious CCP espoused the same Leninist structure – Party dominance of the state. As Perry's review of the study of Chinese politics asserts:

> The historical work offered a newfound appreciation of the significant parallels between the Nationalist and Communist regimes ... To the degree that the modern Chinese state was a product of revolution, then, the revolutionary roots needed to be traced back beyond the Communist wartime base areas — at least to the 1920s, if not as far as 1911. (Perry 2005: 5)

The CCP's adherence to Leninist principles, therefore, reflects the circumstances of its foundation. In a hostile world, socialism could only be achieved if the leadership could count on obedience. So, even today, CCP members are expected to abide by the Party's position regardless of their own views. The core principle is 'democratic centralism'.

The state as a tool of the party is still the dominant characteristic of the Chinese governance, despite some attempts, notably in the 1980s, to emphasise their separate roles. Indeed, in the logic of a Leninist party, the CCP must be as deeply embedded in the delivery of policy as in its formal articulation. This imperative is, ironically, even more strongly felt by the CCP as its legitimacy becomes more firmly enmeshed in its ability to secure material benefits to all the people. As Wong affirms: 'strengthening public sector performance is clearly seen as a critical component of the reforms needed to ensure an effective and credible government leading China into the 21st Century' (Wong 2008: 5).

To do this in the context of market reforms, some economic levers of the command economy have had to be abandoned, the reach of government moderated and much economic management turned over to market forces. As a result, the government's share of GDP has reduced and more resources are in private hands. So, as Saich puts it: 'the vertical and cellular boundaries of the traditional Leninist system have become more porous' (Saich 2002: 75). Nevertheless, to understand the governing of the Chinese state, it is necessary to appreciate the pervasive role of the CCP. As Perry asserted in 2005: 'nearly three decades after Mao's death and more than fifteen years past June Fourth [the Tiananmen Square massacre], China remains a Leninist party-state' (Perry 2005: 7).

To understand the governing of the Chinese state in this context of change, this chapter will examine briefly the role of the National People's Representatives Congress (NPC) and then the State Council and the associated structures of central government departments. The central government's relationship with provincial and local authorities is also outlined. For the individual Chinese citizen, the courts and system of law enforcement are also clearly significant aspects of the state apparatus and these will be looked at briefly.

Internationally, the exact list of tasks undertaken by government in terms of the services provided or the activities routinely and directly under government control varies from state to state. Indeed the composition of the list has become controversial in Western countries where, after years of seemingly inexorable expansion, politicians on the right have come to portray government itself as a problem rather than the answer to difficult social or economic issues. In China, the scales are still tipped toward an expansion of the role of state provision albeit primarily at sub-national levels but, as shown in Chapter 1, the guarantees of security and status, referred as the 'iron rice bowl', that were a feature of the PRC before its change of economic direction, are no longer given. The pressure on the state is to expand social welfare provision but, as will be discussed below, the structures for doing this are currently rather fragmented. The PRC has experimented with all kinds of service delivery from direct provision by central government to decentralisation to local government to contracting out to the private sector and public/private partnerships. Some observers present this broad range of methods as a sign of 'weakened administrative capacity' (Lo, Lo and Cheung 2001: 45) but it is also a product of the pressures of adaptation and expectation identified above. Indeed, on occasions, the process of adaptation is self-consciously begun via local experiments:

> initiated from individual 'experimental points' ... and driven by local initiative with the formal or informal backing of higher-level policy-makers. If judged to be conducive to current priorities by Party and government leaders, 'model experiences' ... are disseminated ... for emulation to more and more regions ... Importantly, the mode of experimentation practiced in the PRC is focused on finding innovative policy instruments, rather than defining policy objectives, which remains the prerogative of the Party leadership. (Heilmann 2008: 2)

Thus, for example, though anticipated for a while because of the potential for a housing market bubble, the State Council introduced property tax in 2011 in just two Chinese cities, Shanghai and Chongqing, and then on a tentative basis.

The exact definition of a civil servant is changed periodically but, as Brødsgaard shows, the trend is definitely up: 'in 1978, there were 3.73 million bureaucrats staffing the governing system in China. In 2004, the number had increased to 9.51 million' (Brødsgaard 2008: 81).

If the Chinese people do have misgivings about the state machinery, it is not about its size but its probity. Polls and other research testify to the pervasiveness of political corruption and, in surprisingly blunt terms, the leadership of the CCP has joined in recognising its danger to the regime.

National People's Representatives Congress

The gap between formal status and actual power in the PRC's machinery of government is clear in relation to the NPC, a unicameral legislature, which is constitutionally the highest state body. Its 3,000 members meet for two weeks each year in the grand setting of the Great Hall of the People in Beijing but its proceedings are very largely pre-scripted by the CCP which makes up around 70 per cent of its membership.[4] The current NPC is the Eleventh and runs from 2008 to 2013. The NPC, together with the more broadly based CPPCC of

2,238,[5] with which it also meets each year, provides a platform for policy pronouncements by the CCP leadership. The NPC has been very 'productive'. As Lu and Zhang stress: '[It] promulgated approximately a total of 185 laws during the nineteen years from 1978 to 1997, which was seven times the total number of promulgated laws ... during the twenty-seven years from 1950 to 1977' (Lu and Zhang 2005: 368).

Though it is easily presented as a symbolic but powerless rubber-stamp legislature, the NPC's constitutional position does ensure that state office holders and the party leadership do have to defer to it to the extent of explaining their performance and proposals. Premier Wen Jiabao's key speech, for example, is pre-approved by the CCP's senior leaders and takes a couple of hours to deliver. It both reviews of the previous year's events and announces plans for the coming year. It is the result of months of research, bargaining and drafting at high levels inside the CCP. In 2011, Wen Jiabao reportedly entertained a group of 'ordinary people' to hear their views on its content.[6]

At the 2010 meeting, fairer income distribution, unaffordable housing and reform of the *hukou* (户口), or household registration system, were the headline agenda items. Indeed, the *hukou* reform gave rise to an unusually public clash between the government and the generally quiescent state media on the fringes of the NPC. If the Party's priorities are not clear, the debate in the NPC can be part of the consensus forming process. Thus, for example, proposals to ban the sale of cat and dog meat were effectively long-fingered after rumblings of discontent ahead of the 2010 meeting. In 2011, Premier Wen Jiabao's 'work report', a central feature of the proceedings, tried to link the perennial discussion on corruption to wider institutional development. Compared to work reports from previous premiers, for example Zhu Rongji's version in 2001, the accounts given in recent years have been detailed and frank.[7] In these respects, the NPC can be placed on a continuum of legislatures even if at the less powerful end. It is also similar to other 'parliaments' in that its main power is exercised by its Standing Committee of approximately 150 members, which meets bimonthly between full NPC sessions.

The role of the CPPCC is also to be a forum for new ideas but its composition is broader, its remit less clear and the ideas floated there often speculative. For instance, in 2011, it discussed making calligraphy a compulsory subject in primary schools to counter the 'writing crisis' in the increasingly computerised world. Some of the CPPCC's members also used the 2011 meeting to highlight the yizu or 'ant tribe' (蚁族), a term coined to describe the unemployed and low-income recent college graduates who live in the PRC's rural-urban fringes. Just before their formal meeting, three representatives paid a visit to Tangjialing, a village in the Beijing suburbs, to draw attention to the plight of this potentially disaffected group. The yizu 'now number more than one million nationwide, and an estimated 100,000 live in Beijing alone'.[8]

As with other legislature, the drafts that the NPC debates and turns into law are prepared by the 'cabinet' – the State Council which has a vast resource of expertise at its disposal in the ministries, commissions and other agencies. By the time votes are taken, either in committee or plenary session, the legislation has already been vetted by all the interested CCP and other stakeholders so amendments are rare and rejection even more so.[9] Nevertheless, defeats have been known and the State Council may be reluctant to make proposals on which there are strong misgivings in the NPC. The appearance of harmony is important and unanimous votes are no longer assured so an orchestrated expression of concern by a relatively small group can secure a proposal's delay or amendment. In the end, however, though compromises and adjustments may be made, the NPC is controlled by the CCP.

State Council and central government departments

The intimate work of most governments is shrouded in secrecy with the political leaders trying hard to manage the public's perception of the way decisions are made. Often, it is not until memoirs are written or once-secret documents are released that it is possible to understand the tensions, divisions and coalitions that really characterised decision-making. In China, the core processes are even more opaque and impenetrable than usual. The state compound Zhongnanhai (中南海) in central Beijing has come to symbolise this hidden government. Nevertheless, the complexity of modern government and accounts from other political systems suggest that it is useful to conceive of the upper echelons of the state as networks – collaborative groups in which informal organisational working arrangements are at least as important as the formal hierachy of power.[10] The enhanced intra-party democracy at senior levels, the significance of patron-client ties based on personal connections and the importance attached to political stability indicate the need for accommodations and compromise in the policy process.

> Apart from the formal relations built in to the process of policy-making, personal friendships and loyalties between high officials . . . are also a vital

feature in understanding policy-making in China. The presence of this aspect of *guanxi*, which involves more than solely functional relations between people, is hard to overestimate. (Zheng *et al.* 2010: 414)

Though the term 'cabinet' was used loosely above to refer to the State Council, chaired by Premier Wen Jiabao, it should not be assumed that this is the top decision making body of the Chinese executive. It is more accurately seen as a part of the ruling élite's closed network, which includes the CCP's top leadership and the People's Liberation Army (PLA). Ultimate control of all state, military and political activities lies with CCP and at the apex is the Communist Party Secretary, Hu Jintao, who chairs both the Politburo[11] and its powerful executive group, the Politburo Standing Committee. This standing committee is at the very core of the PRC's political system and places on it are highly sought after. In anticipation of the 2012 reshuffle, an unusually open 'campaign' for a place was waged by Bo Xilai, the party secretary of Chongqing. He sought to position himself as a candidate by using nostalgia for the less materialist values associated with the Cultural Revolution (1966–76). This radical departure from the usual backroom jockeying for position involved reviving Maoist songs, dances and slogans. Bo was, however, toppled by a scandal and he failed to displace fellow 'princelings' Xi Jinping (习近平) and Li Keqiang (李克强) for the two top posts. Their advancement has been signalled in the traditional way by key appointments and the patronage of the incumbents. Xi Jinping, for example, in 2011 the sixth ranked member of the Politburo Standing Committee, has been favoured by Hu Jintao and is likely to be his successor as General Secretary and President.

The centrality of the Politburo Standing Committee was illustrated during the ethnic crisis in the far Western Xinjiang region in July 2009. When Hu Jintao rushed back to China from a G8 conference in Europe, it was this body that he chaired which decided the state's reaction. The Politburo, in turn, is supported by the CCP Secretariat. Hu Jintao also presides over the Central Military Commission – in effect, the control of the military by the CCP is complete. Again, this was clear during the 2009 Xinjiang crisis. 'As chair of the central military committee, Mr Hu is the only civilian able to give orders to the armed forces' (Fenby 2009b). The State Council's role in the network is to run the central government ministries, commissions and other agencies and to supervise sub-national governments. At its core is the Standing Committee. Its membership varies between 5 and 9 but it includes the president, premier, head of the NPC and other senior figures. Though its members are officially ranked and their number always odd to avoid deadlock, the Standing Committee seeks to work by consensus.

As in other states, some have tried to distinguish between policy and implementation as if governing could move from statements of purpose to non-political administrative actions. In this formula, the State Council is charged with implementing CCP policy. In practice, the distinction is unhelpful because all government is political – every level influences the outcome. The network of which the State Council is part includes members with different formal roles but a shared understanding of their interdependence and direction. Information and opinion are pooled and responsibility diffused and, while formal roles are specified, power is shared. Some observers have even sought to demonstrate consistent patterns in the discourse among China's top leaders – 'competitive comrades' in this model (Shirk 1982) – that can be seen as the green shoots of bipartisan politics.

> The differences between these two coalitions are reflected not only in their leaders' distinct personal careers and political associations, but also in the socio-economic groups and geographical regions they represent ... the 'elitist coalition' ... [t]he core faction is the so-called Shanghai Gang ... represent the interests of entrepreneurs, the emerging middle class, and the economically advanced coastal provinces ... The other coalition ... [is the] 'populist coalition' ... The core faction ... is the Chinese Communist Youth League ... [it represents the interests of] the so-called 'vulnerable social groups' such as farmers, migrant laborers and the urban unemployed. (Li 2005: 2–3)

While this might be an overdrawn image, it is highly likely that both policy and its implementation are the subject of bargaining, compromise and contestation within the central organs of government.

> The groups compete with each other on certain issues but are willing to cooperate on others. Factional politics is no longer a zero-sum game in which the winner takes all ... [It] also makes 'bipartisanship with Chinese characteristics' a sustainable proposition for the near- to medium-term future. (Li 2009: 26)

The development of the machinery of the state is strongly influenced by two broad imperatives. One is the need to allow government officials to improve their knowledge and skills in particular areas of policy and provision by specialising. The other is to ensure coordination and control so that the different agencies of the state act in concert. The demands of specialisation and coordination are reflected in China by the frequent rearrangement of the central bureaucracy – currently the 'coordinators' have the upper hand.

The PRC's state bureaucracy, which acts under the State Council, is divided into various functional ministries and commissions. According to the Constitution, ministers are nominated by the Premier and confirmed by the NPC or its Standing Committee. The bureaucracy has always been very hierarchical but since 2008 the ranking has become more explicit as the latest in a series of reforms sought to 'establish a socialist administration system with Chinese characteristics by 2020' (Yeo 2009: 729).

There are now five 'super ministries' as Hua Jianmin (华建敏), secretary general of the State Council, described them in an address to the NPC in March 2008. They are industry and information, human resources and social security, environmental protection, housing and urban-rural construction, and transport and, importantly, the National Development and Reform Commission (NDRC), a macroeconomic management agency formed in 2003.[12] The NDRC itself performs an important coordinating role in various policy areas but, reflecting the issues new-found centrality, it lost energy management to the new National Energy Bureau (NEB). The new body moved to new offices and did other things to assert its autonomy but in 2010 it too lost its prominence with the establishment of a new institution under the State Council—the National Energy Commission. This new body is chaired by Premier Wen Jiabao and has Li Keqiang, his likely successor, as vice chair – a further sign of the policy area's significance. Still macroeconomic concerns are the major driver of policy and, in this area, the NDRC, the dominant player, is joined by the Ministry of Finance and the People's Bank of China.

This institutional restructuring, an important part of China's overall plan to deepen reforms in its administrative system, is the fifth major government reshuffle since the 1980s. Despite its announced aim of reducing turf wars, the reforms have not reduced the number of bureaucracies reporting to the State Council by much: there are about 28, but it has signaled policy priorities. For example, as noted above, it is clear that economic development and energy management are crucial but may now share their central place with environmental protection.[13] Similarly, the Ministry of Health, though not itself classified as a 'super-ministry' has been given the function of overseeing food and drug safety, a symbolically important change reflecting the increasing significance of this issue. Indeed, food safety was brought even further up the agenda in early 2010 when the State Council established a national food safety commission headed by Li Keqiang.

Again, to the extent that institutional changes signal policy preferences, it is possible to see the transformation of the Ministry of

Construction into the Ministry of Housing and Urban and Rural Development (MOHURD) as part of the harmonious society strategy. The new body, which interestingly has taken some responsibility for major construction projects from the NDRC, has been charged with increasing the stock of low-income housing. According to the first head of MOHURD, Jiang Weixin: 'adding the word "housing" into the ministry's name reflected the Central Government's stress on improving people's living conditions as well as the government's changed perception on how it should satisfy people's housing needs in a market economy' (quoted in *Beijing Review*, 8 October 2009). MOHURD lost urban public transport management functions to the new Ministry of Transportation.

The new Ministry of Human Resources and Social Security (MOHRSS) brings together the former ministries dealing with personnel and social security issues. Its formation signals a broadening of the Chinese government's concern with human resources and the decline in the context of market disciplines of the labour allocation function of government. It will tighten the implementation of labour regulations – an important issue for inward investors. MOHRSS also represents an attempt to unify policies and principles for urban and rural labour markets. During the economic downturn of the late 2000s, it intervened to try to prevent and control large staff reduction especially in labour-intensive industries. As income inequality increases MOHRSS has been criticised, even in the official media, for inaction on pay rates that might exacerbate tensions between workers and employers (quoted in *China Daily*, 28 May 2010). With the official trade unions not fulfilling a bottom-up role in industrial relations, MOHRSS has a direct function in maintaining the balance between employers and workers. In the unusual public criticism in May 2010 the *China Daily* accused it of achieving 'little progress so far in drafting an amendment to the current wage regulation due to strong opposition from employers' (quoted in *China Daily*, 28 May 2010). The new ministry has also taken over the function of civil service recruitment. In October 2009, for example, it advertised 15,000 new positions in central government and, reflecting wider government policy, declared a preference for: 'people with at least two years of working experience at the grassroots level ... and young people who finish their service in the government programmes of working at remote and less developed regions and villages after college graduation' (quoted in *China Daily*, 12 October 2009).

Under Mao, civil service recruitment had class background as a criterion and educational standards were low. Today, the PRC civil service imposes merit criteria through rigorous and highly competitive recruitment processes:

> China's civil service is known as a 'golden rice bowl'. Around 1 million people around the country are expected to take the [2010 entrance] exam for 15,000 positions ... About 84 per cent of the positions require a bachelor's degree. [Others] require a master's degree at minimum. And the notoriously difficult exam is just the first part. There are interviews, a physical and often a background check, for political reliability and solid family background. (Quoted in *Shanghai Daily*, 23 March 2010)

Nevertheless, the CCP's most powerful instrument in controlling the machinery of government is the *nomenklatura* system as discussed below. This gives it a dominant say over personnel decisions (Tsao and Worthley 2009).

Central/local relations

Central government has three instruments for coordinating the system: (1) the State Council, meeting either in plenary or various executive committees; (2) task focused coordinating bodies under the State Council; and, (3) less frequently but for urgent issues specific authority given to the premier, vice-premier or a state councillor. The line of command can, however, be very long and the standard of policy implementation equally varied.

> Beijing's ability to unilaterally impose its will throughout China is ... highly limited ... The leadership has to gauge carefully what it can and cannot get away with vis-à-vis local authorities; how much political capital will be required to enact controversial policies at local levels; and how much discretion to allow local authorities in policies set at the national level ... Even when Beijing issues more categorical commands, local compliance is far from certain. (Bergsten *et al.* 2008: 75)

In China, even more than in democratic states, the focus on the stage managed events in the capital filtered through official news channels can make politics seem like endless theatre of politicians, celebrity journalists and news reporters that compete with the 'soaps' and sport for popular attention on the television and in the papers. Another way to experience politics, however, is to suffer the delays caused by under-invested or poorly run hospitals, to enjoy subsidised theatre or public parks or to seek permission to build or extend a house. In China, in recent decades, for the average citizen, politics has concerned issues such as massive traffic delays and unclean air. In other words, politics is about almost every aspect of life where public agencies provide benefits, impose duties or redistribute resources from some citizens to others through taxes, charges etc. As Pomfret, columnist with the *Washington Post*, identified the concerns of a high income Chinese gated community for US Senate Committee members: 'trash collection, zoning issues, and a fight against the often massive ripping off of their interests by developers and their friends in the Communist Party'.[14]

For far less privileged citizens, he might have added the increasing problem of adequate clean water supplies. It may also be the level of their wages:

> [As the] minimum wage level is extremely decentralised in China. Each city or even a district in a city can set its own minimum wage based on a formula provided by the central government. This takes into account the cost of living in the locality, the prevailing wage, the rate of inflation etc., and it is adjusted each year.[15]

In June 2010, in response to an increasing number of disputes and worker riots, 'which pose a grave challenge to social stability' according to the official quoted by the *Financial Times* (Anderlini 2010), Jiangsu, Zhejiang, Shanghai and other provinces increased their minimum wages by 10 to 17 per cent. In this political process, Beijing is only part of the story. As Table 4 shows, the chain of command is long.

Table 4 Administrative hierarchical delegation

Hierarchical delegation in China
Central government ⇒ provinces
Provincial government ⇒ municipalities
Municipalities ⇒ counties
Counties ⇒ townships
Townships ⇒ villages/farms

Source: Wong 2007: 16.

The everyday pattern of public provision, in education and health in particular, is the responsibility of more local governments and agencies. Nearly three-quarters of all government expenditure takes place at sub-national levels though local governments collect just 45 per cent of total government revenue. The mismatch of expenditure and income is a very significant influence on the level of service in different parts of China. As the management of emergencies, such as food scares and the avian bird flu crisis, demonstrate:

> [T]here exist many incoherencies and inconsistencies both between different levels of government and with government bureaucratic

agencies ... The roles and responsibilities of government are ambiguous, with many jurisdictional gaps and contradictions ... Government and agency action under such a system is often fragmented and ineffective. (Kaibin 2007: 93)

Nevertheless, sub-national provision is becoming even more important since the central government reforms discussed above devolved more power from the centre. For example, the final approval of the NDRC is no longer needed on major construction projects as that body moves away from micro-management of the economy towards a focus on macro-regulation. The power to award investment contracts and other licences increasingly rest with provincial governments and even lower levels. These changes may, in effect, recognise *de facto* local control but they are a significant indicator of the importance of sub-national government and the increased reliance of the centre on macroeco-nomic policy levers (see Table 5). In other policy areas too, it is important to appreciate the impact of complex centre-local relations. For example, as Lo and Frywell point out:

> The *enforcement* of environmental regulations ... is considerably more problematic than their promulgation. Indeed, for the past two decades. China has been aggressively passing environmental laws, many of which have been very progressive and which mandate harsh penalties for non-compliance ... [I]t appears that the bulk of these regulations are *not* being uniformly implemented across China and that many of the country's environmental problems appear to be getting worse. (Lo and Frywell 2005: 558–9; emphasis original)

Table 5 Distribution of budgetary expenditures, by level of government, 2006 (%)

	Budgetary expenditures	*Education*	*Health*	*Social welfare and relief*
Central	25	6	3	1
Province	18	15	22	10
Municipalities	23	18	31	27
County + township	34	61	44	64

Source: Wong, C. (2009: 944).

In many areas, policy can be quickly enacted at the centre without the need for lengthy legislative and consultative delays. The recognition of technical glitches, the need for local accommodations and the reso-lution of conflicts all come at the later stage and are played out in the local government arena. Most important among the sub-national entities are the provinces, prefectures and counties. This latter category include an array of types of unit at city, county and other levels but in this chapter the emphasis will be on the general pattern of central/local relations and service provision.

Provincial government

The provinces of China were established during the Yuan Dynasty and from an original 10 their number has increased to 23.[16] Some have populations of over 100 million and their administrative capacity is quite varied. The most recently formed are Chongqing (1997) and Hainan (1988). They have populations approaching 32 million and 9 million respectively. Scholars differ on the extent to which provincial loyalty is a threat to a collective Chinese identity but it is clear that provincial patriotism is an important element in the politics of the PRC.

The PRC is a unitary state and the CCP is no more welcoming of opposition to its lead role at provincial level than centrally. Nevertheless, the literature on provincial government often focuses on the possibility that China might display nascent democratic tendencies. This is particularly the case in reports on the Provincial People's Congresses (PPCs). Thus, for Cho: 'deputies since the early 1990s have progressively become more representative than before, even without the radical change of the Chinese party-state and its legislative system' (Cho 2003: 197).

The PPCs exhibit the same hierarchical and working characteristics as the NPC: a small chairperson's committee meeting almost weekly, a larger standing committee coming together every couple of months and a large annual gathering of all the representatives.

The CCP nominates about 10 per cent more candidates than places for the standing committee so there is a potential element of choice and the chair's committee is selected from the successful nominees. This latter group effectively exercises the PPC's power as the annual meeting passes only broad legislative measures and each member chairs a specialist committee. Almost invariably, CCP members hold these executive posts. As with its national equivalent, the provincial bureaucracy is responsible for the preparation and delivery of policy measures and is organised along functional departmental lines. Interestingly, many of the senior PPC members are former government officials so the expertise gap may not be as pronounced as at NPC level. Again, consensus on legislative measures is seen as important and this explains some of the divergence between central and local policies.

National policies, particularly when they impose new regulatory burdens, are often changed significantly to address local conditions especially to minimise their impact on economic growth.

It would be hard to characterise the PPCs as the green shoots of democracy though, as with the NPC, they do afford a certain amount of structured contention, compromise and consensus building. PPC members can also fulfil an ombudsman-like role for aggrieved citizens. Formally, there is also a degree of budgetary supervision but this function is very constrained both practically and legally. Indeed, much of the concern about corruption in the PRC is at the provincial level. Nominations for the PPC come from the lower levels of government, such as cities, and from some public organisations, such as trade unions, but CCP control is not compromised. PPC membership reflects party priorities and is often a reward for loyalty or service. The end result is less a destablising trend to democracy and more a bulwark for the *status quo*. As O'Brien puts it: '[Local people's congresses] ... are not a 'rival show' or a 'rubber stamp' but partners in governance ... less to do with responsiveness and altered state-society relations and more to do with state-building, restructuring bureaucratic ties, and making Party rule predictable and effective' (O'Brien 2009: 131).

The PPCs are no more the political power centres of the provinces than the NPC is of China as a whole. The CCP, particularly the Party Secretary, is still at the core but it is important to recognise that the party itself reflects significant local power variations.

> The economic reforms ... have transformed the Chinese polity in far-reaching ways ... There has been a progressive decline in direct state control over the economy [and l]ocal governments have been accorded greater control over local economic activity and the redistribution of economic rewards. (Saich 2002: 75)

In general, the eastern provinces enjoy more autonomy from Beijing than those in the west and some, such as Shanghai and Guangdong, are noteworthy centres of power. These provinces command significant economic and political resources and their citizens' lives reflect this reality. In education, for example, in 2002, spending per student was Rmb 5,500 in Shanghai but only Rmb 600 in the southwestern province of Guizhou. Wong's figures reproduced in Table 6 illustrate the gap starkly.

Table 6 Growing disparities in per capita budgetary expenditures, by province[a]

	1990	1994	1998	2002	2004
Highest (1) Shanghai	609	1,207	3,337	5,516	7,875
Lowest (2) – Henan	104	130	362	680	899
Ratio of (1) to (2)	5.9	9.3	9.2	8.1	8.8
Average	254	374	861	1,684	2,066
Absolute gap	505	1,076	2,976	4,835	6,977
Coeff. of variation	0.57	0.71	0.75	0.75	0.75

Source: Wong (2007: 8).

Note: [a] Deflated to 1990 Rmb, and excluding Tibet.

A redistribution scheme aimed to help poorer provinces has had relatively little effect.

> Few resources are being transferred from the center downward, making it more difficult for some lower level governments to provide basic education, health care, unemployment insurance and other centrally mandated services. At the same time, some of the relatively prosperous provinces are able to manifest greater independence from Beijing than in the past, making it difficult for the central government to ensure that its policy objectives are put into action. (Whiting 2007: 4)

The fiscal reforms of the early 1980s made local governments largely self-financing, though debt is now a significant issue for some local government units at every level. Research published in March 2010 estimated outstanding municipal debt of Rmb 11.4 trillion (quoted in *The Economist*, 11 March 2010). The decline in the share of the states revenue commanded by central government has 'created pressures at all levels ... to meet recurrent costs from the locally generated revenues. This means that local resources and power structures increasingly determine political outcomes. Within the same province and even in adjacent counties one can see radically different socio-political outcomes' (Saich 2002: 76).

Some authors speak of a *de facto* Chinese federalism[17] (Tsai 2004), though Beijing is keen to counter any such trend and, for example, it removed the city boss of Shanghai in 2006 to assert its primacy. Nevertheless, the major cities exercise considerable autonomy in areas such as economic management, environmental protection and social welfare provision. Ironically, the five autonomous regions[18] with provincial status are the least independent of Beijing. The prosperous provinces benefit from the impact of economic growth as well as their ability to generate 'off budget' income which is not available to central government for redistribution across the country. Nevertheless, Saich and Kaufman caution that: 'while the accounts of localities avoiding or deflecting central policy are many, the Center still sets many tasks that must be carried out and imposes burdens to be met' (2005:8).

To maintain its control over the whole country, it is important for the CCP to counter 'localism', including attempts to impose effectively local economic protectionism or shelter businesses violating intellectual property rights. The NDRC, clearly with Party approval, emphasised its opposition with strict new regulations on anti-competitive practice introduced in 2009 (quoted in *China.daily*, 13 August 2009). Obviously, however, this kind of localism is covert but anecdotally:

> Stories run from lending biased support to local enterprises to erecting barriers to outside enterprises (including central enterprises). It seems that there has been a regional/local consensus nationwide that often different government agencies, such as those involved with business licensing, the courts, and public and health inspection, act in a coherent and coordinated way to lend support to local enterprises and to bar outside enterprises from gaining access to local market. (He 2008: 27)

As suggested above, this is easier in the prosperous and powerful provinces. To counteract local protectionism, the Politburo and its Department of Organisation keeps a tight rein over the selection and appointment of provincial party secretaries and governors. There is always a tendency for the senior officials to see themselves as lobbyist for their region in Beijing but the party discourages too great an identification with locally vested interests, particularly in the ethnically distinct provinces.

> The center has retained the authority to appoint top provincial officials who serve as agents of the center rather than being captured by local interests. This *nomenklatura*-based power over the allocation of personnel explains why the center has generally been able to enact macroeconomic stabilization policies that may harm the short-term economic interests of certain localities. (Tsai 2004: 19)

The 'cadre exchange system' seeks to counter localism through regular exchanges in appointments between key cadres of different localities (Zheng 2009: 198). In any event, Chinese officials are not accountable to the citizens but to the party-state apparatus at the next higher level. Their performance is assessed for its contribution to the aims of the political élite. Thus, for example, the politburo's decision to introduce an Obama-style 'stimulus package' in the face of global economic conditions in December 2008 led to an immediate response:

> When a provincial governor confided ... [to a Beijing based economist] his greatest political achievement ... [his] chest swelled on news that bank lending in his province had outpaced the national average ... China's ability to reflate its economy says much more about the Chinese Communist party and the power ... [It has to fulfil] the Politburo's orders ... according to which their future promotions will be judged. (McGregor 2009)

Further, because data on social indicators and service outputs are often quite unreliable and performance, therefore, difficult to measure, local cadres need to be viewed as 'apparently' fulfilling their role. For a party secretary, mayor or other local government official a successful career is built on a hierarchy of approval and may involve transfers between quite different parts of the government machine or state-owned enterprises. The performance measures, known as the Cadre Responsibility System (CRS), set goals on a scale of importance: soft targets, hard targets and priority targets. Failure on the last negates other successes – a priority target represents a major imperative. The CRS explains why officials enforce even unpopular policies with enthusiasm – the key to success is meeting targets set by the hierarchy not the people.[19] Officials in Puning county, Guangdong province, for example, anxious not to miss family planning targets, detained the elderly relatives of parents to force them to submit to sterilisation. For a 20-day campaign in April 2010, the county set out to sterilise 9,559 women or their husbands who were suspected of planning to have a second or third child (Macartney 2010). This prioritising of targets also accounts for major changes in policy emphasis when the incentive structure is altered. Thus, for example, climate change has become a high priority of provincial and prefectural governments after being roundly ignored.

> Until mid-2007 no local government, right from the provincial to the most local level, expressed serious interest in working on climate change ... Economic growth typically helps the political promotion of local government officials ... Climate change was not a factor in the performance evaluation system, and mitigation efforts were believed to slow economic growth. (Qi *et al.* 2008: 380)

Then, the move of climate change up the political agenda signalled in part by the central government reorganisation discussed above, together with a change to the performance measurement applied to local officials encouraged: 'dramatic institutional developments on climate change from the central down to the provincial, prefectural, and county levels' (Qi *et al.* 2008: 384).

As Bo found in his study of provincial government from 1949 to 1998 (Bo 2002), poor performance figures can bring on demotion or retirement – a pattern confirmed also by Li and Zhou's research (2005). Nevertheless, this reward system does not prevent rivalry in fulfilling the targets set as: 'local officials are only evaluated based on their performance within their jurisdiction ... Provincial officials will not be rewarded for helping increase the industrial output in another province; nor will they be punished for polluting the air or water in neighboring provinces' (Zhan 2009: 448).

In many areas of public policy, such as food safety or coal mining regulation, centrally set standards and procedures are bypassed in the interests of rival provincial economies. The career importance of readily measurable policy outcomes means that less quantifiable policies are neglected. In this respect, Chinese public management reflects bureaucratic practice in most other jurisdictions. Indeed, as Guo shows, local officials in China time their performance output with reference to crucial career decision points, in their case promotion rounds, in the same way that, in more democratic systems, elected decision-makers adjust monetary and fiscal policies to the dates of local ballots. 'The Chinese *nomenklatura* system coupled with incomplete information and retrospective economic accountability create incentives for local officials to produce political budget cycles to signal competence to party committees at upper levels' (Guo 2009: 624).

Prefecture and county government
The prefecture-level of government, also referred to as the municipalities, is that between the province and county levels, i.e. the second sub-national stratum in the PRC. It will be discussed here in general though technically, there are four kinds of prefecture-level divisions: prefectures, prefecture-level cities, autonomous prefectures and leagues. There is some ambiguity in the status of prefectures because the constitution of the PRC envisages provinces ruling counties directly. The prefectural level is supposed to facilitate provinces in dealing with issues of size and scale but critics suggest that, if provinces were smaller, this tier of government could be abolished. See Box 2 on the next page.

Though it resonates with more ancient divisions, this level is a relatively recent form of government reflecting the scale of the provinces and the practical issues of governance. The same pattern of people's congresses applies. As with provincial congress delegates, the prefecture bodies are elected by congresses one level down – the link to ordinary Chinese voters is indirect and tenuous. Nevertheless, the

---

Box 2 Prefecture-level government

17 Prefectures: formerly dominant second-level division, largely replaced since 1983 by *prefecture-level cities*. Mostly in *Xinjiang* and *Tibet*

283 Prefecture-level cities: urban centre and surrounding rural areas

30 Autonomous prefectures: contain one or more designated *ethnic minorities*, mostly in Western regions

3 Leagues: in *Inner Mongolia*, prefecture equivalent, mostly replaced by prefecture-level cities

---

rules at county level do call for grassroots experience as a qualification for those assuming leadership roles. The provincial people's congress appoints the prefecture's head officials. CCP control is not compromised by this process, 'in every congress at every level, a majority of delegates are Party members' (Manion 2008: 618).

Counties, of which there are over 3,000, are the lowest level of government and, unlike, prefectures, are relatively old dating back to the Warring States Period, from 476 BC to the unification of China by the Qing Dynasty in 221 BC. This historical lineage gives the counties a central role in most plans for reform of local government in the PRC. The reformers wish to see the administration levels reduced from five to three, i.e. province, county and village. Such a change, it is felt, would reduce administrative costs and corruption.

As with the provincial level, the economic resources available to individual prefectures and counties vary considerably. It is interesting to note, however, how significant rural local authorities have been in stimulating entrepreneurial activity – not always within the official economy. For example, Hengshan county officials, in Shaanxi province, secretly invested in shares in local mining companies and were able to thwart attempts at closure by higher authorities (Martinsen 2009). Not that all these local enterprises are illegal. Whiting's study of township and village enterprises (TVEs), for example, shows how important local government was as a spur to industrial development. She also highlights the way in which fiscal reforms, in particular revenue-sharing requirements, encouraged local government to keep much of the resulting profits 'off the books' (Whiting 2000). An example of how local officials test the boundaries of their discretion in order to raise local income is afforded in the 'grey market' for imported food. Because tax revenue from these commodities would otherwise have to be shared with central government, provincial and county officials collude to categorise the food as 'local'.

> If a port is located in a region, the benefit to the local government from products imported through this region is significant ... Many facilities have been developed by local governments that actually assist grey channel activities. This is especially true of wholesale markets for imported foods near borders where imported products can be redistributed to other provinces of China. (Collins and Sun 2010: 69)

Clearly, central government is aware of this revenue loss but county governments, in particular, lack adequate revenues to finance the wide range of public goods and services they are obliged to deliver (see Table 7).

Table 7 Fiscal trends for government, by level (%)

Revenues	1993	1998	2004	2006
Central government	22	50	31	25
Provinces	13	11	20	18
Municipalities	34	20	21	23
Counties	16	20	22	29
Township	11	8	7	6

Source: Wong C. (2009: 944).

> The intergovernmental fiscal system has been characterised by distrust and mutual blame ... [It highlights] the central government's distrust of local governments to implement tax policy. During the long fiscal decline, local officials often complained of higher level governments 'grabbing' revenues and 'pushing down' expenditures ... [E]vidence ... [supports] the local government complaints: while revenues were increasingly concentrated at higher levels, expenditures were going in the opposite direction. (Wong 2008: 20)

The disparity between the central government's prescriptions and the level of service on the ground is not just a matter of finance – important though that is. Local officials also have policy priorities that gain expression despite higher-level disapproval.

> [Central government] control over social outcomes ... is at best attenuated, and compliance with central policies is not always assured at the local levels. Even when the central government injects resources to support local services, these resources pass through provinces and municipalities before reaching counties. Leakages can occur at each level,

and at present the central government has few levers for holding local governments accountable. (Wong 2007: 15)

Wong was referring especially to rural China but the potential for policy deviance is broader. For example, the central government is very concerned about the widening social and economic gap between migrant workers, overwhelmingly from rural China, and established urban dwellers. The former group lack the residential registration to access public services provided by local governments, one in six of the citizens of the PRC is working away from their registered home.[20] Thus, for instance, their children cannot readily go to public schools. A much inferior under-regulated private school system is in place but even this is beyond the means of many migrant parents. The Chinese government believes that the local education authorities should be responsible for migrant children but, fearing the impact of facilitating outsiders on local social and economic conditions, the central policy is effectively obstructed. Quite instructively, one of the most obdurate local governments on migrant provision is Beijing (Wang 2008). As Wong writes, the central government has to adapt to local realities 'until the incentive structure for government agencies and public institutions ... is fundamentally altered, this top-down reform of the public sector will likely have only limited effect' (Wong 2008: 7).

The incentive system Wong refers to includes the practice throughout the Chinese public service for bureaucrats to increase their own income via both 'the proliferation of arbitrary charges' (Tsui and Wang 2004: 73) and related enterprises. Many local government bodies have associated businesses. The economic reforms facilitated the restructuring of SOEs and introduced employee ownership. In many cases, however, the impact has been that provincial and local governments have become the owners of such businesses in their own areas. For local government, SOEs are a major source of revenue and, despite the formal rules, officials too profit. As the World Bank *Quarterly Update* for December 2008 suggests diplomatically:

> Institutional reforms can be introduced to give local decision-makers stronger incentives and better tools to pursue rebalancing [to more service and consumption stimulus]. A key is to strengthen accountability, especially via the performance evaluation of local officials and enforcement of laws and regulations. (World Bank 2008: 18)

The problem for those overseeing the Chinese machinery of government is that the lines of communication and control are often both long and fractured. Further, the CCP's *nomenklatura* system of personnel management can provide a disincentive to accurate reporting of local policy. The chief local official, the secretary of the party committee, and the top administrator in charge of the day-to-day management are subject to a similar set of evaluation criteria so share similar policy imperatives. As Lieberthal suggests local officials have responded to the economic reforms often by becoming themselves 'a bureaucratic, capitalist political apparatus that is highly entrepreneurial … [O]fficials get engaged, enterprise by enterprise, to use political power to advance the fortunes of individual enterprises' (Lieberthal 2004: 2). The result has been impressive growth but the dangers of corruption, neglect of other policy areas and local protectionism are very evident.

Other levels of government

As noted above, sub-national government in the PRC has many layers and variations and in this chapter the focus has been on provincial, prefecture and county levels. In much of the Western commentary on China, however, the township and village are seen as particularly interesting. In part, this is because the 'frontline soldiers of the CCP' are exceptionally vulnerable. For example, the media have in recent years been given some leeway in reporting critically on local government performance but 'the exposure of local misfeasance has been limited to below provincial level' (Zhan 2009: 451). The further from provincial government levels journalists report, the more freedom they enjoy. Unsurprisingly:

> Leading cadres in China's rural townships have a bad reputation. Many farmers loathe them, Chinese academics tend to blame them for much of what goes wrong in the villages, journalists write reports about their corrupt local kingdoms, and in television programmes you can see them trying to explain away their latest blunders … villagers tend to trust central and provincial level Party committees, but are more sceptical about the county level and have even less confidence in township and village leaders. (Thøgersen 2008: 414)[21]

But it is not just because they are the front line for many citizens that the lowest government level interests observers. It is because of the experiment at these levels with competitive elections. The township is particularly interesting for those who seek to divine the start of a competitive democratic system in the PRC because it is part of the state structure, and comes under the Party's *nomenklatura* list. Indeed, for this reason, the direct elections of the heads of townships are seen as unconstitutional and, though widespread, they are conducted on a project or experimental basis. Nevertheless, various devices have been put in place to broaden the CCP selection process with candidates making speeches and having to persuade a broader cross-section of the local population than just party members. The nearest to open elections, however, are those to the head post in the village administration.

Village elections in China are conducted to an uneven standard of openness with the Party still controlling the process of compiling the register, checking candidate eligibility and counting the votes. In more democratic political systems than that of the PRC, elections offer a significant feedback mechanism for government at all levels. Similarly, complaints, protests and, traditionally in China, petitions give authorities a sense of the impact of policy decisions. Though each of these mechanisms is highly constrained, Chapter 4 will examine them for signs of democratisation in the PRC.

Courts and law enforcement

All political systems require individual citizens to acknowledge constraints of different kinds, seek permission for certain activities and to accept adjudications in disputes between individuals or the state. The more willingly and routinely citizens adhere to the laws, the more efficient the system. In the absence of voluntary compliance, the state has to employ various means of enforcement through agents, such as the police, and punishment via the courts. Each individual citizen does not need a detailed knowledge of the law, comparative research suggests that, as with other aspects of the political system, the level of information on laws, courts and punishments is low. What is important is a generalised sense that the law is fair, its enforcement proportionate and the adjudication in disputes or alleged transgressions is just. Most countries, therefore, seek to assure the public through adhering to established constitutional procedures for making laws, even if in reality these steps are merely token, and by ascribing to the court system an independence that is designed to insulate it from undue influence. In the PRC, the same reassuring characteristics are trumpeted through the role prescribed to the organs of the state by the Constitution and the ideal of the 'rule of law' concept:

> The rule of law signifies that a political civilization has developed to a certain historic stage ... it is desired and pursued by people of all countries. The Chinese people ... know well the significance and value of

the rule of law, and thus cherish the fruits they have achieved in building China into a country under the rule of law. (IOSCPRC 2008)

Given the significance of the ideal, it is hard for any political system to accept that it falls short of international best practice. The PRC is, therefore, very sensitive of criticism of its court and law enforcement systems and points to the ways in which they reflect what happens elsewhere. Chinese legal scholars observe that the country has had a written, codified and nationally enforced system of law since ancient times though they acknowledge the turmoil caused by both foreign interference, including attempts to impose alien systems, and domestic upheavals like the Cultural Revolution. It is important to note, however, that in China: 'courts are like other administrative organs rather than distinctive kinds of institutions ... [and] that law is basically an instrument of governing rather than a restraint on government' (Gewirtz 2003: 618).

A core dilemma for Chinese jurists, discussed further in Chapter 4, is to reconcile the rule of law with the leading role of the CCP. As affirmed in the Chinese White Paper on 'rule of law': 'the legal system of China ... conforms to the basic conditions of the primary stage of socialism in China. It is in line with the basic tasks of socialism, and has distinctive Chinese characteristics' (IOSCPRC 2008).

There are four levels of courts in China and the higher-level supervises the judicial work of the next-lower level.

- Supreme People's Court, highest judicial level, plus appeals cases from below[22] (1);
- higher-level People's Courts, the provincial level, plus appeals cases from below (29);
- intermediate level, important sub-provincial cases,[23] plus appeals cases from below (337);
- basic-level People's Courts, county and district level, minor cases (2,902).

Both civil and criminal cases are heard at each level. Various special courts, such as military and maritime ones, also operate. Except in cases involving state secrets and certain sensitive family issues, the courts are expected to operate in public and, unusually in comparative terms, local politicians vet the process and control court finances. Except in simple civil or minor criminal cases, in which a judge acts alone, the court operates with a panel of judicial officials, not all of whom are career lawyers or judges. The court level above that giving the initial ruling hears appeals, unless the Supreme Court is that of first instance or the death penalty is involved. The Chinese system seeks where possible to deal with minor civil cases through mediation and to discourage litigious citizens from pressing their 'rights' when an accommodation can be reached.[24] Indeed, in August 2009, authorities issued a regulation to encourage parties involved in conflicts to mediate for resolution following what it saw a rapid increase in lawsuits. 'The move is an attempt to bring social organizations into play at an action's early stage to ease public discontent and prevent aggravation of resentment and tension. It is in accord with the new objective of a harmonious society outlined by the Communist Party of China and the government' (quoted in *China Youth International*, 5 August 2009).

The PRC state prosecution or procuratorial service is headed by the Supreme People's Procuratorate and is replicated at each judicial level with the higher level directing the work of the next-lower level. The Procuratorate is charged with ensuring that crime is investigated, deciding if prosecutions are brought to court and overseeing the carrying out of sentences. It shares responsibility for some aspects of policing with the Ministry of Public Security and local government but coordination is tight and the Procuratorate can assume direct responsibility for any cases it chooses. It also monitors the operations of people's courts, prisons and other penal institutions. The Procuratorate can appeal sentences it considers too lenient. High on its formal list of duties is to be vigilant in cases that threaten to: 'dismember the State and other counter-revolutionary activities, and strike at counterrevolutionaries and other criminals, so as to safeguard the unification of the country, the system of proletarian dictatorship and the socialist legal system'.[25]

Though the Procuratorate is obviously politically charged, its main strength is in gaining public respect by imposing standards of conduct in the legal system.[26] The close link between the agencies of law enforcement means that once a trial begins its outcome is seldom in doubt. In 2004, 99.7 per cent of all criminal trials ended in conviction (Yardley 2005).

In China, the experience of capricious arrests and arbitrary punishment is quite recent and the PRC leadership understands that economic modernisation and social stability are undermined if the legal system loses the confidence of the people. By the same token, 'one by-product of the current economic reform is the increased criminal activity' (Cao and Hou 2001: 88).

Since China began moving towards a market economy, it witnessed a sharp increase in criminal activities ... Official statistics reported an increase of a total crime incidence of 340 per cent and a ten-fold increase in serious crimes from 1979 to 1990 ... New offenses, especially offenses related to economic activities (e.g., counterfeiting currency and credit card fraud), emerged and exploded. (Lu and Zhang 2005: 368)

Confidence in the legal system is something of a barometer for attitudes to the process of government as a whole. Although scholarly evidence is sparse, it seems that general public confidence in the legal system is improving as reforms in legal training,[27] supervision of the police and the transparency of the court system take effect. As Yang suggests in his blog: 'legal reforms take time. While some of the reforms ... have been fully implemented, others ... are still only being introduced. Nevertheless, the scope of the reforms has already helped boost public confidence in the judicial system' (Yang 2001).[28]

Support for the police, in particular, is strongest among the more settled, urban and prosperous sections of society that may, in effect, condone 'tough' policies such as:

Detaining migrants arbitrarily. Police stations consider this a profitable business, because bail, fines and forced bribes, also imposed arbitrarily, can amount to several hundred yuan. Even neighbourhood committees that have no power of detention get into the act. Some have been detaining migrant workers and charging bail. (Chan 2003: 47)

The central government does not approve of such practices. It has tried to improve the rights of migrant workers and the CCP leadership has been increasingly concerned about discontent among them. The experience of those perceived as political dissidents, on the other hand, is unrelentingly harsh. As in other authoritarian regimes: '[they] are seldom arrested, placed on trial, sent to gulags, exiled, or murdered, though all these things may still happen from time to time. Today's authoritarians usually employ legalistic or bureaucratic methods' (Puddington 2009: 75). The Procuratorate and the other security agencies may be less prone to use violence, which attracts outside interest, but they are 'determined to marginalise or eliminate all perceived sources of opposition power and dissent' (Puddington 2009: 75).

Charges such as 'endangering state security', defined in Chinese Criminal Law to include acts such as separatism, espionage and armed rebellion, carry the possibility of life imprisonment and capital punishment. They rise at sensitive political periods and places. So, for example, Xinjiang Uyghur Autonomous Region saw a surge in cases amid preparations for the Beijing 2008 Summer Olympic Games (US Congressional-Executive Commission on China 2008). Similarly, though the public may support it, the police response to increasing crime has also been to initiate anti-crime campaigns that short-circuit official procedures and address political imperatives (Liang 2005). For example:

> [In 2002, the CCP] suggested ... that the ongoing severe strike [anti-crime] campaign ... should be carried forward to ensure a stable and good social environment for the forthcoming Sixteenth Party's Congress. This call clearly showed how crime control and the legal system were both subject to political purpose as tools. (Liang 2005: 395)

Similarly, the imposition of the death penalty, which is prescribed for a wide range of offences in China, is also subject to political considerations. As a review by Lu and Zhang reports: 'the actual application of the death penalty in China was not merely a legal matter, but reflective of political and social climate of the time' (Lu and Zhang 2005: 370).

The economic reforms have to a great extent weakened some of the social and ideological framework that underpinned the legal system and the PRC is experimenting with many of the same public order policies tried in other jurisdictions. The changes have been profound. 'When the People's Republic of China started its economic reform and open-door policy in 1978, there was a trend toward formal social/crime control over the Confucianism based informal control that had dominated for more than two thousand years' (Jiang, Lambert and Wang 2007: 261).

The modernisation process also makes it important that foreigners have confidence that the legal system is consistent, fair and comprehensible. In 2009, for example, the Anglo-Australian mining company Rio Tinto had four of its China-based staff arrested on suspicions of stealing state secrets but the process of investigation and charging was opaque, making many foreign investors wary. In this case, foreign observers were left with the impression that the legal moves were designed to bolster negotiations on mineral prices. After nine months of obscure legal proceedings, the four employees entered guilty pleas to bribery charges. Commenting on the case, the *Financial Times* (23 March 2010) suggested that:

> In the short run, the lesson of the trial may be that China can do what it wants: its market is simply too big to ignore ... [A]ttempts by Beijing– or indeed Rio – to pass the trial off as a routine judicial affair ring hollow ...
> The truth is that much of Chinese business is conducted in a legal grey zone, often policed by corrupt officials. That leaves all market participants – Chinese or foreign – in constant danger of a crackdown.

Regulation is another important area of misunderstanding. Much of the political tension that surrounds regulation in dialogue between China and its trading partners, particularly in the EU, arises from the belief that the legal process is invoked for commercial reasons (Yang and Clarke 2005). Nevertheless, as Gewirtz notes: 'the role of legal reform in China's economic development is widely recognized in China. China's leaders see developing its legal system as an important element in its economic development by providing rules of the game to guide transactions and institutions to enforce those rules' (Gewirtz 2003: 64).

China's legal system is under pressure, therefore, to follow international legal norms and to develop legal arrangements that parallel those of its trading partners in areas such as the protection of intellectual property and product safety.

Conclusion

'Even casual observers of events in the PRC note that the leadership of the Chinese Communist Party must decide all matters of any significance. Administrative reform is no exception' (Straussman and Zhang 2001: 411).

Straussman and Zhang sought to place the recent experience of the PRC in a comparative context. They show how trends to centralise in one period have been followed by attempts to do the opposite later in a cyclical pattern. This search for the correct balance, like that between specialisation of function and integration, is a common feature of government. Straussman and Zhang show that: 'the PRC is not immune from worldwide trends to decentralize responsibility to lower level governments and administrative units, promote mechanisms that enhance accountability and responsiveness, and borrow from 'best practices' across sectors and across countries' (Straussman and Zhang 2001: 419).

These 1990s international trends, often bundled together with the ascription New Public Management (NPM), have had varied impact in many different countries including China. They are, however, presaged on a series of axioms about 'running government like a business' that are particularly tested in the PRC. Crucially, NPM suggests that it is possible and desirable to separate the machinery of government from politics. Its advocates present administration was the neutral application of value-free techniques to politically determined policy aims. In China, the influence of NPM can be seen in the use of customer satisfaction surveys, performance measurements, service agreements between public sector providers and other techniques. The PRC also adopted e-government, a key component of the reforms internationally. Since the roll out in 1999 of the Government Internet Programme, Chinese citizens can apply for permits, access routine information and register for civil service examinations online. Overall, however, every aspect of the machinery of government is explicitly political. Not only is the CCP's interest in all aspects of government clear but also the links between the output of the state and its legitimacy have never been more significant.

The PRC is a unitary state with a centralised political system but, in all areas of public policy from fiscal to legal, localism can have a real impact on the experience of individual citizens and businesses. This reality is a significant problem for the CCP centrally as favouritism and corruption undermine the working of the 'harmonious society'. The PRC has seen important changes to its machinery of government in recent years as both a prelude to and consequence of its path of economic development. In part, this has given rise to a diminution of the direct role of the state in people's lives but two problems remain for the ruling party. The legacy of a more all-embracing socialism has identified the state as the guarantor of individual welfare while the experience of growing economic rewards has raised expectations. The CCP's response can, in part, remain ideological but it must also provide state services that satisfy ever increasing material demands.

Notes

1 There are several influential civilian and military think tanks in the PRC but they operate far less independently than their Western equivalents often being sponsored by government departments. The heads of these bodies can have a high rank and notable influence in the CCP.

2 There was also significant domestic pressure to drop this proposal.

3 'China's Rare Earths' (editorial) *Financial Times* (London) 7 July 2011, p. 12.

4 In terms of population, the rural representation has been lower than the urban. Draft regulations brought forward in 2010 will end this inequality.

5 The CPPCC includes some members from the eight 'democratic parties' as well as well-known individuals co-opted from various sectors of society. The number of members varies and the figure here is as of 2008. See www.cppcc.gov.cn.

6 *BBC News* 5 March 2011, sourced at www.bbc.co.uk/news/world-asia-pacific-12548685.

7 An interesting comparison can be found at Andrew Browne 'Premier's Work Report: The Difference a Decade Makes?', *Wall Street Journal*, 5 March 2011.

8 Source China Media Project report at http://cmp.hku.hk/2010/06/25/6376.
9 For example, a property law, prepared in draft in 2004, after years of discussion, and expected to pass in 2006, was delayed until March 2007 because of strong opposition.
10 See for example Liao (2006).
11 Membership is between 19 and 25; its Standing Committee varies between 5 and 9.
12 The Ministry of National Defense is outside the super ministry framework and is subordinate to the Central Military Commission. It does not exercise command authority over the military.
13 According to Elizabeth Economy, senior fellow for China and director of Asia Studies at the Washington-based Council on Foreign Relations, China's central environmental protection agency, the state Environmental Protection Administration, has only 300 full-time staff. 'China's Transition at a Turning Point: Crises, Challenges, And Opportunities', Carnegie Endowment for International Peace, Asia Studies Program, Council On Foreign Relations, 24 September 2003.
14 'China's Transition At A Turning Point: Crises, Challenges, And Opportunities', Carnegie Endowment For International Peace, Asia Studies Program, Council On Foreign Relations, 24 September 2003.
15 *Ibid.*
16 China has 31 provincial-level administrative units, including 23 provinces, 5 autonomous regions and 4 cities, excluding Hong Kong and Macau as well as the 'claimed province' of Taiwan. The four provincial units desig-nated as 'centrally administered municipalities' are Beijing, Shanghai, Tianjin and Chongqing (since 1997). Though the provinces have their origin in dynastic China, the PRC has created new ones.
17 Tsai (2004); Tsui and Wang (2004); He (2008).
18 Tibet, Guangxi, Xinjiang, Inner Mongolia, and Ningxia – each home to a significant ethnic minority.
19 Barry Naughton and Dali Yang (2004: 9) point out that 'China has retained a core element of central control: the *nomenklatura* system of personnel management' and argue that 'this nomenklatura personnel system is the most important institution reinforcing national unity'. On the importance of the nomeklatura system during the 1980s, see Huang (1996).
20 See Ray Brooks and Ran Tao (2003), China's Labor Market Performance and Challenges, IMF Working Paper, sourced at www.imf.org /external/pubs/ft/wp/2003/wp03210.pdf.
21 See also Li (2004).
22 All death penalty sentences, which in China is a wide range, are reported to the Supreme People's Court for final approval.
23 Cases of endangering national security, common crimes that carried a maximum punishment of life imprisonment or death, and crimes committed by foreigners.

24 Similarly, Chinese citizens have the right to petition central government to seek redress for local grievances that dates back thousands of years and the State Council has recently sought to encourage its use as a 'safety valve'. Local officials, however, actively discourage petitioners in fear that complaints may cost them promotions and jobs, or trigger investigations. See Wong (2009).

25 Organic Law of the People's Procuratorates of the People's Republic of China, Article 4, sourced at www.asianlii.org/cn/legis/cen/laws/olotppot-proc656/.

26 For a discussion of recent reforms from a Chinese jurist perspective see Guangzhong Chen and Mei Liu (2007); for interdisciplinary research see Diamant *et al.* (2005).

27 Between 1979 and 1999, law schools increased from 3 to 200 and lawyers from 3,000 to 100,000.

28 See also He (2007).

4

Political change and its limits:

democratisation with Chinese characteristics

Many countries claim to be democracies and the criteria for inclusion in the democratic category are necessarily very broad. They must accommodate a plethora of institutional and cultural circumstances. Variations include political systems centred on parliaments, presidencies and popular initiatives. The reason that democracy is invoked so often as an ideal is that it confers legitimacy on the exercise of power which, in turn, obliges citizens to comply even in the absence of coercion (Buchanan 2002). Governments that can claim to be carrying out the will of the people, expressed either directly or through representatives in accordance with the accepted constitutional rules, are more secure and effective.

In this chapter, the analysis of political change and especially democracy in China will try to avoid the twin problems of conceptual stretching, i.e. using a term so loosely that it has little meaning, and of imposing inappropriate standards based on the experience of particular states. Collier and Levitsky, who focus particularly on Latin America, usefully suggest:

> A 'procedural minimum' definition [of democracy] that presumes fully contested elections with full suffrage and the absence of massive fraud, combined with effective guarantees of civil liberties, including freedom of speech, assembly, and association ... [adding] the criterion that elected governments must have effective power to govern. (Collier and Levitsky 1997: 430)

Similarly, Weale, again keeping the bar low, offers: 'in a democracy important decisions on questions of law and policy depend, directly or indirectly, upon public opinion formally expressed by citizens of the community, the vast bulk of whom have equal political rights' (Weale 2007: 18).

A common theme in most models of democracy is the idea of choice through competitive elections and accountability to the electorate. In the analysis here, the mutability of opinion, i.e. almost all opinions are acceptable and can compete for majority status, is taken as implied by freedom of speech. In democracies, therefore, there is an almost infinite number of combinations of views and opinions vying for support.

Invariably, in democracies as envisaged here, the instruments for articulating and aggregating peoples' views into a manageable number of alternatives are political parties. Direct democracy, where the people as a whole make decisions through referendums or similar methods without elected representatives, is infrequently practised. Eventually, following debate and contestation within and between parties, the wish of the greater number is translated into laws, regulations etc. which the machinery of the state enforces equitably. In the long run, the popular will prevails though a degree of forbearance has to be assumed as people wait for the changes they want to be put into effect. This method of governing a country does not allow permanent majorities, particularly none which base their claim on privileged insight, so democracy is seldom compatible with one-party rule or state-sponsored ideology. These conditions make it difficult for the PRC to meet the ideals of democracy fully because of the 'leadership' role assigned to the CCP. There is much interest, however, in the extent to which China approximates to some of the conditions or shows signs of moving towards them.

Democracy is not simply to be seen as the existence of multiple parties but also as the multiplicity of inputs to public policy by affected citizens. So Dahl's characterisation of polyarchy has encouraged a broader appreciation of the development of democracy. Of course, Dahl's ideal democracy includes free elections and competing parties but, acknowleging that all systems fall short in some respects, he points to the importance of multiple centres of political power impacting on public policy (Dahl 1971). Some commentators discern such a tendency to wider influence on policy-making in the PRC. Additionally, advocates of 'deliberative democracy' look for structured and influential community discussion on policy priorities as a harbinger of democratisation and so moves in this direction will also be examined here. As deLisle affirms, 'whether democratic politics can lastingly take hold in China [...] is a venerable question. Some conclude that democracy is impossible there, others that it is inevitable, still others that it is possible but far from certain' (deLisle 2004: 193).

The literature on what is often termed 'democratisation' in China is vast and much of it based on the idea that a version of democracy that has evolved in the West will inevitably prevail. Proponents of this view point to the demise of communist regimes in Europe and elsewhere and their replacement with multi-party systems with competitive elections and the need for governing parties to seek re-election or be replaced. An interesting non-European example within the same tradition is offered by Dickson who compared the CCP with the KMT in Taiwan, where democratisation has made substantial strides (Dickson 1997). Alternative opinions suggest that this comparative model reflects the particular conditions of Western countries both in historical and cultural terms and that choice, accountability and the attributes of democracy can be secured in other ways that steer clear of the organised partisan conflict characteristic of liberal democracies.

In this chapter, neither approach is assumed but current Chinese practice, rhetoric and aspirations are examined to assess whether politics in the PRC is becoming recognisably more democratic or not. There are a number of areas of Chinese politics where, some observers argue, features of democracy, as it exists or developed elsewhere, have emerged since the 1990s and that may be viewed as the beginning of 'democratisation' in China. Critics suggest that changes in these areas are superficial or marginal and have not significantly altered China's political system in the direction of democracy. Some of these aspects of politics in China will be examined. These are:

- constitutional principles and the role assigned to the CCP;
- protests and petitions;
- development of civil society including experiments in deliberative techniques;
- use of democratic rhetoric and intra-party democracy;
- rule of law.

Constitutional principles and the role assigned to the CCP

According to its constitution, the PRC is a democratic dictatorship of the proletariat (人民民主专政) and adheres to the principle of demo-cratic centralism. The CCP defines itself as the vanguard of the advanced forces in society: 'it is the core of leadership for the cause of socialism with Chinese characteristics and represents the development trend of China's advanced productive forces, the orientation of China's advanced culture and the fundamental interests of the overwhelming majority of the Chinese people' (cited in *China-embassy.org* 2007).

As was noted in Chapter 3, constitutions are not always accurate guides to where power lies in any state but they remain important touchstones on some issues. There is no disputing, however, the centrality of the CCP to Chinese politics – the state it controls can enforce its writ notwithstanding sustained challenge from ethnic minorities, regional separatists and religious movements. Unlike other authoritarian regimes, the risk of removal from power by the military is negligible as the defence forces adhere to the Maoist maxim that 'the party controls the guns'. Where ready acceptance of the state's will is lacking, force is effectively employed. Nevertheless, as has been stressed in previous chapters, an efficient state is one that steers clear of using repression and assumes routine compliance with its policies even when they involve redistribution of wealth, postponement of consumption or involuntary restraint. This is easiest when those in power, inevitably a small minority, can persuade the much larger number that they rule in its interest. The CCP does this in many ways but, important to the Party's ability to bring the people with it, is the assertion that it is attentive to popular opinion – it is to this extent 'democratic'.

While it may be attentive, the CCP does not experience the same short to medium term pressures to be responsive. It does not, for instance, have to factor elections into its decision-making. The Party eschews elections except at the most grassroots level.

> Election procedures in rural China have improved greatly over the last 20 years and a good number of reasonably free and fair elections have been held. But changes in the 'exercise of power' have not kept up with changes in the 'access to power'. In many communities ... social forces (such as clans, religious groups, and underworld elements) continue to impede democratic rule. (O'Brien and Rongbin 2009: 359)

Research on these very local elections presents a mixed picture.[1] The consensus is that village elections have no real influence on policy and often fail to meet even moderate criteria of fairness and transparency. For example, Tsai reports from her study in four provinces that: '[v]illage officials were also comfortable reporting interference – even by themselves personally – in the pre-election process, even though such interference goes against official state regulations, as well as failure on their part to implement officially required procedures for voting and the operation of villagers' representative assemblies' (Tsai 2007: 357). Nevertheless, the system has been rolled out in a few areas at the level of township and even county, i.e. where some policy discretion is exercised. On the whole, however, the great majority of Chinese officials are not subject to even indirect electoral accountability and report to their superiors rather than to the people.

Protests and petitions

In China, aggrieved citizens sometimes resort to direct means of pressure to bring issues into the public domain. For example, in June 2009, protesters in Nankang, Jiangxi province, overturned police cars and blocked roads over plans to enforce payment of taxes more strictly while others delivered a petition to a local government office. Such protests are not unusual and are, as in this case, capable of wringing concessions. Even the prospect of large protests can bring significant accommodations of local views. This was illustrated in May 2007 when the residents of Xiamen, a city in Fujian province, blocked construction of a chemical plant with a text message campaign. Opponents of the facility circulated nearly one million mobile phone messages to urged people to join a protest rally (*news.bbc.co.uk* 2007). As Su says, 'although still authoritarian at its core, the communist state's political changes are nothing short of extraordinary if measured by the ever-growing numbers and types of popular protest' (Su 2009: 465).

While officials may not be subject to much pressure from the electorate, Chinese citizens do have access to protests and petitions as a way of influencing politics. In other countries, notably England from 1689 on, such methods have been the precursor to parliamentary and democratic reforms and, as deLisle suggests: 'the prospects for durable democratization and the nature of democracy in any polity reflect the lingering influences of pre-democratic political institutions and early steps down the road of democratic change' (deLisle 2004: 200). Zaret warns that the archaic appearance of petitioning, for example, belies:

> The historical significance of petitioning for the origins of democracy, especially for its 'public sphere' ... This development superseded norms of secrecy and privilege in political communication; but it was a practical and not a theoretical innovation ... petitioning reveals democracy's practical origins, when public opinion ... began to mediate between the state and civil society. (Zaret 1996: 1497)

It is, therefore, worth considering their role as well as that of protest in the PRC. Similarly, the development of civil society will be examined below for signs of democratic development.

Protests are often taken in the non-Chinese media to be signs of regime weakness but Lorentzen argues that:

> Deliberate toleration of narrow economic protests serves the Chinese government's purposes in two ways. First, it allows the government to identify and defuse discontented groups. Second, it provides a useful signal of local government corruption that can be used to supplement and direct limited administrative monitoring resources. This mechanism

became particularly useful to the government of contemporary China as the processes of decentralization and market reform made identification and investigation of local corruption more difficult. (Lorentzen 2004: 13)

This is not to imply that Beijing encourages rioting, the reverse is clearly true, but that viewing politics as a system, protest is not without a role and, where not an assault on the CCP's legitimacy, may increase responsiveness and accountability. In any event, there are many thousands of incidents of protest and even rioting officially recorded every year (Lum 2006). The issues range from environmental concerns to employment insecurity but an important thread is high-handed or corrupt officialdom.[2] In addition to the streets, protest can be found in factories, house churches and, despite attempts to control it, in cyberspace. The key to the response to protest lies in its scale, leadership and intent. So far, according to Brady, the Party's tactics are succeeding:

> In the post-1989 period, there have been many demonstrations in rural and urban areas over various local issues ... but these have never evolved into a social movement critiquing the whole system as the protest movement of 1989 did. Freedom to debate and explore is greater than ever before, as long as it is 'kept within the tent', the tent being maintaining the political status quo of the leadership of the CCP in Chinese society. (Brady 2009: 452)

Ironically, the Chinese leadership has even colluded with some robust street protests when, as for instance in relations with foreign countries, it wants to seem under pressure from spontaneous public indignation. The recent Sino-Japanese relationship can almost be measured by the tolerance or repression of street protest in China (Reilly 2009). The caution with which such protests are employed and the pre-emptory way in which they are sometimes called off demonstates the danger of unleashing too much free expression in an authoritarian state.

In general, protests and protestors are treated tolerantly if the incidents are localised – any sense of coordination across the state is viewed as threatening. Similarly, any threat to the integrity of the territory of the PRC triggers unremitting repression. The numbers of participants in protests and the deployment of security forces can be very high. In November 2004, for example, in Sichuan province nearly 100,000 farmers protesting over a hydroelectric project and related land confiscations confronted more than 10,000 troops and police. The leadership of the protests are often dealt with harshly by local security forces but the central government is only concerned if the organisers appear to represent a sustained challenge to the Party. Indeed, scapegoating local officials and seeming to address local concerns is a favoured central government response once the protest has been contained.

As Thornton shows, this creation of local villains, a cast including corrupt officials, local bullies, evil gentry and counter-revolutionary cadres, in order to present the state as the hero is a Chinese narrative dating back to the late Qing reign of the Yongzheng Emperor (1723–35) at least (Thornton 2007). Finally, the smaller the scale of protest the more indulgent is the response.

The most infamous protest in China was itself ostensibly about democracy so how the PRC handles public expressions of discontent now may be a measure of the progress since 1989. A worrying trend for the authorities, however, is protests that seem unconnected with any specific cause but, some authors suggest, represent general and unfocused discontent and which take shape spontaneously through text messages and the internet. As Jianrong posits: 'anger-venting riots are often devoid of specific issues, or quickly become divorced from the original issue. These riots devolve into behavior such as smashing, looting and burning. Caught up in the action, participants commit acts that are out of character' (Jianrong 2008: 77). Similarly, as discussed in Chapter 2, monitoring of internet activity and the associated censoring of political comment on the web displays a concern about uncontrollable or spontaneous expressions of discontent. The phenomenon of internet vigilantism, notoriously known as the 'human flesh search engine' (人肉搜索) in China, is, therefore, a potential concern for the CCP as its arousal of widespread and very rapid public anger may spill over from its victims to the authorities (Cheung 2009). As well as cheating spouses and other offenders against popular morals, corrupt officials are a popular prey.

In relation to its reaction to protest generally not all commentators agree that, judged by the yardstick of other authoritarian regimes, the PRC should be considered as one of the most repressive. Peerenboom suggests, for example, that the proportionate number of people against whom harsh action is taken for political dissent is quite small (Peerenboom 2007). It is difficult to know how this performance indicator is constructed but it is hardly one the CCP itself will be trumpeting. Indeed, such is the lack of control by central government of policing that it may be impossible for the Party to know the extent of actions taken in its name: 'local Party leaders, while pursuing their own security interests, frequently order police actions that inadvertently undermine the centre's strategies for refurbishing regime legitimacy and maintaining social control' (Tanner and Green 2007: 645).

Much more in the Chinese tradition is the use of petitions, an ancient system dating from the imperial age. In the post-Mao period, the PRC's strengthening of the petitioning system was seen as a harbinger of democracy. It is still the subject of much analysis and conjecture. 'Indeed, collective petitioning is one of the most common and important forms of transgressive – or at least moderately disruptive – collective action in China today' (Hurst, Liu and Tao 2009: 4).

For both central and local authorities, petitioning as a form of collective action should be more acceptable as it implies some level of deference to established institutions. It should be more easily contained than rioting while offering the same signalling benefits. O'Brien and Li (2006) show how provincial and central governments use petitions and other forms of protest to monitor and discipline village and county officials. The evidence on the coordinating role of social organisations, such as churches, army veterans or tenants groups, is mixed though it is clear that some petitioning is a spontaneous response to a local grievance. After all, 'submitting petitions to the Offices of Letters and Visits ... that exist at every level of government is legal and incurs little risk' (Lorentzen 2008: 9) compared to more violent or confrontational protest.[3] The legal provision for petitioning is, in fact, quite restrictive if enforced, for example the maximum size is five signatures.

Bypassing levels of government, though frequently done, is forbidden. It is clear, however, that petitioning is especially significant in rural China both in the poorer provinces where local government resources are less easily mobilised to address popular grievances and in the wealthier ones 'where land requisitions and compulsory development projects are concentrated' (Hurst, Liu and Tao 2009: 10). Estimates of the proportion of petitions that are addressed by the authorities are very low but the numbers of them submitted shows a steady rise (US Congressional-Executive Commission on China 2006). So petitioning as a form of collective and organised action, particularly if facilitated by established social institutions, should represent a positive development. For Chinese Marxists, however, the idea of civil society as a prior entity to the state is challenging especially as in Eastern Europe it was, in effect, a vehicle of resistance to communism. Even in Confucianism, civil society in opposition to the state is problematic (Cho 1997). The CCP's tolerance of this form of public expression is conditioned by its concern with any protest that moves beyond the very local, specific and contained. Local officials, whose careers can be jeopardised by critical protest, also monitor petitioners closely and actively try to contain their efforts, sometimes resorting to threats and intimidation. For example, Li Ruirui, a 20-

year-old from Anhui province with a grievance against her former school, was held in the store room of a Beijing hotel with other petitioners from Henan province by thugs hired by local government officials. The case came to light after she was raped by a 'guard' (cited in *People's Daily Online*, 13 August 2009). There are also reports of petitioners being sent by local officials for long periods to psychiatric hospitals to suppress their protests.[4]

The pattern of trust that Chinese citizens have in their government structures is quite different from the pattern in liberal democracies where the more local and accessible institutions usually score most highly. In the PRC, the central government in Beijing is ranked much more favourably than the various layers beneath it with the most local being the least trusted. This is a particularly marked trend among rural dwellers. Petitions to Beijing itself are, therefore, a sign of faith in the system. It is significant for the CCP that:

> trust in the central state among rural dwellers who came to Beijing to petition fell from 95 per cent to 39 per cent after just a week of petitioning. The per centage that agreed with the statement that 'the central authorities fear peasants' rose from 7 percent to 59 percent. (Holbig and Gilley 2010: 10)

As Dickson warns:

> Ostensibly [petitions] provide a conduit for citizens ... to correct grievances and injustices, but the efficacy of this channel is doubtful. Although the number of cases presented ... has skyrocketed, the number of successfully resolved cases remains miniscule ....The growing use of this system, combined with frustrations created when people cannot get the relief they are entitled to, presents a potential challenge to the state. (Dickson 2005: 5–6)

The seriousness with which the CCP centrally takes petitioning was confirmed in Wen Jiabao's 'work report' to the NPC in 2011. He particularly mentioned those petitioners who travel to Beijing complaining of abuses or misconduct by local officials.

> We will strengthen the work related to the handling of petitioners' letters and visits ... and effectively solve problems that cause great resentment among the masses, such an unauthorized expropriations of arable land and illegal demolitions of houses.[5]

Much more directly challenging, however, are petition-focused groupings such as Charter 08, a manifesto signed by over 350 intellectuals and human rights activists advocating political reform and democratisation. The leading petitioners were variously prosecuted, harrassed and marginalised. Liu Xiaobo, a principal author, was charged with trying to subvert the state and sentenced to 11 years imprisonment. As one of the best-known dissidents, his imprisonment sent a strong message to Chinese intellectuals that the CCP would not tolerate organised dissent. The authorities appeared unaware of the Charter 08 initiative until the last minute despite the prominence of its authors. It represents the coordinated, multi-centred and broad challenge that the regime feels it has to suppress comprehensively. In 2010, Liu Xiaobo was awarded the Nobel Peace Prize, a distinction for the jailed dissident that greatly annoyed Beijing and confirmed how dangerous he could be. Even less directly challenging petitioners, such as members of a group seeking the return of ancestral houses confiscated in 1956, are viewed with suspicion because of their attempts to organise across the state (HRIC 2009).[6] For some members of the Politburo Standing Committee, the political instability in North Africa and the Middle East in 2011 was a signal that any decline of vigilance in respect of nationally organised protest would 'plunge the country into the abyss of internal chaos' (Xinhua News Agency, 10 March 2011).[7] This wariness of nationwide challenge but willingness to compromise with local, even very disruptive, protest was illustrated again in April 2011. A strike by hauliers over fuel prices that effectively closed the Shanghai port of Baoshan resulted in the elimination or reduction of a range of port fees and the calling off of the drivers' action. At the same time, fear of political unrest across the state, linked by some in the CCP to events in the Middle East, precipitated a crackdown on dissidents. The key leaders of the Shanghai protest will eventually be quietly punished to discourage future organised unrest by them and news of their action has been suppressed. Nevertheless, their challenge to the government triggered the search for a short-term solution rather than recourse to repression.

Development of civil society

From the perspective of democratisation, Western theorists from de Tocqueville on have seen the emergence of an active civil society as a prerequisite to a working democracy. The role played by civil society in the PRC has undoubtedly increased and scholars who search for signs of democratisation point to this as a positive development. Cham Li tracked the enormous increase in group formation in the agricultural sector as a corollary of market liberalisation:

The rise of civil society ... is considered one of the pre-requisites for political democracy in contemporary China ... On sheer economic grounds, the Chinese Government has no alternative but to be receptive to and tolerant of the rise of autonomous organisations and corporate groups in rural areas ... [F]or optimists, the Party's acquiescent attitude towards the development of such associations may hint that economic rationality has at last prevailed over political dogmatism in China. (Wong 2006: 163–4)

Some see in the emerging market economy, the basis for a sizeable middle class, the genesis of civil society in many liberal democracies. Already it is clear from survey evidence that, as in other political systems, 'the citizens in the richest quintile and officially registered urban residents demonstrated a higher willingness to complain formally, that is through official channels' (Brixi 2009: 27).

Clearly, the authorities need to be aware of potential state-wide grievances around which protests of various kinds could be rallied. Perhaps the most threatening one is reaction to environmental degradation that increasingly effects most Chinese urban citizens in terms of clean air and water. 'The effect on the population is alarming. Already more than 400,000 people die each year as a result of ... air pollution ... and an estimated 190 million people drink water so contaminated that it makes them sick. Some 40 million people have had to migrate because their local ecology can no longer sustain them' (Economy and Lieberthal 2007: 89).

Environmental degradation could lead to social unrest. Currently there is an increasing number of small environmental protests, of which some have been violent. If an emboldened environmental movement looked like a focus for nationwide discontent, it could represent a test of CCP control. For the moment, however, it is not.

NGOs in a Western sense (that is, those that are financially and administratively independent of government ...) are virtually non-existent ... Recently ... some green groups ... are ... emerging, albeit primarily at the city and local levels ... [I]t will take some time before such groups become a genuinely independent popular force ... Friends of Nature and the China Environmental Protection Foundation, the only two organisations that have a measure of national-level exposure, have purposely kept a low profile ... [avoiding] confrontations with the government on controversial environmental issues. (Lo and Frywell 2005: 563)

The increasing importance of the middle class, entrepreneurs and professionals in part explains their new role in the CCP. Similarly, the Chinese authorities have also incorporated many new groups of social activists through quasi-governmental civil society.[8] The state also requires all groups to register as civil society organisations (CSOs) of which there are more than 410,000. These include trade associations, charities, professional groups, social and welfare organisations, advisory centres, legal aid groups, environmental groups and foundations. The law in relation to the different types varies. The law also differs across the PRC:

> [Most] recent developments [have] occurred at the local or provincial level ... Thus, although the Five Year Plan that ended in December 2010 spoke of strengthening social organizations, very little has happened with regard to creating new national level laws or regulations ... in the face of political tensions about 'civil society' and what it means for China. (Simon 2011: 3–4)

To register, CSOs need a state partner and clearly articulated goals and intentions. Their activities are monitored regularly and lobbying activity is very constrained. As a 2009 World Bank survey revealed:

> Mechanisms to support citizens' empowerment and voice are yet to be fully established ... while many citizens share their discontent informally, very few feel empowered to complain formally and seek any redress. In recent years, there have been signals of gradual improvement ... citizens lack [a] sense of empowerment relative to service providers. (Brixi 2009: 40–1)

A successful campaign by a registered CSO on an issue of public policy will be largely confined to information provision. It also needs to be non-confrontational and, usually, involves working closely with some part of the established political élite. Shock revelations are taboo. Criticisms are couched as constructive recommendations though successful actions usually feature media and information campaigns. Of course, not all CSOs are registered[9] but those that are not are also constrained by the need to avoid confrontation. Most are small, under funded and dependent on government money. Often their existence is a function of their carrying out some social, environmental or educational function in collaboration with a state agency. The conclusions of a study of CSOs in the health field also speak to the wider picture: 'Chinese CSOs – particularly unregistered, grassroots organisations – operate under a mixed set of cross-cutting pressures; indeed, they exist in a limbo of only partial legitimacy and nascent, fragile capacity, rife with both risks and opportunities' (Gill, Morrison and Lu 2007: 3).

It is clear that the civil society sector is currently a minor player in China but, because of its importance as a feature of democracy elsewhere, it is the focus of much attention. As Cham Li hints above, there are two broad scenarios sketched for the development of CSOs in

China that each address their importance for democratisation. One suggests that the CCP and the state more generally will maintain such a level of suspicion towards any hint of independent focuses of influence and popular support that CSOs will remain marginal players for the foreseeable future. The alternative view is that many aspects of Chinese development will inevitably escape state control as a wealthier China with a rising middle class and more complex economic structure challenges the CCP's capacity for omnipresence. Further, more intense pressure from class inequalities, environmental degradation and the like will turn CSOs from potential threats to invaluable partners for the state which is downsizing and decentralisation.

> Central government is coming to realise that organised societal support ... could make a positive contribution to environmental protection, particularly in regulatory control, by reporting and disclosing 'acts violating environmental laws and regulations'. Consequently, there is some room for such groups to become allies of environmental agencies and their officials to counter bureaucratic resistance in order to get environmental regulations more strictly enforced. (Lo and Fywell 2005: 563)

Clarke, similarly, points out the dependency that Western governments have on business associations for the bottom-up development of a workable regulatory framework and asks why financial interests: 'seem oddly to have more faith in the ability of Chinese politicians, who after all have much less direct experience of a market economy and the workings of civil society, to put their prescriptions into effect' (Clarke 2007: 583).

In this view, there will be an inexorable increase in the space and influence accorded to civil society that will be exploited by politically savvy organisations. The state will need more sophisticated, accurate and timely information to manage public policy and, as happens elsewhere, organised interests will fill the void.

As discussed in Chapter 3, the policy process in the PRC is characterised by more voices – if not of dissent, at least expressing diverse interests. 'In China today, political life is marked by an increasing competition among group interests, which is a fundamental shift in the policy process and in state-society relations' (Teets, Rosen and Gries 2010:18).

It would be stretching the notion of democracy unhelpfully to suggest that diversity and openness to new sources of information and opinion in the policy process signalled a fundamental shift in the political system. Nevertheless, several authors have seen in this development signs of a new pluralism.

> [Chinese] elites agree on the need for more pluralistic avenues for
> interest articulation and mechanisms to deal with social conflicts arising
> from a modern economy. While these ideas of political reform fall far
> short of electoral democracy, they are nevertheless an attempt to make
> the single-party regime more attentive to social tensions and flexibly
> adapt to a more pluralistic socio-economic stratum. (Lewis and Teets
> 2009: 19–20)

Of course, the CCP holds the trump cards but the Party itself increasingly needs to balance divisions between, in broad terms, advocates of
socialist policies that stress equity and public ownership and more free
market proponents of private entrepreneurialism and property rights.
The policy process exhibits various political compromises and accommodations that mirror more open democratic systems to some degree.

An important reality for China is the market economy albeit with
Chinese characteristics. The market assumes the postponement of
consumption and the presence of choice to ensure investment and
assure profit for innovators and entrepreneurs. In such circumstances,
there is the danger that politics will become the most obvious area of
the life of the citizens that does not offer choice or respond to people's
expressed wishes. The Party, therefore, employs many of the techniques of the market to monitor people's opinions. Many of these have
been outlined in Chapter 2 and involve using marketing tools such as
opinion polls and the internet to measure the public's preferences or
attitudes. In addition to these and more self-consciously in line with a
policy of political engagement are various experiments in deliberative
polling. In best practice, these methods involve a randomly selected
microcosm of the public being briefed on and discussing some policy
issue and then expressing their views on behalf of their community.
The key values of this testing of public opinion are participation and
deliberation. Its proponents suggest that it is more meaningful than
representative democracy, i.e. allowing elected officials to decide on
the community's behalf, especially at a local level. The experiments in
'scientific earnest democracy discussion meetings' have created some
interest in the CCP for engaging citizens at a local level though they are
still very isolated and circumscribed. The most prominent experiment
is in Zeguo, a township in the coastal city of Wenling in Zhejiang
province where the public works budget was allocated using deliberative polling (Siu and Fishkin 2009).

Use of democratic rhetoric and intra-party democracy

'We must act in accordance with the overall requirement of democracy and the rule of law, fairness and justice, honesty and fraternity, vigour and vitality, stability and order, and harmony between man and nature and the principle of jointly building and sharing' (Hu Jintao, quoted in the *Shangai Daily Online*, 15 October 2007).[10]

The claim that China is democratic is important for the CCP and, in terms of rhetoric, it is central to its appeal. The terms democracy or democratic were used 60 times in President Hu Jintao's report to the Seventeenth Party Congress in 2007 (Freedom House 2009). In the Party's view, the form of democracy offered is appropriate to Chinese conditions with all its ethnic complexity, territorial scale and stage of economic development. The model offered by the West is, for the medium term at least, unsuitable. Indeed, rhetorically the term 'Western' is often used to dismiss calls for specific reforms. For example, in September 2009, Hu Jintao, addressing the Chinese People's Political Consultative Conference (CPPCC), warned: 'developing social democracy should draw on the fruits from the entire human civilization, including achievements made in the political sphere, but can by no means indiscriminately copy the Western system' (cited in *People's Daily Online*, 29 September 2009).

There are officially eight democratic parties in addition to the CCP but they are part of the 'united front' (Gottwald, Sandschneider and Zhang 2008: 555–6) and they accept the leading role of the CCP.[11] As a White Paper issued by the State Council Information Office entitled *China's Political Party System* put it: 'the political party system China has adopted is multi-party cooperation and political consultation under the leadership of the Communist Party of China, which is different from both the two-party or multi-party competition systems of Western countries and the one-party system practiced in some other countries' (quoted in *China.org.cn*, 15 November 2007).

In the Party's view, China is suited for democracy with 'Chinese characteristics', the code for a claim to Chinese exceptionalism. In March 2010, Li Fei, a senior official of the NPC, told *China Daily* that:

> The current priority is to perfect existing direct elections at county and township levels ... Whether in terms of justice or fairness, a society must pay more attention to 'substantial democracy', which in China means that there should be representatives from all areas, ethnic groups and walks of life ... Western-style elections ... are a game for the rich ... As a socialist country, we cannot simply take the Western approach. (Zhu 2010)

The CCP offers socialist democracy, a brand that can encompasses elements of Marxism-Leninism and Maoism with nationalism. The Party's organisational principle is democratic centralism as part of the dictatorship of the people.[12] As Tang's study of public opinion demonstrates (Tang 2005), the ideological orientation of different social strata in China should not be dismissed, the CCP still puts a lot of effort into what in Chinese terms is known as 'propaganda and thought work' (Brady 2009).

> A strong case can be made that Marxist-Leninist ideology and its various Chinese permutations are irrelevant in today's China ... The CCP, however, does *not* and *cannot* agree ... for the very reason that it is a communist party ... To reject the underlying ideology is to reject the party's raison d'être itself ... [The CCP] is left with three alternatives: embrace the ideology ... , ignore the ideology, or finesse and adapt the ideology ... What it has done is to fully embrace the third option. (Shambaugh 2008: 104–5; emphasis in original)

The current leadership of the Party is aware of the dangers of an over-reliance on the economic boom the country is enjoying for, while modernisation has taken almost 400 million citizens out of poverty since 1990, 415 million Chinese still live on less than US$2 a day (Chen and Ravallion 2007). Democracy is a lesser goal than freedom from hunger. As well as ensuring prosperity, they seek to appeal to the patriotic, populist and philosophical values of the Chinese, as discussed in Chapter 2.

> The great banner of socialism with Chinese characteristics is a banner for the development and progress ... Emancipating the mind is a magic tool for developing socialism ... Scientific development and social harmony are the basic requirements ... and building a well-off society in an all-round way is the party's and the state's goal for 2020. (Hu 2007)

The Party is practised at the use of popular media to emphasise its role in safeguarding China's values. Eschewing 'a long tradition of ideologically sound but mind-numbingly dull Party propaganda' (Foster 2009), it is increasingly using new media and making more imaginative use of the traditional outlets. Thus, for example, part of the celebrations of 60th year of the PRC took the form of an epic film, *The Founding of the Republic*, for which 172 major Chinese stars, such as the Hong Kong kung-fu hero Jackie Chan, vied for cameo roles. In the film, produced by the state-owned China Film Group, Mao and other revolutionary heroes are given lines that affirm the stance of the current leadership on the role of the market, democracy etc. (Foster 2009).

In some respects, the CCP is offering a worldview that juxtaposes the precepts of Western democracy with a set of 'Asian values' encompassing some influences of Confucianism, in particular loyalty towards the family and nation and the sublimation of personal freedom for the sake of society's stability and 'social harmony'. 'The rhetoric of a harmonious society is aimed at demonstrating the government's commitment to the construction of a socialist *market* regime on behalf of 'the people' (as opposed to a re-emergent *capitalist* class). In using the rhetoric of the harmonious society, the Party-state seeks to reassure 'the people' that it is responsive' (Smyth and Qian 2009: 42; emphasis in original).

The Party has promoted these ideas claiming that strong and stable leadership, respect for social harmony and the privileging of collective well-being over individual rights are more grounded in local experience than the structured conflict of pluralism. As deLisle says, 'this vision of human rights relativism typically included democracy—at least of a liberal, contentious, 'Western' sort—among the alien values that Asians need not or should not embrace' (deLisle 2004: 194).

The CCP, it is posited, offers security and efficiency, both of which underpin its claim to be advancing democracy. Further, Dickson reminds those looking for signs of reform: 'greater democracy is not the immediate goal of China's leaders . . . The CCP is pursuing a variety of political reforms that are intended to enhance the capacity of the state to govern effectively, if not democratically' (Dickson 2005: 1–2).

In part, this stress on effectiveness has facilitated some democratisation within the Party. Notably, the relatively smooth leadership transition from the third to the fourth generation of leaders of the PRC.[13] The highest levels of any authoritarian regime are always conscious of potential political instability or the loss of their own privileges so renewing the top position, the function of elections in liberal democracies, is fraught with danger. The process used to take place secretly within the state headquarters Zhongnanhai, or at the summer resort Beidaihe (北戴河). The CCP has, however, innovated with more intra-party democracy through sharing power within the Party élite and allowing limited electoral competition at the highest levels.

> These measures are aimed at enhancing the Party's art of leadership and raising its capacity to resist corruption, prevent degeneration, and withstand risks. No signs indicate that the new leadership is going to change the one-Party ruling system or discard the principle of democratic centralism for the foreseeable future. The preexisting rules have provided both constraints and opportunities for political actors in a new round of the game. (Lin 2004: 274–5)

Hu Jintao's election in November 2002 as general secretary and in March 2003 as president was the first smooth power transfer in the PRC. It was not prompted by death or political crisis. The same procedure has been signalled for choosing his successor and analogous means of political élite selection have been institutionalised from the top to the basic levels, i.e. more candidates than seats. Additionally, the CCP's regulations now provide criteria for convening Party congresses, the selection and retirement of officials, fixed term limits and other measures to make it more 'democratic'. As discussed in Chapter 3, Provincial People's Congresses (PPCs) and other local government bodies have seen increased level of electoral challenge within the Party and some improvement in their representativeness. As Hu Jintao himself explained at an event to mark the CCP's 88th birthday: 'the realisation of inner-party democracy must rely on the guarantee of all Party members' democratic rights to know, to participate, to vote and to supervise in all internal affairs of the Party' (cited in *Xinhua News*, 30 June 2009).

The result of this intra-party democracy is more stable leadership with the emphasis on administrative-technical experience as a pathway to the top. According to Zang:

> Political technocracy is a very stable polity not only because of elite inter-dependence, but more importantly because of its ability to co-opt intellectuals and professionals into the power circle. The CCP offers ambitious intellectuals opportunities to climb up the political hierarchy ... thus leaving few in a state of discontent. The formation of the political technocracy has diminished dissent among Chinese intellectuals significantly ... China's political technocracy will stay in power for the foreseeable future. (Zang 2001: 74)

Rhetorically, the greater democracy within the CCP is encompassed by the 'three represents' – the principle that the Party should be representative of advanced social productive forces, advanced culture, and the interests of the overwhelming majority of the people. The three represents may be poorly articulated but it is much more embracing than the idea of 'Dictatorship of the Proletariat' which it effectively replaced. Greater democracy is also facilitated, as are other reforms, by the recasting of China's foreign policy to encourage a calmer international environment (see Chapter 6).

More pressing for the Party, at least in its democratic rhetoric, is reform within the organisation itself and it is at this level that there are signs of change. The CCP has, as outlined in Chapter 2, embraced the new entrepreneurial class, institutionalised the élite succession process, improved the calibre of its membership and still retained the symbols of its revolutionary past.

Even in liberal democracies, political parties, ruling factions and governing élites do not give up power without resistance and they always seek to scan the horizon for threats to their position. The CCP does the same and its leaders have set out to adapt to anticipated change. The future, they assert, will be different with hunger conquered, prosperity assured and national unity unchallenged. New forms of democracy will be developed.

Rule of law

'The rule of law' has transformed from a governing instrument to a fundamental goal of reform. Chinese reformers have taken the legal system more seriously than ever before. They realised that their legitimacy and governance must have a legal and constitutional foundation. Numerous new laws have been enacted and put into practice. But China still has a long way to go before solidly establishing the rule of law. (Liu 2008: 550)

The rule of law is almost as ambiguous a term as democracy but its essential elements are that the same rules apply to all citizens regardless of their social position and that the application of law is predictable rather than vicarious. There must be meaningful limits on the arbitrary exercise of power by state actors and effective ways in which citizens can challenge state action. The law should be unbiased and judicial hearings held in public. While some states have reneged on the principle in times of severe national crisis, none can retain the ascription democratic if they routinely do so for short-term political reasons. In China, the self-identification of the CCP's interests with those of the nation have made the rule of law a testing concept to apply. Diamond stresses the scale of the task:

If the Communist Party truly intends to build a rule of law, it must tie its own hands in an irretrievable way. This means giving up the power to appoint these various officials and entrusting the appointment and supervision of these bodies to some source of authority that is truly independent of politics. Only in that circumstance could a 'rule of law' system be credible in China. (Diamond 2003: 325)

Nevertheless, especially since amending the constitution in 1999, the leadership of the CCP have sought to embrace change and there have been reforms to the laws on administrative litigation, state compensation and legislative procedures. For China, the path may be typified by the shift from 'rule by law', a common feature of authoritarian regimes (Schedler 2009: 11), to an aspiration to rule of law as a source of political legitimacy. As the title of Peerenboom's study suggests, it is *China's Long March toward Rule of Law* (2002)[14] and, though it is unlikely to follow Western course directly, the constitutionally ascribed ambition of establishing a 'socialist rule of law' should not be completely dismissed. Peerenboom sees the 'rule of law with Chinese characteristics' as a model or 'thin theory' that promotes clarity, consistency, stability and enforcement. It may fall short of Western ideas but it does presage a 'government in tune with the law'. This is, in part, for economic reasons. 'In order to deliver sustained economic growth, Asia's leaders also rely increasingly on foreign direct investment, which requires predictable transparency, governance, and the rule of law; this is particularly true for China' (Green 2007: 20).

Foreign and local firms are increasingly pushing the boundaries of the Chinese legal system, for example, to defend their intellectual property. In an opinion article in the *New York Times*, the chairman of the American Chamber of Commerce in China suggested that:

> [China is] a country with a legal system vastly improved from a generation ago, particularly in the area of business law ... Evidence that China has benefited from an increasingly robust legal framework is clear. China's rapid economic development has stemmed both from relaxing state control over the economy and also its move toward a law-based society. (Watkins 2009)

There are also political motives such as countering the alienation of citizens who feel their rights have been trampled. Despite this, there is strong resistance from within the Party, the bureaucracy and state-owned enterprises. The rule of law can be seen as irksome and restrictive when 'action' is needed. For example, during the SARS crisis: 'to guarantee social stability and to limit what it saw as especially harmful social behavior, the state did not stop to think about rule-of-law injunctions against Mao's instruction, 'policy is the soul of law' (政策是法律的灵魂). It quickly resorted to a newly expanded political-legal principle of 'flexibility'' (Keith and Lin 2007: 407). New regulations, punishments and restrictions were created to meet the crisis without reference to laws or due process. Officials felt no inhibitions and feared no sanction in bypassing existing laws.

The separation of executive, legislative and judicial powers that underpin the rule of law elsewhere are effectively absent in the PRC despite aspirational statements in the constitution. As Backer puts it, 'separation of powers doctrine differs significantly from that understood in the West' (Backer 2009: 129). The regime does discipline its members, for offences such as corruption, and they can be subject to the normal legal process following party enquiries but it is clear that much of this application of the law is heavily influenced by the factionalism and demonstration-needs of the CCP. Similarly, the prosecution and harassing of politically active individuals outside the Party is generally conditioned by the perceived threat to the government rather than the application of legal principles and processes.

A major dilemma for the CCP in relation to any ambition its leaders may have to embrace the rule of law in some form revolves around the control of the police. In effect, the police are allowed a great deal of autonomy because they display strong loyalty to the Party: 'the political role of the police acts as a double-edged sword. After obtaining loyalty, a political party can only give the police more free discretionary power and political influence, and this threatens the goal of the rule-of-law society that the CCP wishes to promote' (Weifang 2007: 672).

Up to the highest level, the police hierarchy takes precedence over the judicial and the independence of the courts is highly circumscribed. As O'Brien and Li's study shows, China's judicial system 'remains deeply embedded in politics' (O'Brien and Li 2005: 31). Their research in rural China also demonstrates that: 'litigating is expensive, getting a case accepted is difficult, and long delays are common. Even when rural complainants manage to win a lawsuit, they often face uncertain enforcement or retaliation' (O'Brien and Li 2005: 31).

Nevertheless, if there are signs of democratisation in the PRC, they must be supported by parallel developments in the legal system. As Diamond's conclusions suggest, the rule of law goal presents China with a dilemma: '[It] will not achieve a truly vigorous rule of law, and bridge the widening chasm between the people and the ruling élite, unless it also develops, however gradually, democracy' (Diamond 2003: 331).

There may be a vicious circularity about this argument but legal scholars[15] suggest that, if the legal system is disaggregated, the rule of law ideal is beginning to influence some branches of law and that incremental changes will have a cumulative effect.

> The ongoing struggle for the rule of law should be regarded as a long-term struggle within the mutating, but still critically important, institutional dimensions of China's particular 'political legal system' ... the Party still sees its own leadership as 'organic'. Its approach to social stability requires a 'socialist rule of law' that serves the interests of the people. (Keith and Lin 2007: 419)

Conclusion

For the Chinese leadership, having recently left behind the ravages of Mao's charisma and evil genius and survived the traumatic state-society confrontation of 1989, democratization at the national level has not been a priority. Instead, ... the foremost concern for China's leaders has been the maintenance of political order and the promotion of effective governance. (Yang 2006: 143–4)

Chinese progress towards democracy and the rule of law, if actually occurring, may give rise to a new model that is *sui generis*. It may not, therefore, copy Western models. For an assessment of democratisation in China, however, some reasonably universal criteria have to be employed. Here, following Weale, the bar for describing a system as democratic was set low and asked that important public decisions depend, directly or indirectly, on structured expressions of public opinion buttressed by equal political rights (Weale 2007: 18). The PRC is still short of this standard but, in some respects, there are signs of moving towards it. If one's definition of democracy includes not only public influence on decision-making and policy but also political rights (such as freedom of speech and assembly) together with formal and real limits on the state's power over it citizens, China is probably much further from democracy. It is important, however, to avoid assuming that the Chinese path will be modelled on the European. Nevertheless, Chinese conservatives, who advocate slow institutional reform, frequently call on the Irish philosopher Edmund Burke's warnings of chaos and instability in the rush to democracy in the Europe of his day.

Notes

1 See *Journal of Contemporary China* (2009), Special Issue 'State of the Field: Assessing Village Elections in China', Vol. 18, No. 60.
2 Some officials experiencing conflicting localist and official loyalties collude in protests though tight controls on open political protests are retained. See Perry and Selden (2003).
3 The PRC has high levels of literacy across the state; see Hannum and Park (eds) (2009).
4 See *British Medical Journal*, 25 June 2010.
5 http://news.xinhuanet.com/english2010/china/2011–03/15/c_13779521 _24.htm.
6 Source: Human Rights in China, an NGO promoting human rights in China.
7 The quote is from the 2011 Legislative Work Report of the NPC Chairman Wu Bangguo (吴邦国), a Politburo Standing Committee member.

8 Sometimes referred to in the literature as GONGOs, government organised non-governmental organisations.

9 Some register as businesses to have a legal status but avoid the official CSO procedure.

10 Hu Jintao, General Secretary, opening the 17 CCP National Congress in Beijing, on 15 October 2007.

11 The 17 CCP National Congress in 2007 appointed 2 non-CCP ministers.

12 Article 1 of the State Constitution describes China as 'a socialist state under the people's democratic dictatorship'.

13 In chronological order, Mao Zedong (ruling years: 1931–76), Deng Xiaoping (ruling years: 1976–89), Jiang Zemin (ruling years: 1989–2004), and Hu Jintao (ruling years: 2004–). See Table 1.

14 For a contrary view, see Lubman (2000).

15 See Heuser (2003).

5

The national question in
Chinese politics

The exact shape and size of a state is the result of many factors ranging from royal inter-marriage to conquest. In many parts of the globe straight-line borders suggest arbitrary imperialist deals and pragmatic compromises. Nevertheless, once the lines are drawn, they are hard to change. Each political system once established lays claim to the concept of sovereignty, i.e. supreme authority within a territory, which since the Peace of Westphalia in 1648 has defined the state as the core political institution. It is not that states refer often to this European settlement directly. Individual countries construct their own versions of history that justify the *status quo* and the defining claim that each state has ultimate control of all those who live in its territory. Nationalists, in particular, encourage narratives that suggest that the current shape is the playing out of a manifest destiny reflecting ancient loyalties, ethnic ties and cultural affinities.

> The homeland becomes a repository of historic memories and associations, the place where 'our' sages, saints and heroes lived, worked, prayed and fought. All this makes the homeland unique. Its rivers, coasts, lakes, mountains and cities become 'sacred' – places of veneration and exaltation whose inner meanings can be fathomed only by the initiated, that is, the self-aware members of the nation. (Smith 1993: 9)

So it is with China – the 'Central Kingdom' and 'the realm under heaven' (Li 2008c: 323).

The PRC occupies its current territory and even claims rightful jurisdiction over some adjacent areas. It rebuffs any suggestion of secession or reallocation of land based on rival claims. Nevertheless, as Lin asserts, 'as late as the mid-twentieth century, the very definition of "China" remained an unresolved issue' in the minds of Chinese officials (Lin 2007: 203). The official history, often accepted uncritically even by foreign commentators, is that for five thousand years a

Chinese state existed with much the same footprint on the globe as the PRC. It is suggested that this historical reality is further grounded in archaeological evidence from 250,000 to 2.24 million years ago. As Tu affirms: 'the idea of a cultural core area first located in the Wei River Valley, a tributary of the Yellow River, and later encompassing parts of the Yangtze River has remained potent and continuous in the Chinese consciousness' (Tu 1991: 3).

The essential unity of the Chinese people over time is attested to in this interpretation by the continuity of the written language, standardised by the first emperor of China, Emperor Qin Shi Huang who unified China in 221 BC. As with many other nationalisms, the core beliefs are impervious to evidence – it is the strength of the conviction that matters.

Whatever ambiguities may exist at the periphery, the core area and claimed common ancestry are essential to being Chinese. Though the idea of nationalism is itself adapted from a Western notion of territorially grounded social solidarity and claims of national sovereignty, it has been employed by the Chinese state in various guises since the 1920s. As outlined in Chapter 1, the May Fourth Movement, which in 1919 began with student demonstrations against the Treaty of Versailles' transfer of Chinese territory to Japan and many of the leaders of which helped form the CCP, is identified as a key turning point. In all nationalisms, foreigners are always a touchstone of self-identity but, in China, the nationalist discourse draws heavily on the experience of a century of humiliation at the hands of outsiders. At first, Chinese nationalism was essentially based on the Han, the overwhelmingly dominant ethnic group, but has been broadened to include all the other peoples that live in what official PRC ideology describes as a multi-ethnic state. This idea is reflected in the concept *Zhonghua minzu* (中华民族) that is used to express a Chinese nationality transcending ethnic divisions. It is taken to be inclusive of all ethnic groups in China and is similar in scope to the assertions of a conscious national identity developed in several European states in the nineteenth century.

> This suggests that, whatever else it may be, what we mean by 'national' identity involves some sense of political community, however tenuous. A political community in turn implies at least some common institutions and a single code of rights and duties for all the members of the community. It also suggests a definite social space, a fairly well demarcated and bounded territory, with which the members identify and to which they feel they belong. (Smith 1993: 9)

The most recent consolidation of the current Chinese territory and its reunification, following a period of warlord rule over its constituent parts, was achieved by Chiang Kai-shek in the late 1920s. Historically, Chinese dynasties have ruled both much larger and smaller tracts of land sometimes as united political systems and at other times as forms of federations or rival kingdoms. The loss to the PRC of Taiwan following the civil war did not affect the claim of jurisdiction over the entire territory or, indeed, the reciprocal assertion by the exiled Kuomintang of ownership of the same land mass. So the current Chinese state as controlled by Beijing occupies a vast area with extremely varied terrain and a population of over 1.3 billion. Despite the heroic national narrative of unity, however, the state must actually deal with significant issues of diversity. Central to these challenges are the different ethnic groups and nationalities, the worldviews of which may diverge from the official one. This chapter examines the nature of the tests the Chinese state faces in dealing with ethnic and nationalist issues and how it deals with them.

Ethnic politics

There is clearly no hard and fast division between what constitutes either an ethnic or a nationality issue. In the literature on the PRC, particularly where it relies on ethnographic research, the terms 'nationality' and 'ethnic group' are used almost interchangeably. Interestingly, this ambiguity can, in part, be attributed to Sun Yat-sen who borrowed a Japanese term, Mínzúku, which is itself ambiguous, when defining his five-fold categorisation of the Chinese people during the nationalist revolution at the beginning of the twentieth century (Wang 2004). For many Chinese, their ascribed ethnicity is less significant than much more local affiliations. For example, Kaup reports that in her fieldwork among the Zuang, 'when speaking in Mandarin, respondents would use the word 'nationality' (*zu*) when referring to their zhìxì' (Kaup 2002: 876),[1] a more local territorial and linguistic division. It is important to note, however, that for the Chinese state all distinctions are essentially ethnic. As Gladney explains,

> The Communists incorporated the idea of Han unity into a Marxist ideology of progress, with the Han in the forefront of development and civilization. The more 'backward' or 'primitive' the minorities were, the more 'advanced' and 'civilized' the so-called Han seemed, and the greater the need for a unified national identity. (Gladney 2009)

Though the state acknowledges different nationalities, it recognises no rival nationalist claims, which it typifies as 'splitism' or 'secessionism'.

The newly assertive nationalist ideology in China shares with previous formulas the idea of a cohesive, unified people forming a single indissolvable nation, as outlined in the PRC's constitution. As Bulag affirms: 'minorities and their culture … do not exist in their own right, but as part of the Chinese nation' (2003: 243).

The task of identifying the ethnic make up of China was given to a commission shortly after the foundation of the PRC. It was tutored by an analogous process previously undertaken in the Soviet Union under Stalin and which developed criteria around language, region, economic life and ascribed psychological characteristics. 'It is clear that the realities of China's ethnic groups have to be tailored to fit the socialist Russian theory' (Wang 2004: 161).

Applying the official PRC definitions, there are 56 distinct ethnic groups. This figure was arrived at in 1982 after adjustments to the previous classifications that set the total at 41 in 1952 and 53 in 1964 (Leibold 2010a). By far the largest is the Han, which is 92 per cent of the population. The other 55, though only 8 per cent, still represent large numbers of people and are often concentrated in particular areas. All citizens of the PRC are obliged to state their ethnicity on their personal identification cards and other official documents. The application of the one-child policy has resulted in a large increase in the proportion of non-Han citizens, not just through natural growth but also inter-ethnic marriages and legal redesignation. Ethnic minorities were only 6 per cent in 1953. They are afforded some legal autonomy in areas of marked concentration. This is a long-standing policy to protect diversity and currently more than 71 per cent of China's minority population lived within one of the over 1,328 autonomous provinces, prefectures, townships or villages covering 64 per cent of the PRC (Leibold 2010). Table 8 lists the largest official ethnic groups though the categories suggest clearer definitions than are possible given internal migration and settlement patterns. (See Appendix A at the end of the chapter for a complete list.)

> The differences among regional and linguistic subgroups of Han Chinese are at least as great as those among many European nationalities. Han Chinese speak seven or eight mutually unintelligible dialects, each of which has many local subdialects. Cultural differences (cuisine, costume, and custom) are equally great. (Worden, Savada and Dolan 1988)

Nevertheless, intra-Han distinctions are less important than the identities they share. By the same token, some other ethnicities do not represent major divisions either. In practice, for example, the Hui are very similar to Han Chinese except for their Islamic religion, and the

Table 8 Largest official ethnic groups

Ethnic group	Population	Distribution
Zhuang	15,489,630	Guangxi, Yunnan, Guangdong, Guizhou
Manchu	9,821,180	Liaoning, Heilongjiang, Jilin, Hebei, Beijing, Inner Mongolia
Hui	8,602,978	Ningxia, Gansu, Henan, Xinjiang, Qinghai, Yunnan, Hebei, Shandong, Anhui, Liaoning, Beijing, Inner Mongolia, Heilongjiang, Tianjin, Jilin, Shaanxi
Miao	7,398,035	Guizhou, Yunnan, Hunan, Guangxi, Sichuan, Guangdong, Hubei
Uyghur	7,214,431	Xinjiang, Hunan
Yi	6,572,173	Sichuan, Yunnan, Guizhou, Guangxi
Tujia	5,704,223	Qinghai, Gansu, Hunan, Hubei, Sichuan, Guizhou
Mongolian	4,806,849	Inner Mongolia, Xinjiang, Liaoning, Jilin, Heilongjiang, Qinghai, Hebei, Henan, Gansu, Yunnan
Tibetan	4,593,330	Tibet, Sichuan, Qinghai, Gansu, Yunnan
Bouyei	2,545,059	Guizhou

Sources: www.agenceglobal.com/ accessed 26 July 2010.

Hakka, officially an ethnic group, are of Han nationality (Zhang 2007). For the political system, these finer distinctions are easily accommodated by sensitivity to religious or cultural differences. For instance, the enforcement of food safety regulations is attuned to Halal practice in Ningxia Hui Autonomous Region despite more stringent state rules. Indeed, as Kaup demonstrates in her study of China's largest ethnic minority, the Zhuang with around 18 million members, variations in provincial and other sub-national governments' policies can significantly impact on the extent to which ethnicity is a salient political cleavage (Kaup 2002).

The central planks of Han unity are the written language, which has produced a shared canon and discouraged regional self-consciousness or nationalism, and the centralised imperial state.

> Being Han, even for illiterate peasants, has meant conscious identification with a glorious history and a state of immense proportions … The legacy for modern Chinese society has been a strong centralized government that has the right to impose its values on the population and against which there is no legitimate right of dissent or secession. (Worden *et al.* 1988)

The really significant issues arise where ethnic groups are so distinctive linguistically, religiously and racially that they may seek political expression outside the official bounds of multiculturalism. The concentration of potentially dissident citizens reinforces the problem. Most of the minority ethnic population in China is found in the border regions and over 50 per cent live in the Western regions. In these areas, the Han dominance is challenged by both a major diversity of languages and the range of religious beliefs.

The PRC's pattern of population, with a central dominant group sharing the state with others that enjoy pre-eminence in parts of the periphery, is not uncommon. In such circumstances the centre often seeks to encourage loyalty through education policies that assume that the lot of minorities would be better if they could conform more closely to the lifestyle of the majority. Thus, in China, while ethnic minority culture is officially celebrated, the Mandarin-speaking Han in practice assume their language and relative secularism to be more advanced culturally. 'In spite of periodically encouraging bilingual education, the CCP still holds firmly to the belief that the backwardness of ethnic minorities can be overcome by stressing the importance of the Chinese language as the means to gain access to Han culture' (Yi 2007: 935). Even more than language, religion has the potential to anchor the ethnic minorities in their 'backwardness'. It is presented in the educational mainstream as a hindrance to development and it is given no place on the school curriculum (Postiglione 2006). For minorities, the achievements of the Han are represented as a road map for modernisation. As Yi affirms: 'minority communities are thought not to be fully in concert with the presumably advanced socialist system in either social or economic terms, though they supposedly are in political terms' (Yi 2007: 938).

Despite this, schools have been assisted in the presentation of the official multi-ethnic China narrative by 'several powerful editors': 'who transformed the non-Han peoples in Chinese history from non-Chinese others into an integral part of the Chinese self by changing the content, language, and organization of previous textbooks' as Baranovitch stresses (2010: 87).

Attention to the version of history taught in schools is a feature of most political systems and in the PRC it is also part of the state's strategy of reinforcing the official ideology. The lessons of the break-up of the Soviet Union and Yugoslavia on ethnic grounds are not lost on the CCP. Indeed, for modern Chinese nationalists, they mirror the dangers identified by their KMT predecessors looking at the Austro-Hungarian Empire. Earlier, the Republic of China formed in 1912

used a five horizontal-striped flag representing the five major nationalities of the one China – Han, Hui, Manchu, Mongol and Tibetan. This
was a self-conscious effort to counter the idea that being Chinese and
Han were the same. The boundary cases for national identity for the
PRC are Tibet and Xinjiang, where the Han are in the minority. As well
as being geographically peripheral from a Beijing-centric view, each
has rival and assertive self-identity, which challenges the core precepts
of Chinese nationalism. These two border areas are also important
economically being rich in natural resources, such as grassland, forests,
oil, gas, minerals and precious metals. (See Box 5 for a brief discussion
of Hong Kong and Macau.)

Tibet

'An internally cohesive group, the Tibetans have proven the most
resistant of the minority groups to the government's integration efforts'
(Worden *et al.* 1988). Since the 1951 invasion of Tibet, the PRC's
control over the region has become complete with Chinese officials
holding all the 'positions of influence and trust' (Patterson 1961: 81).
The bureaucracy and government machinery reflect the Chinese
pattern and only token gestures are made to Tibetan sensibilities. A
new governor of the Tibet Autonomous Region, Padma Choling, an
ethnic Tibetan and long-time PLA officer, was elected in 2010 vowing
to 'oppose all attempts at succession and put national unity as a top
priority' (quoted in *UPI Asia.com*, 18 January 2010). The most
powerful official in Tibet, however, is the CCP party secretary Zhang
Qingli, a Han Chinese with only a few words of the Tibetan language
(quoted in *Spiegel Online International*, 16 August 2006). The 'real'
Panchen Lama, second highest-ranking Lama after the Dalai Lama,
was rumoured in 2010 to be dead while the Beijing appointed equivalent was elected an honorary president of the Buddhist Association of
China. The violence that occurred in March 2008 has not been
repeated on any appreciable scale and the police and military clearly
have the upper hand. Despite this apparent hegemony, however, the
Chinese government remains concerned about 'splitism' and Chinese
nationalists remain strident about the status of Tibet as an integral part
of China.

The Chinese nationalist narrative places Tibet as part of China since
the thirteenth century Yuan Dynasty. This history features harmony
among ethnic groups, despite upper-class separatists plotting with
foreigners to drive the Han Chinese out of Tibet before the peaceful
liberation in 1951 with entry of the PLA. Post-liberation, Tibetan

Box 3 Special Administrative Regions

The PRC has two Special Administrative Regions (SAR) with the status of provincial-level administrative divisions – Hong Kong and Macau. These two SARs are both former colonies that were returned to China in 1997 and 1999 from the UK and Portugal respectively.

The SARs represent an important development in Chinese politics. Not alone did their return represent the end of a period of 'humiliation' for China with part of its territory still occupied by European colonial powers but the new institutional arrangements provide a possible template for reunification with Taiwan. Both SARs enjoy considerable autonomy and their status is reflected in the principle 'One country, two systems' originally proposed by Deng Xiaoping.

Hong Kong

Much about Hong Kong reflects the impact of 150 years of British rule and English shares with Chinese the status of official language. It is 1,104.3 sq km with a population of 7.0 million, 95 per cent Chinese. Its constitution, known as the Basic Law, is not democratic but affords the Executive Council an advisory role for the Chief Executive as well as an influential role to the elected Legislative Council (LegCo), the electorate for which is divided into geographical and functional constituencies. The geographic constituencies' elections are by universal suffrage using a proportional representation method. The other constituencies employ various methods with an electorate based on vocational groups.

The Chief Executive is elected by the Election Committee - approximately 800 Hong Kong residents representing major interest groups plus members from the PRC.

Despite misgivings about its future after British rule and the influence of the PRC, Hong Kong is a free and open society in which the rule of law applies. Its democratic credentials are more likely to improve than be lessened in the foreseeable future. Similarly, its economic characteristics are those of a developed country and there is little reason to suggest any marked change. Hong Kong's foreign affairs and defence are the responsibility of the PRC but it still operates independently on trade and other economic issues on the international stage.

Macau

Macau SAR was returned by Portugal to China in 1999 and enjoys a similar high degree of autonomy to Hong Kong. It is only 29.2 sq km with a population of approximately 543,000. Macau's political system is somewhat less democratic than that of Hong Kong but its legal system is independent and robust. While competition in Hong Kong is keen, Macau's elections are sometimes uncontested and civil society is underdeveloped. It is the only part of China, other than (quite recently) Taiwan, in which casino gambling is legally permitted and the gaming sector contributes more than 50 per cent of Macao's GDP and 70 per cent of government revenue. The 'casino capitalism' of Macau has been associated with corruption and increasing income inequalities that have at times undermined the legitimacy of the government. 'The current global financial crisis is seen to offer an "opportunity" to rethink Macau's profit-driven and consumption-oriented image construction for the sake of a more balanced consideration for visitors and residents alike' (Chung and Tieben 2009: 11).

feudal backwardness is combated by the Chinese government building roads and bridges and providing medical treatment to grateful locals, whose religious freedom and ethnic traditions are well preserved.

> Tibet had long been a society of feudal serfdom under theocratic rule, a society which was even darker than medieval society in Europe ... The serfs and slaves, ... 95 per cent of the total population, suffered destitution, cruel oppression and exploitation ... The long centuries of theocratic rule and feudal serfdom stifled the vitality of Tibetan society, and brought about its decline and decay. (IOSCPRC 2009)

With schemes such as the China Western Development Strategy,[2] the PRC is demonstrating its benevolence and patriotic solidarity with Tibet and other backward regions that need to share in the prosperity and higher living standards enjoyed by fellow Chinese. The only reason for discontent is the pernicious scheming of exiles that had once so cruelly ruled their own people as serfs. Chief among the mischief-makers is the Fourteenth Dalai Lama. Thus, for the CCP party chief, Zhang Qingli: 'the comfortable-housing programme and job creation in the countryside were an essential foundation for keeping 'the upper hand in our struggle with the Dalai clique"' (quoted in *The Economist*, 4 February 2010). Much the same narrative is repeated in the 2011 White Paper *Sixty Years Since Peaceful Liberation of Tibet*.

The rival version of history, which features a small distinct nation with a history stretching back nearly two thousand years subsumed by its powerful neighbour through force and chicanery, is given much credence outside China where the Dalai Lama is fêted as a spiritual leader of global significance. Half of Tibet has been annexed directly to China while the rest, including the capital Lhasa, are now the Tibet Autonomous Region of the PRC. In 1959, an attempt to end the occupation and reestablish the traditional order was crushed and the remnants of Tibetan self-government dismantled. Since then, there has been an effort to undermine the religious, linguistic and cultural identity of the Tibetans together with an infusion of Han Chinese calculated to weaken the nation's distinctive character. Central government development projects, such as new highways or railways, are for the benefit of Han business interests. As well as their exclusion from most senior-level government post, Tibetans also complain of Han domination in commerce. The restoration of traditional buildings is similarly motivated by tourism considerations. In this narrative, Tibet is more like a colony than an autonomous region.

Both stories have ambiguities and contradictions but, to understand the politics of the PRC, what is important is less their accuracy than their currency. While the international support is clearly extensive, the level of support for Tibetan nationalism within the Autonomous Region and the annexed territories is hard to assess. Violent protests in Lhasa in March 2008 were, according to media reports, largely directed at Han settlers. The authorities placed responsibility for this and other protests by Tibetans in the Autonomous Region and in the provinces of Sichuan, Yunnan, Gansu and Qinghai[3] on separatists loyal to the Dalai Lama and external agitation. Dewan and Srivastava, on the other hand, report widespread local alienation from the PRC despite impressive economic development (Dewan and Srivastava 2009).

Both sides engage in propaganda, much of it rival interpretations of historical agreements and key events. The authorities exercise surveillance over the internet, music and religious practice for signs of separatist activity. Clearly, elections, opinion surveys or other measures are not available. The level of state security activity, heavily monitored media reportage and the intelligence sources of exiled activists have to be taken as measures of discontent. The reasons the Tibetan case is so important for the PRC, however, are ideological, economic, strategic and, possibly of increasing significance, environmental. As President Hu Jintao, himself a former party secretary in Tibet, told a high level CCP meeting in January 2010:

> More efforts must be made to greatly improve living standards ... in Tibet ... building a well-off society in an all-round way, establishing a national ecological protective screen and realizing sustainable development ... The work is also vital to ethnic unity, social stability and national security, as well as a favorable international environment. (Quoted in *English.xinhuanet.com*, 22 January 2010)

Though there are intermittent negotiations with representatives of the Dalai Lama, the central government has to view any concessions it might make to Tibetan demands in the context of ethnic and territorial disputes elsewhere. Controlling the border areas is of particular importance to retain the integrity of the PRC just as it was to former Chinese political regimes and, though buffer zones were sufficient until the Qing dynasty, assimilation is now the preferred *modus operandi*.

Xinjiang

> Religious communities are often closely related to ethnic identities ... For the greater part of human history the twin circles of religious and ethnic identity have been very close, if not identical. (Smith 1993: 6)

Xinjiang, a vast territory representing one-sixth of the PRC's total land area, is another politically sensitive frontier region that challenges the Chinese nationalist idea of a single China. Its main ethnic minority, the Uyghurs account for 45 per cent of the population. They have a common ancestry with diaspora in several Central Asian states. The most relevant shared characteristic is the adherence to the Sunni Muslim religion. The Xinjiang Uyghur Autonomous Region has borders with Russia, Mongolia, Afghanistan, Pakistan and India as well as Kazakhstan, Kyrgyzstan and Tajikistan. It is these newly independent Central Asian states that the PRC fears could be role models for its unsettled Muslims;[4] though the Uyghurs, unlike the smaller groups, such as the Kazakhs and Tajiks, do not have such an adjacent mentor, the Chinese are even more concerned about pan-Turkic aspirations. For this reason, Becquelin suggests that:

> Of all its borderlands, Xinjiang has always remained the most important ... Its geographic position ... and its history of violent opposition to Chinese rule made it a permanent strategic concern ... Hence, ... Xinjiang continued to resonate with the key elements of the Qing state project, namely the overlapping objectives of political integration, diffusion of ethnic and religious tensions, promotion of Chinese immigration and reclamation of land, cultural assimilation ... and economic self-sufficiency of the territory. (Becquelin 2006: 489)

Rudelson likens PRC policy to 'an attempt ... to turn the region into an internal colony'. He gives three reasons – the vulnerability of the borderlands; the danger that separatist gains there would encourage other potential claimants; and, access to rich natural resources[5] (Rudelson 1997: 34). Though oil, lead, zinc and gold are often cited as the key strategic assets for China in the region, the military, through the Xinjiang Production and Construction Corps (XPCC), still have major agricultural interests in Xinjiang, long after similar ventures were ended elsewhere in the PRC. It serves as:

> A powerful colonizing force, reclaiming land to settle new immigrants from interior parts of China; securing the territory with a string of cities, farm complexes and industries; attracting demobilized soldiers to settle in Xinjiang; and consolidating territorial control – all of which are elements closely associated with the objectives of the campaign to Open Up the West. From the outset.., the XPCC has been vested with an important role. (Becquelin 2004: 366)

Partly due to XPCC efforts, Xinjiang, which means 'New Frontier' in Mandarin, has a sizeable Han population (41 per cent up from 6 per cent in 1949). Recent violence has centred on the dominance of Han in politics and commerce and, what Uyghurs regard as, cultural encroachment. The influx of Han was encouraged by Beijing through 'comprehensive engineering of economic and social incentives to increase Han migration ... in order further to alter the ethnic balance' (Becquelin 2004: 358).

These policies facilitated the rapid economic growth in the west generally[6] but exacerbated community tensions. The rioting of July 2009 was particularly ethnically charged and ended with 156 dead, thousands injured, and 1,500 arrested (Gladney 2009). The incidents provoked 'a rare public challenge by Han Chinese to the ruling Communist Party in the region' (quoted by *BBC News*, 24 April 2010) and the regional police chief and the CCP secretary of Ürümqi, the provincial capital which is over 75 per cent Han, were removed from office.

Like Tibet, the official and local nationalist narratives characterise the PLA's arrival in 1949 as either liberation or invasion, brief periods of independence are accorded little or crucial significance and PRC modernisation projects are either signs of Chinese solidarity or Trojan horses. The official history dates the incorporation of Xinjiang with reference to the Han Dynasty (206 BC–220 AD), which set up military and civil institutions in the region. The Party message, as used in its relentless propaganda in Xinjiang, is also similar to that used in Tibet:

> It paints the opposition as vanishingly small in number, extreme and completely misguided in outlook, socially isolated, and doomed to fail ... The people are the vast majority, sensible and noble in worldview, closely linked with the Party and the military, and bound to win in their never-ending quest to tie Xinjiang more tightly to China. (Bovingdon 2002: 42)

Unlike its southern counterpart, however, Xinjiang's periodic violent protests at Chinese rule have, at least according to PRC accounts, often involved a militant separatist group. The East Turkestan Islamic Movement (ETIM) is said to seek an independent, Islamic state of East Turkestan, though its very existence is disputed.

> Not one significant terrorist attack against any strategic infrastructural target ... has ever been documented, nor have any incidents been verifiably identified with any international Uyghur or Islamic organization ... Such as they are, China's Uyghur separatists are small in number, poorly equipped, loosely linked, and vastly out-gunned by the People's Liberation Army and People's Police. (Gladney 1996: 6)

Nevertheless, the ETIM has allowed the PRC, especially since the terrorist attacks on New York and Washington in 2001, to represent its security operations in Xinjiang as part of an international anti-terrorist effort. In 2001, China was the initiating member of the Shanghai Cooperation Organisation (SCO) with Russia, Kazakhstan, Kyrgyzstan, Tajikistan and Uzbekistan though which it seeks to encourage joint action against the 'three forces' (terrorism, separatism and extremism). It has used the grouping to effect the extradition of suspected Uyghur separatists to China. In August 2002, the American government listed the ETIM as a terrorist organisation. It sent a group of militant Uyghurs captured in Pakistan and Afghanistan to its detention facility in Guantánamo Bay. A US court ordered the release of the suspects several years later but they were not extradited to the PRC.

As well as security measures, China denies freedom of assembly or speech to putative ethno-nationalist groupings in its jurisdiction so it is difficult to assess the extent of popular rejection of the Chinese nationalist ideology except via exiled groups and reported violence (HRW 2005). Bovingdon suggests, however, that:

> Since it [the CCP] prohibits active political resistance, the contention that in democratic polities might be conducted in the public realm is forced onto other terrains. Uyghurs' struggles are confined to the cultural realm. They cannot directly resist the form of social and political life into which they are born, so they resist its representation. (Bovingdon 2002: 46)

He paints a picture in the 1990s of widespread Uyghur discontent 'in their homes and restaurants, out of ear-shot of Han superiors and coworkers' (2002: 46). Bovingdon enumerates Uyghur attitudes as a: 'rejection of the assimilationist formula of the Zhonghua mínzú, repudiation of the CCP's claim that all mínzú enjoy political and economic equality, critiques of the system of autonomy in Xinjiang, and open wishes for independence' (Bovingdon 2002: 46).

If the extent of hidden hostility and the breadth of discontent with the PRC are accurate, it is unsurprising that violence could be triggered by rumour and supposed ethnic slights. The ethnic tension is also influenced by the Han settlement pattern, which is concentrated in the major urban centres. For example, the southern part of Xinjiang is still 90 per cent populated by Uyghurs. In such areas of Uyghur concentration assimilation efforts have been stepped up since the 2009 riots. Especially since September 2009, schools have been merged, curriculums revised and teacher training enhanced to promote Mandarin. The authorities wish to rebalance the influence on young Uyghurs of schools compared to their families (Hille 2010).

> While this is seen as a way to improve the standard of Mandarin among minority graduates entering the work force, the emphasis on teaching Mandarin in schools has reduced the status of mother tongue, and raised concerns among ethnic minorities about its effect on the sustainability of mother tongue and local culture. (Strawbridge 2008: 6)

As in Tibet, the official PRC narrative on the tensions in Xinjiang feature a non-domicile troublemaker – Rebiya Kadeer, now based in Washington, DC. She was once a delegate to the NPC but baulked at what she regarded as the assimilationist policies of Beijing and, despite her prominence, was jailed on charges of betraying state secrets. While she does not have the international status of the Dalai Lama, Kadeer offers a focus for Uyghurs abroad, especially in Turkey Western Europe and North America where the ex-patriot community is concentrated (Chen 2010).

Conclusion

The exact boundaries of even the longest established states are to some extent arbitrary and so most political systems employ a range of policies to cope with potential ambiguities in the loyalty of marginal groups. In the PRC, the official 'one China' policy is backed by ideological, economic and security policies that try to foster unity but accommodate ethnic tensions. In common with other states, China has established autonomous regions to protect both its:

> Territorial integrity and the fragile rights of minorities. But all autonomy regimes privilege territorial integrity over absolute responsiveness to the demands of the autonomous group: they are a compromise between (a) states, which want unabridged sovereignty and homogeneous populations; and (b) peoples that want self-determination ... Thus we should

not be surprised to find both state actors and autonomous groups pressing for renegotiation of their agreements. (Bovingdon 2004: vii)

For an understanding of the national question in Chinese politics, Xinjiang and Tibet are the boundary cases. To a lesser extent, Inner Mongolia also presents similar issues and there were serious violent clashes there in 2011. Ethnic tensions are not, however, confined to these areas and are a significant issue in the PRC more generally though media reporting of them is discouraged. In October 2004, for instance, a minor traffic altercation between members of the Han Chinese and Hui Muslims in Henan province exploded into serious violence in which at least 15 policemen were killed before paramilitary troops were deployed. Fellow Han and Hui from neighbouring provinces were rallied by text messaging etc and many civilians were killed and injured. The uneven pattern of economic development has increased tensions that often surface as the grievances of migrant workers. Further, the language difference of, for example, the Hokkien-speaking employer in prosperous coastal Xiamen and the Tu migrant worker, from the north west using her own language, accentuates the ethnic social cleavage (Guo and Zhang 2010). As Zang illustrates using data from a 2001 survey conducted in Lanzhou, capital of Gansu Province: 'minority ethnicity is the main determinant of labor market discrimination, controlling for educational attainment and other key characteristics' (Zang 2008: 2341).

The central government's quest for a harmonious society via increased living standards for all and concerted direct state investment in the Western provinces is aimed in part at this problem.

> It is the people of the west that have reaped the benefits of this development strategy ... From 2001 to 2008 ... the poverty-stricken population in the Western areas was reduced from 55 million ... to 27 million ... The challenge that hasn't gone away is how to realize sustainable development. Resolving those longer term issues will close the gap between China's west and east. (Qiao 2010)

As Shih shows, however, the efforts of the Han-dominated élite to modernise the backward provinces are not received in the way state propaganda suggests. Indeed, it may give a boost to the assertion of ethnic distinctiveness by the minorities (Shih 2002). Further, Western development and affirmative action may create resentment among the Han. They point, for example, to college entrance examinations, for which the ethnic groups are given preferential treatment, a more tolerant family planning policy and ethnic job quotas.

While the gradual process of acculturation continues to eat away at non-Han identities, these policies have ironically invested minority identities with renewed significance and utility. Hence, ... the policies have backfired ... [by creating] resentment among the majority (especially its non-elite and disaffected elements) who decry the party. (Leibold 2010b: 6)

For some their ethnic identity and resentment towards the various minorities finds expression in Han ethnocentrism, which, though a relatively modern phenomenon associated with China's transition from empire to nation-state, 'remained a distinct problem for Chinese policymakers throughout the twentieth century' (Leibold 2010b: 5). This assertive stance finds contemporary expression chiefly on the internet.

Han nationalists and the CCP both question the basis of the West's interest in their ethnic policies. They suspect that the championing of the cause of the minorities owes more to hostility to China itself than to human rights sensibilities. In February 2010, President Barack Obama met the Dalai Lama in the White House and, though the visit was low key by previous presidential standards, it caused considerable angst in Beijing. The event illustrated again the contrast between Western and official Chinese perspectives on Tibet. It also highlights that, though the government of the PRC: 'has consistently treated the ethnic minority issue as an essential national concern, meanwhile rejecting any foreign criticism on the grounds of protection of state sovereignty ... In reality, ... its ethnic minority problem becomes an international concern for its foreign policy' (Zhu and Blachford 2005: 248).

The international dimension of the relations between the state and its ethnic minorities was well illustrated by the reaction of Chinese people not just in the PRC but also across the globe to pro-Tibetan demonstrations in the West during the Olympic torch relay before the 2008 Games. The Han diaspora closed ranks and identified with the motherland while many outsiders questioned the unity of the PRC for the first time. What it is to be Chinese wherever one lives is, in part, about the perception of foreigners. Indeed, as Bilik put it: 'the connotations of "Han" in modern discourses have been shaped by Chinese interactions with foreigners, and ways of dealing with the minorities in the process of state building' (Bilik 2008).

Too great a concentration on the national question risks underestimating the extent to which China has forged a real multi-ethnic political unity. It also suggests that the minorities are only recipients of Han hegemony and make no contribution to the PRC itself. The competing narratives of both official China and disaffected minorities are important at home and abroad but, in most cases, ethnic or national minority issues do not threaten CCP rule. Similarly, they do not significantly weaken the states territorial integrity. In the cases of Tibet, in particular, and Xinjiang, to a significant degree, there is a fundamental incompatibility between the ethnic groups, which wish for extensive rights and political autonomy at minimum and outright independence at maximum, and the Chinese government. The state views such steps as a fundamental threat to Chinese national integrity. The grounds for compromise between the Tibetans and Uyghurs, on the one hand, and the Chinese government, on the other, are, therefore, rather limited. Nevertheless, relying primarily on repression only stores up tensions for the longer term, while bringing international opprobrium onto China. The PRC could, therefore, achieve its goal of greater harmony more efficiently if it could accept more divergence and expect less gratitude from its periphery.

Appendix A: Official ethnic groups

Ethnic group	Population	Distribution
Zhuang	15,489,630	Guangxi, Yunnan, Guangdong, Guizhou
Hui	8,602,978	Ningxia, Gansu, Henan, Xinjiang, Qinghai, Yunnan, Hebei, Shandong, Anhui, Liaoning, Beijing, Inner Mongolia, Heilongjiang, Tianjin, Jilin, Shaanxi
Uyghur	7,214,431	Xinjiang, Hunan
Yi	6,572,173	Sichuan, Yunnan, Guizhou, Guangxi
Miao	7,398,035	Guizhou, Yunnan, Hunan, Guangxi, Sichuan, Guangdong, Hubei
Manchu	9,821,180	Liaoning, Heilongjiang, Jilin, Hebei, Beijing, Inner Mongolia
Tibetan	4,593,330	Tibet, Sichuan, Qinghai, Gansu, Yunnan
Mongolian	4,806,849	Inner Mongolia, Xinjiang, Liaoning, Jilin, Heilongjiang, Qinghai, Hebei, Henan, Gansu, Yunnan
Bouyei	2,545,059	Guizhou
Tujia	5,704,223	Qinghai, Gansu, Hunan, Hubei, Sichuan, Guizhou
Dong	2,514,014	Guizhou, Hunan, Guangxi
Korean	1,920,597	Jilin, Heilongjiang, Liaoning, Inner Mongolia
Yao	2,134,013	Guangxi, Hunan, Yunnan, Guangdong, Guizhou
Bai	1,594,827	Yunnan, Hunan
Hani	1,253,952	Yunnan
Kazak	1,111,718	Xinjiang, Gansu
Li	1,110,900	Guangdong
Dai	1,025,128	Yunnan
Lisu	574,856	Yunnan, Sichuan

Ethnic group	Population	Distribution
She	630,378	Fujian, Zhejiang, Jiangxi, Guangdong
Lahu	411,476	Yunnan
Va	351,974	Yunnan
Sui	345,993	Guizhou, Guangxi
Dongxiang	373,872	Gansu, Xinjiang
Naxi	278,009	Yunnan, Sichuan
Tu	191,624	Qinghai, Gansu
Kirgiz	141,549	Xinjiang
Qiang	198,252	Sichuan
Daur	121,357	Inner Mongolia, Heilongjiang, Xinjiang
Jingpo	119,209	Yunnan
Mulam	159,328	Guangxi
Xibe	172,847	Xinjiang, Liaoning, Jilin
Salar	82,280	Qinghai, Gansu
Blang	87,697	Yunnan
Gelao	437,997	Guizhou, Guangxi
Maonan	71,968	Guangxi
Tajik	33,538	Xinjiang
Primi	29,657	Yunnan
Nu	27,123	Yunnan
Achang	27,708	Yunnan
Ewenki	26,315	Inner Mongolia, Heilongjiang
Gin	18,915	Guangxi
De'ang (Benglong)	15,462	Yunnan
Uzbek	14,502	Xinjiang
Yugur	12,297	Gansu
Jino	18,021	Yunnan
Bonan	12,212	Gansu
Derung	5,816	Yunnan
Tatar	4,873	Xinjiang
Oroqen	6,965	Inner Mongolia, Heilongjiang
Russian	13,504	Xinjiang
Gaoshan	2,909	Taiwan, Fujian
Hezhen	4,245	Heilongjiang
Monba	7,475	Tibet
Lhoba	2,312	Tibet

Sources: www.agenceglobal.com/article.asp?id=478; http://big5.fmprc.gov.cn/gate /big5/www.

Notes

1 Zhíxi meaning directly related or of one's ancestors and descendants.
2 Launched in 2000, the Western Development Strategy covers two-thirds of the PRC. It applies in Tibet and 11 other provincial-level administrative areas – Chongqing Municipality; Sichuan, Guizhou, Yunnan, Shaanxi, Gansu and Qinghai provinces; and the autonomous regions of Ningxia Hui, Xinjiang Uyghur, Inner Mongolia and Guangxi Zhuang.
3 The majority of the 6.5 million Tibetans in the PRC live in these provinces.
4 See Blanchard (2009).
5 For a more recent strategic assessment of the resources issue, see Bi (2006).
6 Largely attributed to the construction sector, according to Yang and Lahr (2008).

6

Foreign policy

China's rise – the emergence, or more accurately re-emergence, of China as a major power – is the single most important geo-political trend of the early twenty-first century. Its sustained high-level economic growth since the late 1970s has catapulted the PRC from being a very large but relatively poor country with a limited geo-political footprint to being *the* emerging power of the twenty-first century with a major impact on all aspects of Asian and global affairs. China has become the world's second most important power after the US and, according to some projections, may equal or surpass the US in coming decades. What kind of power China is and will become and how it will relate to the outside world are, therefore, questions of major importance not only for the PRC and its neighbours but also for the future of global politics as a whole.

China's leaders argue that their country's dramatic economic development and consequent return to great-power status has benefited and can continue to benefit not only the Chinese people, but also the larger global community. China's economic progress has lifted hundreds of millions of its citizens out of poverty and, through China's integration into the global economy, has contributed to growth elsewhere in the world. At the same time, they argue, China is not an aggressive power with expansionist ambitions. It upholds the key norms of international society, such as respect for other states' sovereignty and borders, and is willing to work cooperatively in addressing international challenges. The Chinese academic Zheng Bijian sought to capture the essence of China's foreign policy and emerging global role with the phrase 'peaceful rise' (中国和平崛起) (Zheng 2005). Even 'peaceful rise', however, was viewed by the Chinese leadership as too provocative a term and Chinese foreign policy is now officially described simply as one of 'peaceful development' (中国和平发展). Similarly, in official discourse, China's vision of global order and commitment to work with other states is described by the term 'harmonious world', which, with its Confucian overtones, parallels the domestic goal of a 'harmonious society'.

In contrast, some observers view China as a threat to regional security and to the existing global order. From this perspective, China is – or will become – an expansionist power set on dominating the Asian region and re-writing the rules of the post-1945 Western-led international order (Bernstein and Munro 1997; Gertz 2000). Clearly, between these two extremes – China's advance as entirely unproblematic for the rest of the world and the emergence of an aggressive new superpower – is a range of more nuanced possibilities.

The extent and impact of China's rise will depend on developments in both China itself and the wider international system. Most projections of China's increased international role rest on the assumption that the country's remarkable economic growth will continue into the medium-term future – the next few decades – and that this will underpin further expansion of its global impact and role. Given that China is at a relatively early stage in its economic development, comparable to that of developed Western states at similar points in their industrial history, the assumption that its economy will continue to grow at quite high rates for some decades is not unreasonable. Nevertheless, the PRC's current economic and political path could be disrupted by a variety of factors. Economic problems could trigger a serious slowing down in growth or even an economic collapse. Politically, a variety of factors could also dramatically alter China's direction. The protests that are a significant feature of contemporary China – see Chapter 4 – could gain a more overtly political character and result in a direct challenge to the CCP's hegemony similar to that of 1989 – resulting either in repression or the collapse of the regime. The fall of the communist system could result in the emergence of a democracy, a period of political instability – in the worst case akin to that between 1911 and 1949 – or some new form of authoritarian state. Alternatively, if facing intensifying economic and political challenges, China's communist leaders could turn to extreme nationalism as a means of legitimising their continued rule. Any of these scenarios would have significant implications for PRC's relations with the rest of the world.

The impact of China's renewed status will also depend on its relative strength *vis-à-vis* the other major powers and the character of its relationships with them. A world in which, by the middle of the twenty-first, China is clearly the world's dominant power will be quite different from one in which it is one amongst a number of major powers. Here, the distinction between a superpower and a great power is a useful one: a superpower is a country which has substantial power across all dimensions (economic, political, military and soft power) and has a significant impact on all global issues; by contrast, a great power is one which has substantial power in only some and has a significant impact within its region but less so globally (Buzan and Wæver 2003: 30–9). By these measures, the US is still the world's only superpower. Most of the other contenders are great powers but not superpowers: they have major influence within their regions but not globally (Russia, India) and/or they are global powers in some dimensions but not others. The EU and Japan, for example, are global powers economically but not militarily. China stands on its own in a category of great powers that appear on a course to become superpowers over the next few decades. Assuming China's power continues to increase, the other big uncertainty is the situation of the US. There is currently debate about whether the financial crisis of 2008, a growing budget deficit and the severe challenges the US has faced in Iraq and Afghanistan signal the beginning of a decisive fall from superpower status. Alternatively, they may be more temporary problems from which the US will recover (Ferguson 2010; Joffe 2009). On balance, it seems that, while the US may be in a relative decline, especially in relation to major non-Western powers such as China, India, Russia and Brazil, it is not in absolute decline and will remain a superpower well into the twenty-first century. The most likely medium-term scenario, therefore, is shift from a world of one superpower to a world of two superpowers (the US and China).

Theories of international relations can help analysis of the implications of China's rise and the prospects for the PRC's relations with the rest of the world. To date, the dominant debate has been between realism and liberalism. Realists and neo-realists argue that, under conditions of international anarchy, patterns of cooperation and conflict are determined primarily by distribution of power in the international system and the responses of states to shifts in the balance of power. From this perspective, the arrival of a new superpower, such as China, is a worrying development: powers in the ascendant tend to chafe against the constraints of the existing international order and usually challenge it; existing dominant powers are threatened by the emergence of a new power and will seek to prevent its emergence or to contain it (Christensen 1996; Callahan 2005; Yan 2006). At minimum, a long-term strategic competition between the US and China – akin to the US-Soviet Cold War – is likely; in the worst case, such a competition can trigger a major war. Other states will face a choice between bandwagoning[1] with China (in order to broker compromises with

China and benefit from Chinese largesse) or joining the US in balancing against China.

In contrast, liberals and neo-liberals argue that the conflict generating effects of international anarchy and the balance of power are mitigated by three factors which facilitate peaceful relations and cooperation between states: economic interdependence, international institutions and domestic politics, in particular democracy. From this perspective, China's deep enmeshment in the global economy and its integration into international institutions, such as the World Trade Organisation and the various Asian and East Asian frameworks for cooperation, generate mutual interests between China, the US and Asian states which make armed conflict between them unlikely and counter-balance pressures for strategic competition (Ikenberry 2008). If China becomes a liberal democracy, it may even become part of the zone of democratic peace – within which wars have become inconceivable – with the major Western powers. Liberalism's focus on domestic politics, however, also directs attention to an alternative scenario: if China descends into extreme authoritarianism and nationalism, this is likely to increase the prospects of an aggressive Chinese foreign policy and conflict with other states (as occurred with imperial Japan and Nazi Germany in the 1930s).

A third school of international relations theory – social constructivism – suggests that states' foreign policies and patterns of interaction between states are the product not primarily of material factors, such as the balance of power or economic interdependence, but rather are constructed through discourse and resultant political action. From this perspective, the key questions are, in light of China's rising power and changing domestic situation, what foreign policy identity and role is China constructing for itself and what patterns of interaction are being constructed with other states (Xiao 2005; Katzenstein 1996).

Chinese foreign policy in historical perspective

During China's long imperial era, relations with the rest of the world were far from central to the Chinese system. Indeed, the notion of foreign policy – in the modern sense of interaction with other states on the basis of sovereign equality – made little sense. As Roy has observed, China viewed 'itself as the political and cultural centre of the earth, the "Middle Kingdom" ... [F]or centuries the Chinese had little or no contact with other peoples ... Foreigners were considered inferior ... since they had little to offer the refined culture and civilization of China' (Roy 1998: 6). To the extent that other nations interacted with China – and such interaction occurred largely between China and its near neighbours – they did so on the basis of an imperial tribute system under which other states paid tribute to China and received certain privileges in return. Tellingly, imperial China had no foreign ministry and relations with the non-Chinese world were dealt with by the Board of Rites or Court of Colonial Affairs (Dryer 2010). This system left China ill-prepared to engage with the technologically and economically superior Western powers, as it was eventually forced to do in the nineteenth century. When the British sent their envoy Lord George Macartney to China seeking trading rights in 1793, Emperor Qianlong (乾隆皇帝) famously responded with a letter to King George III stating that 'I set no value on objects strange or ingenious, and we have no use for your country's manufactures' (quoted in Gelber 2008: 164).

As was seen in Chapter 1, foreign intervention in China was central to the 'century of humiliation' from the middle of the nineteenth century to 1949. The First Opium War (1839–42) set the pattern for much that was to follow: in the early nineteenth century, opium smoking was a major problem in China and the British East India company was responsible for most of the opium illegally smuggled into China. When the British refused to halt the opium trade, the Chinese blockaded the factories supplying opium and boarded British ships. The British responded by sending military forces. The militarily superior British forces took the key southern port of Canton (now Guangzhou) and sailed up the Yangtze. In 1842, the Chinese sued for peace and, under the Treaty of Nanjing, were forced to concede to Britain the payment of a large indemnity, the opening of four ports and the ceding of Hong Kong. The larger issues were access to the Chinese economy for foreign powers and the rights and status of foreign governments and nationals in China. The Treaty of Nanjing was followed by further 'unequal treaties' with others – including France, Germany, Russia, the US, Japan and Portugal – in the middle and latter part of the nineteenth century. After the Second Opium War (1858–60), the Treaty of Tianjin (1860) resulted in the creation of 10 further port cities and permission for foreigners, including Christian missionaries, to travel throughout China. The now second-class status of the Chinese within their own country became symbolised by the apocryphal story of the sign reading 'Chinese and Dogs Not Permitted' on the gate of Huangpu Park (黄浦公园) in foreign-administered Shanghai (Roy 1998: 9).

After the 1911 revolution, China was gradually integrated into the modern international system but the country remained weak and the subject of machinations by the major powers. In the prolonged on-off conflict between the KMT and the Communists, both the Soviet Union and the US played complex games hedging and shifting their support between the two groups. The Americans hoped that China might become a major democratic ally in Asia and sought to build up the KMT to this end. Washington, however, became disillusioned with the KMT's authoritarianism, corruption and failure to establish an effective government and, at various points, made overtures towards the Communists.

Although the Chinese Communists were the natural allies of the Communist Soviet Union and the Soviet Union did provide them with significant support, Moscow also provided support to the KMT, in part because the KMT were an anti-imperial force and appeared more likely to gain control of China, but also because the Soviet Union preferred a weak and divided China over a strong one. Both the US and the Soviet Union also made a number of attempts to broker an alliance between the KMT and the Communists. As was seen in Chapter 1, however, the depth of distrust between the two ensured that cooperation was never more than very short-lived.

The Japanese invasion and occupation of China – beginning with Manchuria in 1931 and extending to much of the rest of China from 1937 – produced not only massive loss of life and appalling human suffering but also left a legacy which continues to shape Sino-Japanese relations and regional international politics into the twenty-first century. With the defeat of Japan in 1945, the US made further efforts to broker an alliance between the KMT and the Chinese Communists, again hoping to establish China as a key democratic ally in Asia but these proved fruitless as the civil war escalated.

Following the Communist's victory in October 1949, China rapidly became drawn into the escalating US-Soviet Cold War. Mao and the Chinese leadership's worldview was shaped by the Marxist ideological assumption that conflict between the communist and capitalist blocs was inevitable. China's political and economic weakness meant that the country also needed external assistance and the Soviet Union was the most likely source of that assistance. Mao declared that, while China was an independent power, it would 'lean to one side' – the Soviet side – in the US-Soviet conflict (Kavalski 2009: 68). Mao visited Moscow for two months from mid-December 1949 to mid-February 1950, resulting in the signing of a Treaty of Friendship, Alliance and Mutual Assistance and a five-year loan of $300 million. Although President Harry Truman announced in January 1950 that the US was ceasing aid to the KMT in Taiwan (Xiang 1995), strong Congressional opposition to the Chinese Communists precluded US recognition of the newly established PRC.

The Korean War (1950–53) consolidated China's position in the emerging Cold War. In response to the North Korean invasion of South Korea in June 1950, the US stationed its Seventh Fleet in the Taiwan Straits to prevent the Communists from taking Taiwan (which they had hoped to do later that year). US, South Korean and allied forces (formally under United Nations command) were initially pushed back deep into South Korea but they successfully counter-attacked crossing the 38 parallel – the border between the two Koreas – and advanced into North Korea in October 1950. Fearing an attack on China itself, the Chinese leadership sent troops into Korea. The Chinese and North Koreans forced the US and South Koreans back to the 38 parallel by the end of the year and the war settled into a stalemate which only ended in July 1953. The US and China were now confirmed enemies. Chinese shelling of offshore islands held by the KMT triggered crises in 1954 and 1958, with the US sending naval forces to deter further Chinese action. The US also concluded a mutual defence treaty with Taiwan in December 1954. In the 1950s and 1960s the Chinese also provided assistance to the Vietnamese communists against the French and then the US (with 320,000 Chinese soldiers serving in North Vietnam between 1965 and 1968), as well as support for revolutionary movements elsewhere in the Third World (Roy, 1998: 25–7).

The Korean War had, however, reinforced China's international isolation. The Chinese leadership thus undertook diplomatic initiatives to build ties with other states, while, at the same time, strengthening China's revolutionary credentials and asserting its independence from the Soviet Union. Chinese diplomacy focused on developing ties with African and Asian countries and opposition to both US and Soviet 'imperialism'. China played a central role in the 1955 Bandung[2] conference of African and Asian countries, a key point in the development of the non-aligned movement, and the new direction in Chinese foreign policy became referred to as the 'Bandung Spirit' (Chambers 2008: 283).

From the mid-1950s and into the 1960s, China's alliance with the Soviet Union began to break down. Historically, relations were far from unproblematic: Russia had participated with the other major powers in exploiting China's weakness in the nineteenth century; there were unresolved border disputes between the two states; and, as was noted above, the Soviet Union had been less than wholehearted in its support for the Chinese communists before 1949. Even when the

Sino-Soviet alliance was negotiated in 1949–50, the Chinese leadership were disappointed at the level of economic assistance they received and the Soviet assumption that the Chinese were very much the junior partners. From the 1950s, ideological and political factors generated increasing tensions between the world's two largest communist powers. After Stalin's death in 1953, the Soviet Union began to pursue more moderate policies at home and coexistence with the West externally. In contrast, Mao continued to press for radical transformation at home and revolutionary activism abroad. An ideological war of words ensued, with the Soviets accusing the Chinese of dangerous extremism and the Chinese accusing the Soviets of betraying Marxism-Leninism.

In 1960, the Soviet Union abruptly withdrew its technicians and much of its economic aid from China. The majority of other communist states sided with the Soviet Union, leaving China increasingly isolated – an isolation further exacerbated by the Cultural Revolution (a period which saw China withdraw almost all its overseas ambassadors, the foreign ministry ransacked and foreign embassies in Beijing attacked). Sino-Soviet ideological warfare intensified. The 1968 Soviet invasion of Czechoslovakia and the Brezhnev declaration, which asserted the right of the Soviet Union to intervene in other communist states in the interests of unity, triggered fears of a Soviet invasion of China. In early 1969 a series of low-level exchanges of fire between troops occurred at points on the Sino-Soviet border. Although the Zhenbao incident did not escalate to a larger conflict, the relations between the two states plummeted.

The collapse of the Sino-Soviet alliance created a new opening for Sino-US relations. For the Chinese leadership, the Soviet Union was now a greater threat than the US and developing relations with America could be a means to counter-balance the Soviet Union. From the US perspective, Sino-Soviet tensions could also be exploited in waging the Cold War against the Soviet Union. In summer 1971, US President Richard Nixon's National Security Adviser Henry Kissinger secretly visited China to discuss the details of a rapprochement: the two countries would put aside their ideological differences in their shared interest of countering the Soviet Union; the US would recognise the PRC as the legitimate government of China and drop its existing recognition of the Taiwanese Republic of China; and, a formula of words was devised under which the US accepted the principle of 'one China'. Nevertheless, the future status of Taiwan was left ambiguous. In February 1972, Nixon himself visited China to meet Mao and seal the new relationship – one of the most remarkable diplomatic coups of modern times (Fenby 2009a). Nixon and Kissinger's diplomacy paved the way for the normalisation of relations between China and the US and the dramatic growth in economic ties in the decades that followed.

At the end of the 1970s and beginning of the 1980s, an even more fundamental shift in Chinese foreign policy occurred. Reforming China's economy, the Chinese leadership concluded, required opening China up to foreign trade and investment, a peaceful external environment and cooperative relations with the world's other major powers, especially the US. As Deng Xiaoping put it in 1980:

> To accelerate China's modernization we must not only make use of other countries' experience. We must also avail ourselves of foreign funding. In the past years international conditions worked against us. Later, when the international climate was favourable, we did not take advantage of it. It is now time to use our opportunities. ... China has opened its door, and will never close it again. (quoted in Roy 1998: 33)

From the early 1980s, China gradually set about implementing this new policy: the country was opened up to foreign investment; export-oriented industries were encouraged; and, initiatives were launched to resolve historic disputes and promote political and economic cooperation with most neighbouring states. The post-1949 goal of promoting revolution elsewhere in the world, already downgraded since the 1960s, was quietly abandoned. The 1989 Tiananmen Square massacre might have de-railed the new direction in Chinese foreign policy. The US, Japan and the EU imposed economic sanctions in response to the Tiananmen Square massacre. Both China and the major Western powers, however, quite quickly made efforts to re-establish relations: sanctions were gradually rescinded, China's integration into the global economy continued rapidly in the 1990s and 2000s and an important symbolic turning point occurred in 2001 when China joined the World Trade Organisation (WTO).

During the 1990s, Chinese foreign policy emphasised the primacy of economic growth and the consequent need to avoid being unnecessarily entangled in disputes with the West or controversial international issues. By the mid-2000s, however, the scale of China's economic growth and the implications for world politics were becoming so great that this policy was increasingly unviable. China's position as the world's leading exporter, its role in global financial markets and its increasing demand for resources and raw materials pushed the country to the top of the global agenda. As Kynge put it, 'quite suddenly, or so it seemed, China became an issue of daily international importance. It is difficult to pinpoint when, exactly, that transition took place; perhaps it was in late 2003, or maybe it was early the next year' (Kynge 2007: 6).

China's growing economic presence has both facilitated and been complemented by an increasing global political activism and self-confidence that amounts to a new Chinese foreign policy. China's reinvigorated international political activism included the first East Asia Summit in December 2005, a major Sino-Africa summit in Beijing in November 2006 and diplomatic efforts to develop ties with states in Africa and Latin America. As discussed in Chapter 5, China has played a leading role in the Shanghai Cooperation Organisation (SCO), which brings together China, Russia and the Central Asia former Soviet republics. In addition, the PRC also has developing relations with a number of countries which the West, in particular the US, views as 'rogue states'[3] such as North Korea, Iran, Myanmar and Sudan.

Zhang (2010) argues that the emerging new Chinese foreign policy is characterised by five elements:

- the pursuit of full partnership with the US, based on an assumption of equality between them;
- 'soft balancing' against the US through the development of strategic partnerships with other states, in particular, but not only, Russia;
- pro-active efforts to re-shape regional orders, in particular in East Asia but also in other regions, such as Central Asia;
- a global economic security strategy designed to secure access to energy; and,
- a sustained effort to enhance China's soft power through the promotion of Chinese culture overseas, of China as a model for other states and of an image of China as a benign power.[4]

While there is debate about the character of the new Chinese foreign policy, it is clear that the old policy of maintaining a low profile and never trying to take the lead has become unviable and is being abandoned and that a new policy is emerging.

The Taiwan wildcard

Above any other issue, Taiwan is a wildcard with the potential to severely disrupt China's relations with the outside world. Since the US recognition of the PRC in the 1970s, the *status quo ante* has prevailed in terms of Taiwan's international status: the US and the majority of other states have accepted the One China policy and do not recognise Taiwan as an independent state, but Taiwan has nevertheless consolidated its *de facto* status as an independent political and economic entity. When the US formally recognised the PRC in 1979, the Congress passed the Taiwan Relations Act. This states that any attempt to resolve the Taiwan situation by force will be viewed by the US as a threat to the security of the Asia- Pacific region and a matter of 'grave concern'. The Act commits the US to provide Taiwan with defensive arms and to maintain America's own capacity to defend Taiwan. Although the commitments under the Taiwan Relations Act are ambiguous, US administrations have consistently sold armaments to Taiwan and sought to maintain the US capacity to deter Chinese aggression.

From the perspective of China's communist leaders, Taiwan is an internal matter and re-unification with the mainland is vital. Indeed, since the recovery of Hong Kong and Macau at the end of the 1990s, it is the final part of the long-term project of re-establishing China's national unity and overcoming the 'century of national humiliation'. Since the 1950s, however, the PRC has refrained from the use of force against Taiwan, reflecting the military superiority of the US and the risks involved in any conflict over the island. Taiwan's KMT rulers have also had to live with the *status quo*: they lack the capacity to overthrow their communist counter-parts on the mainland, but their claim to be the legitimate rulers of China precluded support for Taiwanese independence. From the 1980s, however, democratisation within Taiwan led to an increasing sense of a distinctive Taiwanese identity as well as calls in some quarters for independence (Lee 1999). This trend continued into the 1990s and culminated in the victory of opposition Democratic Progressive Party (DPP) candidate Chen Shui-bian (陈水扁) in Taiwan's presidential elections in March 2000. This was the first time that Taiwan was led by a non-KMT president. The fear that Taiwan was moving inexorably towards independence led the PRC to alter its previous policy of isolating Taiwan, gradually replacing it with a policy of economic and political engagement designed to draw the island into the mainland's embrace – a policy that was arguably having some success by the late 2000s (Banyan 2009).

Taiwan is of much more than simply local or regional significance because of its potential to trigger armed conflict between China and the US. The reality of this danger was highlighted by the Taiwan Straits crisis of 1995–96 (Lee 1999). In the context of parliamentary and presidential elections in December 1995 and March 1996 – in which

Taiwanese politicians were calling for greater autonomy and, in some cases, even independence – China test-fired missiles into the waters near Taiwan, undertook large-scale military exercises and unilaterally closed air and sea-lanes. The US responded by sending two aircraft carrier battle groups close to Taiwan. In the event, the crisis did not escalate further. China was most likely seeking to deter Taiwanese moves towards independence, rather than actually preparing to attack Taiwan, and the military actions were brought to an end. Nevertheless, the risks were clear.

Armed conflict over Taiwan could occur in a number of ways. The PRC could, at some point, decide to use military force to regain control over Taiwan – perhaps if it believes that the military balance has shifted in its favour or if domestic pressures lead it to play the nationalist card. Alternatively, since the PRC leadership have consistently stated that a Taiwanese declaration of independence would be viewed as *casus belli*, were such a step ever taken the PRC would be highly likely to take military action. Finally, in a future crisis like that of 1995–96, misperceptions and action-reaction dynamics could trigger escalation to war. In the event of armed conflict, the US would face strong domestic pressure to live up to its commitment to defend Taiwan. The impact of any such war would be hard to predict but, were China perceived internationally as the aggressor, the result could be a prolonged Cold War between the US (and its allies) and the PRC. Such an outcome would undermine the integration into the global economy which has underpinned China's development since the 1980s and thereby alter the underlying dynamic which has shaped China's relations with the rest of the world. Given the risks involved in any conflict, the more likely scenario is the continuation of the status quo, which, after all, has now remained in place – albeit with the shifts noted above – for more than sixty years since 1949. Nevertheless, so long as its status remains disputed, Taiwan has the potential to severely disrupt China's relations with the rest of the world.

China, the US and the major powers

The United States

The relationship between the US and China – the world's dominant power and the leading rising power – is the most important in the world. The extent to which it is characterised by cooperation will have a major influence on global political and economic stability. Additionally, it bears on the international community's ability to manage global challenges such as climate change, energy security and nuclear proliferation.

Since the end of the Cold War, the Sino-US relationship has been characterised by a complex and shifting mix of efforts to build a sustainable strategic partnership and elements of strategic competition. In both China and the US, there are debates between hawks and doves over their respective policies. As noted above, the mainstream view amongst the Chinese leadership has emphasised the primacy of economic growth based on exports and foreign direct investment and the consequent necessity for good relations with the US. This view is challenged by hardliners arguing, variously, that:

- the US is determined to prevent China's rise;
- China's assertion of its rightful position in the international order requires challenging US hegemony; or,
- the pursuit of particular Chinese interests, such as the reassertion of control over Taiwan, make conflict with the US virtually inevitable.

To date, the less belligerent view has largely won out within the Chinese leadership but, at various points, more assertive, and arguably aggressive, rhetoric and policies have emerged.

In the US, moderates argue that China's rise does not necessarily pose a threat to America, the economic relationship between the two powers is one of mutual benefit and that engaging China is the best means of encouraging it to play by the rules of the international system. In something of a mirror image of their Chinese counterparts, American hawks argue that:

- China's rise poses an inevitable challenge to US hegemony and interests;
- China is a revisionist or aggressive power; and,
- the PRC's authoritarian communist system makes a true strategic partnership with the US impossible.

To date, US policy has been shaped more by a logic of engagement than one of containment.

In the early 1990s, the Clinton administration (1993–2001) came to power arguing for a tougher policy towards China, in particular over human rights. The 1995–96 Taiwan crisis also generated serious tensions between the US and China. Nevertheless, the Clinton administration eventually adopted a policy of engagement towards China. Following a series of top-level visits, the two countries committed to pursuing a 'strategic partnership'. Like its predecessor, the Bush administration (2001–09) began pursuing a tougher approach to China but soon opted for a policy of engagement. Similarly, President Obama's policy reflects continuity more than change in America's relations with China:

> he seeks cooperation on economic recovery, nonproliferation, and climate change. He explicitly downplays human rights issues ... Shared interests take precedence over sovereign ones. (Nau 2010: 31–2)

Despite the rhetoric of partnership and cooperation and efforts on both sides to strengthen bilateral relations, there remain significant areas of tension between China and the US. In the economic sphere, the growth of Chinese exports has produced a growing trade deficit for the US, which American critics argue contributes to economic decline and job losses. It is sustained by what these critics view as an artificially low valuation of the Chinese currency. To date, the US has resisted domestic pressures for retaliatory measures such as tariffs or limits on Chinese imports. Nevertheless, a Sino-US trade war is viewed by some observers as a very real danger.

In East Asia, the Sino-US relationship remains characterised by significant elements of geo-strategic military competition. America's continuing security commitments to Taiwan, Japan and South Korea and its backing for China's South-East Asian neighbours over territorial disputes in the South China Seas are viewed negatively in Beijing. The PRC's desire to regain control of Taiwan and its territorial claims over the South China Seas and the Senkaku Islands[5] are viewed as threatening by the US. Critics argue that it is part of a larger Chinese goal of asserting hegemony over East Asia. The destabilising potential of these tensions was illustrated by two developments in 2010. During 2010, the Chinese defined the South China Sea as a 'core interest' (implying that they might be willing to go to war over control of it) and asserted 'indisputable sovereignty' over the sea. Washington responded by declaring that freedom of navigation in the sea was a US 'national interest' and proposing a legal process to resolve disputes over the South China Sea (Pomfret 2010; Solomon 2010). In September 2010, a clash between a Japanese Coast Guard patrol boat and Chinese fishing vessel near the Senkaku Islands (see below) triggered a minor crisis between the countries. It prompted the US to re-affirm that its commitment to defend Japan under the mutual security treaty extended to territories under Japanese administration including the Senkaku Islands. Neither situation escalated further but the potential for crises between the US and China in East Asia was clear.

There are also significant disputes between the US and China on a range of global issues. On nuclear proliferation, the US has sought to mobilise diplomatic pressure and economic sanctions against Iran and North Korea because of their efforts to develop nuclear weapons. For China, North Korea is a historic ally and Iran has become an important supplier of gas. Beijing is reluctant to pressure either state. On 'rogue states' more generally, America has been strongly critical whereas China has been building economic, political and military ties since the 1990s. In addition, human rights remain an on-going source of friction between Beijing and Washington. Although economics has to some extent trumped human rights, the US continues to criticise China's human rights behaviour – criticism which the PRC views as unwarranted interference in its domestic affairs.

The elements of strategic competition and the various disputes between the US and China are unlikely to go away. Nevertheless, the larger picture is that the two powers have sought to cooperate and to manage or at least contain their differences. As Lampton has put it:

> America and China have made a double gamble ... Washington has bet that as China becomes more powerful it will be socialized into the norms of the international system and, because of interdependence, will become a 'responsible stakeholder' ... Beijing has bet that despite its misgivings ... Washington will not seek to systematically frustrate the growth of PRC power. (Lampton 2008: 274)

As China's power rises, maintaining the viability of this double gamble will pose real challenges of political leadership and diplomatic skill for Beijing and Washington.

Japan

The Sino-Japanese relationship is one of the most important in East Asia. Despite its economic decline since the 1980s, Japan remains a major economic power and a key regional ally of the US. Like the US, Japan did not formally recognise the PRC until the early 1970s. From this point, economic relations between the two countries grew rapidly and China and Japan are now amongst each other's main trading partners.

Relations between China and Japan, however, remain weighed down by the legacy of history. Sino-Japanese tensions emerged in the second half of the nineteenth century, when Japan – following the Meiji restoration of 1868 (明治維新) – moved from isolationism to imperialism. Korea, which had historically been under Chinese suzerainty, became a focus of competition between the two countries. In the First

Sino-Japanese War of 1894–95, both powers sent forces to Korea but China was defeated and was forced to cede both the Liaodong Peninsula in northern China (including Dalian (大连)) and Taiwan. As was discussed in Chapter 1, the Japanese invasion and occupation of China during the 1930s and the Second World War involved massive loss of life and acts of appalling brutality by the Japanese. This history continues to shape relations between the two countries. In China, resentment and fear of Japan remain powerful political forces. In Japan, there is a reluctance to accept responsibility for the events of the 1930s and the Second World War. In both countries, nationalistic – and often racist – views towards the other are commonplace. As a consequence, there has been no equivalent of the post-1945 Franco-German reconciliation within Europe. When tensions or disputes emerge between the two countries, the relationship easily falls into one of mutual recrimination and popular protest against the other state – sometimes stoked by political leaders in one country or both.

The Sino-Japanese relationship is further complicated by Japan's alliance with the US. Since the Second World War, Japan has hosted America's most important forward military bases in Asia and, under the 1960 US-Japan Mutual Security Treaty, the US is committed to defend Japan in the event of an attack. For Japan, the alliance with the US remains the bedrock of its national security policy and an important means of counter-balancing and deterring China. China's attitude to the US-Japan alliance is complicated. At least rhetorically – and to a significant degree substantively – Beijing is opposed to both the US forward military presence in Asia and the US-Japan alliance, viewing them as a part of a larger policy of containing China. At the same time, the US-Japan alliance has facilitated the limitation of Japan's military capabilities as well as mitigating potential Sino-Japanese conflicts. Were that alliance to collapse, Japan would be likely to expand its armed forces, might well develop nuclear weapons and Sino-Japanese tensions would probably increase. China may, therefore, have an interest – albeit largely unspoken – in the maintenance of the US-Japan partnership. The picture is, however, further complicated by efforts to reform the US-Japan alliance, with the US encouraging its ally to play a more proactive military role in the region and Japan participating in US missile defence plans. From the Chinese perspective, these developments both reinforce the character of the US-Japan alliance as a tool for containing China and increase the danger of renewed Japanese militarism.

A particular focus of Sino-Japanese tensions is the East China Sea, which lies between the two countries. They have long disputed the

Senkaku Islands, which have been in Japanese hands since 1895. With Japan's defeat in 1945, the islands fell under American administration. The US returned the islands to Japan in 1972 but China has disputed Japan's control since then. The two countries also challenge each other on the rights to and extent of Exclusive Economic Zones (EEZ) in the East China Sea under the UN Convention on the Law of the Sea (UNCLOS). This dispute has become more important since the early 2000s because of gas and oil deposits, with both countries establishing drilling platforms. The issue has become militarised, with China's growing military power allowing it to extend patrols into new areas and bringing the two countries' forces into regular proximity in disputed territories. Observers fear that the situation could trigger armed conflict between them. In 2008 China and Japan reached a 'political agreement' on exploitation of the East China Sea but implementation of this agreement has proved difficult. The September 2010 incident noted above illustrates the continuing fragility of the situation. US analysts have proposed that China and Japan should negotiate specific crisis management and military confidence-building measures to prevent armed conflict. The larger troubled state of political relations between the two countries makes agreement on such steps difficult (Bush 2010).

The relationship between China and Japan can be summarised as one of substantial economic interdependence but deep political Cold War. The continuation of this Cold War was made clear in the mid-2000s when, in the context of a major debate on UN reform, Japan's bid for permanent membership of the UN Security Council triggered large demonstrations in China (arguably encouraged by the Chinese leadership). Beijing made clear that it would, if necessary, use its own veto as an existing permanent member of the Security Council to prevent Japan gaining the same status. The legacy of history and the strength of nationalism in China and Japan make it difficult for political leaders in either country to take the kind of steps which might move relations beyond their current troubled status: '[R]econciliation, a road not yet taken, awaits leaders with the wisdom and skill to pass through the political and historical barriers that clog its entrance' (Roy 2005: 211).

Russia

Since the 1990s, China and Russia have been establishing increasingly close political and military relations, which the two countries refer to as a 'strategic partnership'. In the 1960s and 1970s, the Soviet Union was viewed by China as the country's greatest external threat and the two countries came close to war. From the mid-1980s, however, the Soviet Union reduced its military presence on China's border and relations between the two countries improved significantly. The break-up of the Soviet Union itself in 1991 further reduced the potential military threat that Russia, as the Soviet Union's successor state, might pose to China. The historical reconciliation between the two countries continued into the 1990s with agreements on further reductions in military forces and on the delimitation of their mutual border. The two countries also found common cause in countering US hegemony: both countries resent and oppose the dominant position of the US and the larger Western-led international order. The rhetoric of the Sino-Russian strategic partnership thus stresses opposition to hegemony and the desirability of establishing a multipolar international order – in which implicitly China and Russia would be two major poles. China and Russia also share largely common positions on issues such as human rights (where both emphasise state sovereignty in order to protect their regimes from external criticism and interference), as well as peacekeeping and intervention (where they again stress the primacy of sovereignty fearing that they might themselves be targets of Western interventions).

China and Russia have developed more concrete elements of cooperation. With China modernising its military and becoming a major energy importer, Russia has become a major supplier of arms[6] plus gas and oil to the PRC. For China, these ties are important to its economic and military development. For Russia, China has become an important source of hard cash. The SCO is in part a by-product of the Sino-Russian rapprochement. In December 2010, Russia expressed its support to India becoming a full member, emphasising the SCO's role in countering terrorism and potential insurgency.

Although the new Sino-Russian relationship is now well-established and quite stable, there are limits to the 'strategic partnership' between the two states (Anderson 1997). From China's perspective, Russia is not a core market for Chinese goods, nor can it offer the investment or the technology of the West. Russia, therefore, does not provide an alternative to the West in terms of economic relations; nor would it be worth deepening the partnership with Russia to the extent that would seriously undermine relations with the West, especially the US. In addition, there are concerns in Moscow about Chinese economic and migratory penetration into eastern Russia: as Lampton notes, the Sino-Russian border 'is only a thin membrane separating seven million Russians in the Siberian-Russian Far East region ... from about one hundred million Chinese in the PRC's three north-eastern provinces'

(Lampton 2008: 201). Although Sino-Russian border issues were essentially settled in the 1990s and 2000s, there are residual fears in Russia about the possible re-emergence of Chinese territorial claims (which, for example, have limited Russia's willingness to sell certain military technologies to China). For both China and Russia, therefore, neither is the other's most important international partner and there are likely to remain limits to their strategic partnership.

India

Malone and Mukherjee describe the Sino-Indian relationship as 'one of geostrategic competition qualified by growing commercial coopera- tion' but also 'a largely reactive relationship' in which 'neither has developed a grand strategy with regard to the other' (Malone and Mukherjee 2010: 137). India achieved independence in the same year that the PRC was established. At this point the two countries shared a common desire to assert their independence from the Western colonial powers. Initial relations between the PRC and India were good, with the 1954 Panchsheel Agreement affirming common principles of respect for each other's territorial integrity and sovereignty, non-inter- ference and peaceful co-existence. India also recognised Chinese sovereignty over Tibet at this point (Norbu 1997). Tensions between the two Asian giants, however, emerged quite quickly, with China providing assistance to insurrections in India's north-east border disputes and the Dalai Lama fleeing to India in 1959. The border disputes led to a brief war in 1962, with India decisively defeated and China gaining control of 90,000 square kilometres of territory previ- ously held by India. A Cold War between the two countries ensued. From the 1970s relations slowly began to improve, with the rapproche- ment accelerating in the 1980s and 1990s. In 1993 an agreement on maintaining Peace and Tranquillity on the Line of Actual Control – the cease-fire line at the end of the 1962 war – was signed. In 1996 Jiang Zemin was the first Chinese head of state to visit India since 1962. Economic ties between the two countries also grew significantly from the 1990s. By the late 2000s President Hu was describing Sino-India relations as 'on a fast track' (Ogden, 2010: 2).

Despite improved relations and growing economic ties, the Sino- India relationship remains characterised by continuing tensions and a significant element of geostrategic competition. The border disputes between the two remain unresolved. China has long backed Pakistan in order to maintain geo-political pressure on India, including by supporting Pakistan's nuclear weapons programme. The need to deter China remains one of the primary rationales for India's own nuclear weapons. India tested a nuclear weapon in 1998, rapidly followed by Pakistan, with both states subsequently consolidating their status as nuclear weapon states.

China and India's economic growth and the consequent likelihood that they will become two of the world's leading powers in the twenty-first century has intensified the element of strategic competition in their relationship. China has pursued the so-called 'string of pearls' strategy in the Indian Ocean, building civilian and military naval ties with Pakistan, Myanmar, Sri Lanka and Bangladesh, including various military bases and facilities. India fears encirclement by China and has sought to counter this by extending its own commercial and military naval influence, developing its own ties with Myanmar and island nations such as Madagascar, Mauritius and the Seychelles. In a mirror image of the view from New Delhi, China perceives India's actions as potentially threatening to its interests (Kaplan 2009).

An additional important factor in the Sino-Indian relationship is the US. As concerns about the implications of China's growing power have intensified, the US has sought to bolster relations with India as a counter-weight to China – approaches which India has been happy to reciprocate given its own concerns about China. These dynamics have facilitated a transformation in US-India relations since the Cold War, when India tended to rail against 'US imperialism' and was a semi-ally of the Soviet Union. This development began in the 2000s under the Bush administration, with the conclusion in particular of a civilian nuclear cooperation agreement with India (previously precluded because of concerns about India's development of nuclear weapons). In November 2010 US President Barack Obama visited India, in what was viewed as a further effort to bolster ties with US allies vis-à-vis China. Neither India nor the US, however, wants to antagonise China by establishing an overt alliance against Beijing: if China is sometimes described as pursuing a strategy of 'soft balancing' against the US, India and the US may be viewed as engaging in a policy of 'soft containment' towards China.

The relationship between China and India is thus characterised by contradictory dynamics. Political relations between the two have improved greatly in the last two decades or so and economic ties have expanded and are growing rapidly. As developing states and victims of European imperialism, the two countries share elements of a common worldview and some important mutual interests such as ensuring that efforts to address climate change do not come at the expense of their economic development. Nevertheless, the unresolved border dispute between the two remains a source of tension, while the two countries' growing power also pushes them towards strategic competition in South Asia and in the wider Indian Ocean region.

China and East Asia

Growing engagement with the wider East Asian region has become an important element of Chinese foreign policy since the 1990s (for basic geography of East Asia see Map 2). During the Cold War, China was relatively isolated from most of its East Asian neighbours. Most of the East Asian states were governed by non-communist regimes and viewed the communist PRC as a threat, particularly as it backed communist parties in Indonesia and other countries. Many of the PRC's neighbours were allied to the US. The Association of South-East Asian Nations (ASEAN), the main regional forum, was, in part, an anti-communist bloc. China maintained bilateral relations with the various East Asian states but these were often problematic – marred by historic tensions, territorial conflicts and disputes over the rights of Chinese minorities. Since the early 2000s, however, as Breslin points out, there has been a radical change and much of the Chinese suspicion of American influence has gone:

> Today, Chinese policy-makers see considerable potential for the progression of Chinese objectives in the region, and China's economic and security interests are perceived as being best served by engagement and cooperation. (Breslin 2009: 817)

This transformation has had a number of dimensions. First, economic ties between China and its East Asian neighbours have grown significantly as the PRC's economic development has intensified. For most of the East Asian states, China has become an increasingly important market as well as a source of investment. Second, China has pursued a 'good neighbour' policy, seeking to resolve territorial disputes and upgrade bilateral diplomatic relations with its East Asian neighbours. Third, China – historically a reluctant multilateralist – has become willing to engage with multilateral regional forums, such as the Asia Pacific Economic Cooperation (APEC) process, set up in 1989, and the ASEAN Regional Forum (ARF), established in 1994. By the mid-to-late 2000s, perceptions of China within the region were shifting, with the PRC increasingly being viewed as a partner to be worked with rather than a problem to be held at arm's length. One indicator of this was the willingness of the other East Asian states to join the East Asian Summit process, a periodic (approximately annual) meeting of heads of state of the ASEAN states plus China, Japan, South Korea, India,

Australia and New Zealand launched in 2005. The East Asian Summit emerged in part from Chinese initiatives and did not, until 2010, include the US, yet the other East Asian states proved willing to join the process.

By the late 2000s, China was increasingly integrated into the wider East Asian economy and into institutionalised East Asian political and security processes. This process has, however, generated its own tensions. From the perspective of the other East Asian states, although mutual trade and investment with China have brought economic benefits, there are now fears of the region being drawn into a Chinese dominated sphere of economic and, consequently, political influence. At the same time, there remained questions over how far China would 'play by the rules of the game' – in terms of the non-use of force and the acceptance of multilateral diplomatic or legal processes – in territorial disputes within the region. The mini-crises in 2010 over the South China Seas and Senkaku Islands triggered fears in East Asia that China might seek to use its growing power to resolve disputes in its favour. In this context, it was no coincidence that the October 2010 East Asian Summit in Hanoi was the first attended by the US and that the US formally joined the East Asian Summit process in 2011. China's relationship with the wider East Asian region has thus shifted from one of isolation to one of integration and engagement but the implications, nature and durability of the new stance remain very much to be determined.

China and global governance

As China's economy has grown and its power has risen so has its impact on almost all global issues. In 2009, China overtook Germany as the world's largest trading nation (*New York Times*, 11 January 2010). In 2006, it surpassed the US as the largest emitter of the greenhouse gases (GHGs) that contribute to climate change. China is already a major energy importer, accounting for 17 per cent of global energy use in 2009, a figure set to rise to 22 per cent by 2035 (Krauss 2010). From the global economy to global security and from climate change to human rights, China will play a major role in global governance.

China was a largely absent partner in global governance after 1945. The US refusal to recognise the PRC meant that it did not join the United Nations (UN) until 1971. China also stayed outside other major institutions such as the General Agreement on Tariffs and Trade (GATT – the predecessor of the WTO), the International Monetary Fund (IMF), the World Bank and the Nuclear Non-Proliferation

Treaty (NPT). Even after it joined the UN the PRC retained a low profile, for example rarely using its veto power as one of the permanent members of the UN Security Council. As the policy of integration with the world economy gained momentum in the 1980s and 1990s, however, China gradually entered the mainstream of existing global institutions, becoming a member of the IMF and World Bank in 1980 and a signatory of the NPT in 1992.

Since the 1990s, China has assumed an increasingly prominent role in institutions of and debates on global governance. Since joining the WTO in 2001, China has become one of a group of developing nations that have challenged the traditional dominance of the US, the EU and Japan in international trade negotiations. In the UN Security Council, China has used its veto power as a permanent member more often to protect allies such as Iran, Sudan and North Korea from Western proposed diplomatic and economic sanctions. In the wake of the 2008 global financial crisis, China assumed a prominent position within the Group of 20 (G20) in efforts to manage the crisis, with some observers talking of China saving the world economy (Powell 2009).

Two key features of China's policies on global governance are notable. One is a strong commitment to the concept of state sovereignty. This reflects China's historical experience as a target of Western imperial interventions and concern that dilution of the principle of state sovereignty could lead to the institutions of global governance being turned against China in areas such as human rights. The second is the issue of how far China is willing to moderate its positions in order to facilitate international cooperation.

In terms of global economic governance, China has arguably benefited massively from a broadly liberal international economic order that has allowed it to build an export-based economy and to access foreign capital and technology. Critics in the West argue that, while China has benefited from access to Western markets, it has failed to play by the rules of the game, in particular by subsidising export industries, creating bureaucratic obstacles to foreign companies operating in China and maintaining an artificially low currency. In the context of debates in the G20 since 2008, China and Western governments found it relatively easy to agree on coordinated stimulus packages to generate economic growth in 2008–09. Since then, as issues of trade deficits and currency valuations have come to the fore, we may have entered an era of more difficult choices, where accommodation between Chinese and Western positions will become more problematic. On both sides, there are calls for protectionist economic measures and more forceful currency policies. Western business leaders are expressing more reservations about investing in China while the PRC itself seeks to secure future energy and raw material supply lines.

In the sphere of global security, questions of peacekeeping and intervention highlight the dynamics and dilemmas arising from China's approach to global governance. Even after it joined the UN in 1971, China did not participate in UN peacekeeping operations and was wary of the idea of peacekeeping. China first contributed forces to UN peacekeeping operations in 1989 and since then China's role in UN peacekeeping has gradually expanded. China has consistently emphasised that peacekeeping operations should not infringe the principle of state sovereignty and should only be authorised by the UN Security Council. Traditional UN peacekeeping operations – which rest on the consent of the state(s) to which peacekeepers are being deployed and do not involve the use of force – are thus compatible with the Chinese view.

Since the 1990s, however, peacekeeping and intervention has moved in new directions, involving situations where international forces may be deployed without the consent of the state to which they are being sent and may use military force. The essential argument in favour of such operations is that there are sometimes circumstances, such as genocide, mass atrocities and on-going civil wars, where it may be necessary to deploy military forces to halt violence even in the face of opposition from the state concerned. China has been prominent amongst those countries countering these arguments and seeking to reaffirm the primacy of state sovereignty in relation to peacekeeping. Thus, China opposed NATO's 1999 intervention in Kosovo. Similarly, in relation to the conflict in Darfur in the mid-2000s, China argued that a UN peacekeeping force should only be deployed with the consent of the Sudanese government and should have a limited mandate. Given its veto power in the Security Council, China was able to circumscribe the scale and mission of the UN force eventually deployed in the second half of the 2000s.

China's role in Darfur also highlighted the interaction between these larger questions of principle and specific national interests. According to American analysis:

> China views [secure supply lines] ... as a national security issue and has linked its military, diplomatic and political efforts in the world to their energy acquisition strategy. They have entered into energy acquisition deals with Iran, Sudan and other nations to ensure their access to energy. In return, they have transferred military equipment, technology, and cash and have agreed to support the political aims of those and other countries. (Wessel 2005: 2)

Thus, national interests almost certainly reinforced China's principled reluctance to support more forceful intervention in Darfur. Given China's increasing engagement in most regions of the world (including areas such as Africa and the Middle East which are the location of many of the world's violent conflicts) and its position as a veto-holding permanent member of the UN Security Council, Beijing is likely to assume a growing role in debates on peacekeeping and to shape the limits of what is possible in this area.

While accepting the idea of universal human rights standards, China's attitude to the global human rights regime is strongly influenced by the concern that international human rights law and institutions may be used to criticise China or, *in extremis,* to justify intervention in its internal affairs. China thus emphasises the primacy of state sovereignty over human rights. China signed the International Covenant on Civil and Political Rights – the key legal instrument guaranteeing political rights – in 1998 but has yet to ratify the treaty and is, therefore, in legal terms, not fully subject to its provisions.

At the UN, China has consistently made common cause with other authoritarian regimes in opposing or watering down criticisms of their countries in relation to human rights. In the United Nations Human Rights Council, which was created in 2005–06 with the objective of strengthening the UN's capacity to review and criticise member states human rights records, China has worked with other authoritarian states to obstruct reviews of these countries' human rights records and prevent criticism of them. In June 2009, as part of its Universal Periodic Review process in relation to human rights, China rejected 70 recommendations by UN member states relating to human rights abuses in China (Human Rights Watch, 2009). Despite a theoretical commitment to universal human rights, there are clearly fundamental differences between China and Western governments on human rights – differences which are unlikely to be bridged in the foreseeable future.

Conclusion

China's foreign policy and world role in the early twenty-first century can perhaps best be summed up as 'rising power, rising impact': China's remarkable economic growth has established it as one of the world's leading powers and, as a consequence, it has a growing impact on almost all aspects of global politics. Unless China's economy collapses or a crisis – most likely over Taiwan – triggers armed conflict with the US, this dynamic is likely to continue. The nature and impact of China's rise is, however, often exaggerated. Jacques, for example, has argued that an era has begun when China will 'rule the world' (Jacques 2009). As Ikenberry has pointed out, however:

> It may be possible for China to overtake the US alone, but it is much less likely that China will ever manage to overtake the Western order ... [W]hen the economic capacity of the Western system as a whole is considered, China's economic advances look much less significant; the Chinese economy will be much smaller than the combined economies of the OECD far into the future. This is even truer of military might. (Ikenberry 2008: 36)

In terms of China's foreign policy, the primary driver and objective from Beijing's perspective has been to facilitate the country's on-going economic growth. This has required integration into the global economy and cooperation with other major powers, above all the US. Until quite recently, the Chinese leadership also placed an emphasis on maintaining a low profile internationally in order to avoid generating conflicts with other states or provoking fears about the consequences of China's rise. Since the mid-2000s, however, this approach has increasingly fallen away. In part this reflects the reality that, as China's economic and political footprint has grown in most regions of the world, it is simply no longer possible to maintain a low profile. At the same time, as China's power has increased, the opportunity for Beijing to assert its national perspective and interests has grown.

China sits at the heart of a complex set of relations with the other major powers. These relationships reflect both the particular historical and political dynamics of China's relations with each of the other major powers and a larger game of multipolar balance of power politics. A somewhat contradictory dynamic can be discerned: both China and the US have compelling interests in cooperating with one another; at the same time, China is also wary of American hegemony and seeks to counter US domination. Similarly, America is circumspect about China's rising power and tries to balance against China through its alliance with Japan and the development of ties with India. Although the specific mix of these dynamics shifts over time, short of a fully fledged Cold War between the US and China, the most likely outcome is the continuation of the current contradictory but arguably relative stable pattern of great power relations in Asia.

Like all states, the PRC faces foreign policy choices and the range of options open to China arguably increases as its relative power grows. One key choice is how China approaches the various historical disputes with its East Asian neighbours, over Taiwan, the South China Sea, the Senkaku Islands and the East China Sea. A situation in which

China seeks to use its growing economic, political and military power to resolve disputes in its favour or to assert hegemony over these regions will be quite different from one in which China works cooperatively with neighbouring states to manage these territories and waters. A second key issue is how China approaches global governance: how far will China abide by the existing rules of the international order and seek accommodation with other states in managing global issues and how far will it seek to re-write the rules or assert the primacy of narrow national interests? In the context of domestic pressures to maintain economic growth and reassert their country's status as a leading power, China's leaders will need great wisdom and political skill in addressing these issues.

Notes

1 Bandwagoning is a term used in realist theories of international relations. It was introduced by Wright (1942) and given greater currency by Waltz (1979).
2 In West Java, Indonesia.
3 Rogue state is a term used primarily in the US to describe states viewed as particularly threatening to global security, in particular because they severely restrict human rights, sponsor terrorism or seek to develop weapons of mass destruction.
4 Soft power refers to the use of social, cultural, economic and other non-military resources to encourage other governments and publics to look on a country favourably. Soft balancing, on the other hand, is the use of non-military means, partnerships with other countries and diplomacy to challenge the hegemony of a strong state.
5 Also referred to as the Diaoyu Islands (钓鱼台群岛).
6 Russia's role as a supplier of arms in part reflects the impact of EU and American embargos.

Conclusion

In this book, we have sought to explore the nature of Chinese politics in the early twenty-first century, as well as the historical trends that have shaped the Chinese political system and China's foreign policy and role in the world. It is clear that the China of the 2000s and 2010s is not the China of 1949 or 1979: the totalitarian system which was established after 1949 has been significantly liberalised; the attempt to control all aspects of people's lives and to re-make them into true socialist men and women has been abandoned; and, the Chinese people now have much greater social and economic freedom in their daily lives than during the Mao and immediate post-Mao era. The traditional communist model of a centrally planned economy has also been radically reformed, arguably completely abandoned.

In terms of politics and the political system, however, change has been both less radical and more difficult to interpret. Three broad alternative interpretations may be advanced. One interpretation is that, at least politically, China remains in essence a communist system, with core institutions, decision-making mechanisms and power relations following the model that was established in the Soviet Union after 1917 and replicated, with local modifications, by other communist states including the PRC. From this perspective, the CCP remains the central institution in Chinese politics, penetrating all state institutions and key economic actors (state-owned companies and other major businesses) and retaining control over all major policy decisions. Other features of communist political systems also remain intact. Political decision-making within China remains strongly centralised, implicitly following the Leninist model of 'democratic centralism'. While there is debate within the CCP, core decisions are taken by the central leadership essentially behind closed doors. Although there is some freedom for provincial and local leaders in implementing them, decisions promulgated at the centre define the direction taken. Survival and promotion within Chinese politics depends on success in achieving the goals set by the central leadership. The CCP also remains intolerant of political dissent: while there is debate over economic and social policy (and to lesser extent 'political reform'), the leading role of the CCP cannot be questioned. Further, while socio-economic groups beyond the Party have grown significantly, any which threaten or are perceived to threaten its leading role are quickly closed down. Individuals calling for an end to the Party's hold on power or reforms along the lines of Western liberal democracies are imprisoned and silenced.

A second interpretation of contemporary Chinese politics is that, with the abandonment of communist economics and totalitarian control over society, China has moved towards 'developmental authoritarianism' (Pei 2006). From this perspective, China is not radically different from many other authoritarian states in the developing world – the key objective of the dominant political class is to pursue the economic development of the country while maintaining political and social stability. The state is a key instrument in this process, directing economic activity and resources to the larger national objective even if no longer controlling them along the lines of the old communist model. The dominant political party, class or élite views the maintenance of its rule as the pre-requisite for national economic development and the maintenance of order. This line of reasoning suggests that contemporary Chinese politics can be viewed as broadly similar to that in other authoritarian states, such as other East Asian states at earlier stages in their development (for example, South Korea and Taiwan up to the 1980s). The PRC also resembles many Middle Eastern states (at least up to the dramatic events of the early 2010s) and Russia and some other former Soviet states since the collapse of communism. In the Chinese case, with the abandonment of old-style communist economics, the distinction between a 'communist' political system and a 'developmental authoritarian' one is a moot point.

A third interpretation is that China is a reforming, liberalising or even democratising political system. The central argument here is that, although core elements of the communist political system remain intact, political reforms have nevertheless been instituted and that these are significant or at least potentially so in their character and implications. Key developments here include: the broadening of the CCP's membership to include representatives of a wider range of economic and social actors; increased interest within the CCP and its top leadership in mechanisms by which citizens can express their views and the Party can identify the concerns of the ordinary Chinese people; and, experiments, albeit limited to date, in competitive elections of officials, deliberative democracy and the like. In addition, it is clear that, since the 1980s, there has at various points been debate within the CCP leadership about 'political reform', with reformers advocating more radical and rapid reforms (even up to the development of a Western multi-party system) and conservatives opposing anything but the most limited reforms. How we should assess these exercises in and debates on 'political reform' is contentious. For some, these may be the beginnings of liberalisation within China which will eventually result in the emergence of a liberal democratic system, with multiple political parties. While such a scenario cannot be ruled out, such reforms as have taken place to date are still very far from producing this outcome. A second argument is that these reforms are a serious project for the CCP but that the outcome is unlikely to be a Western-style liberal democracy. The central logic is that the CCP recognises that it needs to maintain and enhance its legitimacy and, in order to achieve this, it needs to become more responsive to the concerns of the majority of the Chinese people and better at aggregating the competing interests of different socio-economic sectors into sustainable national policies. The outcome cannot be foreseen but the political system that may emerge could be very different both from today's notionally communist system and from the Western model of liberal democracy. A third view is that the political reforms undertaken to date are no more than 'window dressing' and are unlikely to develop into a substantive change to the existing political system within China. The central logic here is that the ultimate imperative is the survival and maintenance in power of the CCP. 'Reforms' may be undertaken as part of efforts to enhance the legitimacy of the Party, but truly significant change would ultimately threaten the Party's monopoly on power and, therefore, will not be permitted.

A second large question relates to the sources of change within the Chinese political system, both to date and potentially in future. Although only expressed *sotto voce*, the failure of the Maoist political and economic system was the central driver of reform from the late 1970s. If the central objective was to re-establish China as an economically viable society and a great power, Deng Xiaoping's key insight was that new economic policies need to be found to achieve this goal. The economic reforms instituted by Deng and his successors, however, themselves generated pressures for political change. The greater freedom both required by and resulting from market economic reforms gave the Chinese people space to express new demands and dissent. Market economic reforms also created new actors, in particular in the form of private business enterprises and businesspeople. The CCP has responded, sometimes with repression, but also by trying to address newly arising economic, social and political concerns and by expanding the membership of the Party and widening its social base. To date this change from within the Party has been both limited and incremental; how far and in what ways CCP initiated reform efforts will evolve remains to be seen.

Another potential source of political change is pressure from outside the Party. Protests, strikes, sit-ins and other forms of disorder are widespread within China, but they are usually localised, rarely include demands for fundamental change in the political system and do not normally have system-wide political repercussions. While such protests are a driver of internal Party-led efforts at political reform, they have not so far become a major source of political change in and of themselves. At the same time, there are explicit calls from some individuals and groups outside the Party for fundamental political change, such as the Charter 08 manifesto and its most prominent signatory Liu Xiaobo (who was awarded the Nobel Peace Prize in 2010, triggering angry protests from the Chinese regime). Such groups and individuals, however, do not appear to have great prominence within China or the capacity on their own to mobilise popular opposition to the CCP.

The greatest concern of the CCP appears to be that popular discontent arising from socio-economic concerns – unemployment, low wages, the poor treatment of workers and the perception that the Party is failing to address the concerns of the ordinary people – could combine with the calls of dissidents to produce a fundamental threat to the regime. Indeed, this is arguably exactly what happened in 1989, when worsening socio-economic circumstances led students, intellectuals and workers to come together in mass protests for political change. The Party leadership is often said to view the maintenance of an economic growth rate of about 8 per cent as necessary to avert the socio-economic problems that might trigger such a scenario.

A further source of demands for political change is ethnic minority opposition to CCP policies and, in some cases, to continued incorporation into the Chinese state altogether. As the violent protests in Tibet and Xinjiang in 2008 and the Chinese government's tough response to these protests indicated these issues continue to pose major challenges for China. Ethnic discontent, however, does not appear likely to be a key driver of demands for political change beyond Tibet and Xinjiang. Almost all Chinese provinces have large Han Chinese majorities and, although other ethnic minorities do have grievances, these are not a basis for strong political mobilisation. Similarly, although there are centre-periphery tensions between the central government/Party and regional governments/Party leaders over some economic and policy issues, these are again not a basis for any more general political mobilisation or advocacy of a truly different political vision from that advanced by the central CCP leadership.

As of 2011–12, two particular developments, one internal, the other external, were shaping Chinese politics. Domestically, as discussed in Chapter 2, the coming shift to the 'fifth generation' of CCP leadership was the main event in Chinese politics. A central element of the new leadership is likely to be the 'party of princelings'. It is ironic that, a century after the 1911 revolution overthrew one dynastic system and sixty years after the communists sought to sweep away all features of the old Chinese system, China's political system appears to be morphing into a new dynastic model. The larger question is what will be the priorities and policies of the 'fifth generation' of CCP leadership? The opaqueness of the Chinese political system makes this difficult to gauge. Some observers suggest that the 'fifth generation' of CCP leadership is significantly shaped by China's 'new leftists', whose politics embrace a greater emphasis on socio-economic equality, a stronger role for the state in the economy, and greater authoritarianism (Miles 2011: 4–5). How far and in what ways the policies of the 'fifth generation' of China's communist leaders will differ from their reformist predecessors remains to be seen.

The new external development impinging on Chinese politics in 2011 was the Middle Eastern Arab Spring – the series of popular protests which swept away long-standing authoritarian regimes in Tunisia and Egypt and threatened to do the same to many other regimes across the region. In the 1980s and 1990s, democratic transitions in Southern Europe, Latin America, Eastern Europe and elsewhere suggested a major global shift towards democracy and made communist China appear a vulnerable outlier. By the 2000s, setbacks to democratisation in some countries and the apparent stability and success of some major authoritarian states (such as China and Russia) suggested that the global political tide was now flowing in the opposite direction. In particular, China's remarkable economic growth and relative political stability despite the large size of the country and many challenges posed by its economic transition made it appear to offer a new model of authoritarian economic development for other developing states. The Arab Spring raised new questions about this analysis. If long-standing regimes which had appeared impervious to political change could collapse so dramatically and unexpectedly, might not the same dynamic occur elsewhere in the world? And, if one central element of the Arab Spring was a contagion effect, reflecting the power of a new generation of dissatisfied young people and made possible in part by new social media such as Facebook and Twitter, might a similar contagion not spread to other regions and countries? Indeed, in 2011 it was clear that the Chinese communist leadership was worried about exactly such a development. When protests with the slogan 'Jasmine Revolution' occurred in China in February 2011 they were quickly suppressed and the regime took steps to block internet searches for 'Jasmine Revolution' (the term was first used to describe the Tunisian revolution at the beginning of 2011, then used by Chinese protestors in February 2011). Indeed, during early 2011 observers detected growing repression in China, with the detention of dissidents, criminal charges against political opposition, beatings and house arrest of those calling for protests and the disappearance of prominent defence lawyers (*The Economist* 2011) – suggesting that China's communist leaders were indeed worried about the possible spread of the Arab Spring to their country. As of 2011–12 a dramatic collapse of China's communist regime similar to those in Tunisia and Egypt appeared unlikely, but it should be remembered that almost no one predicted the Arab Spring and once protests took hold in these countries events moved with breathtaking speed. As China's dramatic transition continues, therefore, the central questions facing the country's political system are twofold. First, how far and in what ways Party-led efforts at political reform will truly alter a political system which still in foundation rests on the communist model established after 1949; and, second, whether political dissent and socio-economic discontent from outside the Party will create pressures for yet more fundamental change.

Bibliography

Agence France-Presse (AFP) (2008), 'China's Communists Call for Intensified Graft Fight', 23 June.

Almond, G. and Verba, S. (1963), *The Civic Culture: Political Attitudes and Democracy in Five Nations*. Princeton, NJ: Princeton University Press.

Alpermann, B. (2009), 'State of Field: Assessing Village Elections in China', *Journal of Contemporary China*, Vol. 18, No. 60, pp. 397–409.

Anderlini, J. (2010), 'China Follows Tigers' Path', *Financial Times* (London), 3 June.

Anderson, J. (1997), *The Limits of Sino-Russian Strategic Partnership*, Oxford: Oxford University Press for the International Institute for Strategic Studies.

Andrew, A.M. and Rapp, J.A. (2000), *Autocracy and China's Rebel Founding Emperors: Comparing Chairman Mao and Ming Taizu*, Lanham, MD: Rowman and Littlefield.

Associated Press (2011) 'China blocks searches for "Jasmine Revolution"', 21 February, sourced at www.ndtv.com/article/world/china-blocks-searches-for-jasmine-revolution-86851.

Backer, L. (2009), 'The Party as Polity, the Communist Party, and the Chinese Constitutional State: A Theory of State-Party Constitutionalism', *Journal of Chinese and Comparative Law*, Vol. 16, No. 1, pp. 101–68.

Banyan (2009), 'A Watched Frog Never Boils', *The Economist* (London), 7 May.

Baranovitch, N. (2010), 'Others No More: The Changing Representation of Non-Han Peoples in Chinese History Textbooks, 1951–2003', *Journal of Asian Studies*, Vol. 69, No. 1, pp. 85–122.

BBC News (2010), 'China replaces top Communist boss in Xinjiang region', 24 April, http://news.bbc.co.uk/2/hi/asia-pacific/8641443.stm.

Becquelin, N. (2004), 'Staged Development in Xinjiang', *China Quarterly*, Vol. 197, pp. 358–78.

Becquelin, N. (2006), reviewing S. Frederick Starr (ed.), *Xinjiang: China's Muslim Borderland*, London: M.E. Sharpe, *China Quarterly*, Vol. 186, pp. 489–90.

Beech, H (2010), 'Asia's New Cold War', *Time Magazine*, 3 October.

Beijing Review (2009), 'Homes of Their Own', 8 October.

Bell, D.A. (2008), *China's New Confucianism: Politics and Everyday Life in a Changing Society*, Princeton, NJ: Princeton University Press.

Bell, D.A. (2009), 'The Confucian Party', *New York Times*, 12 May.

Benn, C. (2004), *China's Golden Age: Everyday Life in the Tang Dynasty*, Oxford: Oxford University Press.

Bergère, M.C. (1998), *Sun Yat-sen*, Stanford, CA: Stanford University Press.

Bergsten, C.F., Freeman, C., Lardy, N.R. and Mitchell, D.J. (2008), *China's Rise: Challenges and Opportunities*, Washington, DC: Peterson Institute for International Economics.

Bernstein, R. and Munro, R.H. (1997) *The Coming Conflict with China*, New York, NY: A.A. Knopf.

Berthrong, J. (2003), 'Boston Confucianism: The Third Wave of Global Confucianism', *Journal of Ecumenical Studies*, Vol. 40, No. 1–2, pp. 26–47.

Bi, J. (2002), 'China's Internet Revolution: the Economic Impact', *New Zealand International Review*, Vol. 27, No. 1, pp. 23–7.

Bi, J. (2006), *The Quest for the Oil and Gas Infrastructure Protection in Central Asia: Time Bombs and Policy Options*, Ottawa: Canadian Centre of Intelligence and Security Studies.

Bilik, N. (2008), 'Han in Three Mirrors: History, Foreigners, and Minorities', paper presented at Critical Han Studies Conference & Workshop, Stanford, CA, 25–27 April.

Blanchard, J.M.F. (2009), 'Economics and Asia-Pacific Region Territorial and Maritime Disputes: Understanding the Political Limits to Economic Solutions', *Asian Politics & Policy*, Vol. 1, No. 4, pp. 682–708.

Bo, Z. (2002), *Chinese Provincial Leaders: Economic Performance and Political Mobility since 1949*, Armonk, NY: M.E. Sharpe.

Bovingdon, G. (2002), 'The Not-So-Silent Majority: Uyghur Resistance to Han Rule in Xinjiang', *Modern China*, Vol. 28, No.1, pp. 39–78.

Bovingdon, G. (2004), *Autonomy in Xinjiang: Han Nationalist Imperatives and Uyghur Discontent*, Washington, DC: East-West Center, Policy Studies, No. 11.

Brady, A. (2009), 'Mass Persuasion as Means of Legitimation and

China's Popular Authoritarianism', *American Behavioural Scientist*, Vol. 53, No. 3, pp. 434–57.

Breslin, S (2009), 'Understanding China's Regional Rise: Interpretations, Identities and Implications', *International Affairs*, Vol. 85, No. 4, pp. 17–35.

Brixi, H. (2009), *China: Urban Services and Governance*, World Bank Policy Research, Working Papers No. 5030, Washington, DC: World Bank Policy Research.

Brødsgaard, K.E. (2002), 'Institutional Reform and the Bianzhi System in China', *China Quarterly*, No. 170, pp. 361–86.

Brødsgaard, K.E. (2008), *Hainan: State, Society, and Business in a Chinese Province*, London: Routledge.

Brødsgaard, K.E. and Zheng, Y. (2006) (eds), *The Chinese Communist Party in Reform*, London: Routledge.

Brooks, R. and Tao, R. (2003), *China's Labor Market Performance and Challenges*, Washington, DC: International Monetary Fund.

Buchanan, A. (2002), 'Political Legitimacy and Democracy', *Ethics*, Vol. 112, No. 4, pp. 689–719.

Bulag, U.E. (2003), 'Alter/Native Mongolian Identity: from Nationality to Ethnic Group', in E. Perry and M. Selden (eds), *Chinese Society: Change, Conflict and Resistance*, London: Routledge, pp. 223–46.

Bush, R. (2010), *China-Japan Security Relations*, Washington, DC: Brookings Institution.

Buzan, B. and Wæver, O. (2003), *Regions and Powers: The Structure of International Security*, Cambridge: Cambridge University Press.

Callahan, W. (2004), 'National Insecurities: Humiliation, Salvation, and Chinese Nationalism', *Alternatives*, Vol. 29, No. 2, pp. 199–238.

Callahan, W. (2005), 'How to understand China: The Dangers and Opportunities of Being a Rising Power', *Review of International Studies*, Vol. 31, No. 4, pp. 701–14.

Cao, L. and Hou, C. (2001), 'A Comparison of Confidence in the Police in China and in the US', *Journal of Criminal Justice*, Vol. 29, No. 2, pp. 87–99.

Chambers, M. (2008) 'The Evolving Relationship Between China and Southeast Asia', in A. Murphy and B. Welsh, (eds), *Legacy of Engagement in Southeast Asia*, Singapore: Institute of Southeast Asian Studies, pp. 281–310.

Chan, A. (2003), 'A Race to the Bottom: Globalisation and China's Labour Standards', *China Perspectives*, No. 46, pp. 41–9.

Chang, I. (1998), *The Rape of Nanking: The Forgotten Holocaust of World War II*, Harmondsworth: Penguin.

Chen, G. and Liu, M. (2007), 'Reform of Criminal Evidence System in China', paper presented at the Twentieth Anniversary Conference of the International Society for the Reform of Criminal Law, Vancouver, Canada, 22–6 June.

Chen, J. and Dickson, B.J. (2010), *Allies of the State: China's Private Entrepreneurs and Democratic Change*, Cambridge, MA: Harvard University Press.

Chen, S. and Ravallion, M. (2007), *The Changing Profile of Poverty in the World*, Washington, DC: International Food Policy Research Institute.

Chen, Y.W. (2010), 'Absence Makes the Heart Grow Fonder: A Social Network Analysis of the Uyghur International Mobilization', paper presented at the Political Studies Association Annual Conference, Edinburgh, 29 March–1 April.

Cheung, A. (2009), 'China Internet Going Wild: Cyber-hunting versus Privacy Protection', *Computer Law and Security Review*, Vol. 25, No. 3, pp. 275–9.

China Daily (Beijing) (2009), 'China Drafts Regulation on Monopoly Price', 13 August.

China Daily (Beijing) (2009), 'China's Central Government to Recruit 15,000 Staff', 12 October.

China Daily (Beijing) (2010), 'Increase Wages', 28 May.

China-embassy.org (2007), 'Full Text of Constitution of Communist Party of China', 25 October, www.china-embassy.org/eng/xw /t375504.htm.

China.org.cn (2007), 'White Paper on China's Political Party System', 15 November, www.china.org.cn/english/news/231852.htm.

Chinadaily.com.cn (2010), 'Online Ballot', 1 June.

Cho, H. (1997), 'The Historical Origin of Civil Society in Korea', *Korea Journal*, Vol. 37, No. 2, pp. 24–41.

Cho, Y.N. (2003), 'Public Supervisors and Reflectors: Role Fulfillment of the Chinese People's Congress Deputies in the Market Socialist Era', *Development and Society*, Vol. 32, No. 2, pp. 197–227.

Christensen, T. (1996), 'Chinese Realpolitk', *Foreign Affairs*, Vol. 75, No. 5, pp. 37–52.

Chung, T. and Tieben, H. (2009), 'Macau: Ten Years after the Handover', *Journal of Current Chinese Affairs*, Vol. 38, No. 1, pp. 7–17.

CINIC (China Internet Network Information Center) (2009), www.cnnic.net.cn/en/index/0O/index.htm.

Clarke, D.C. (2005), *The Chinese Legal System*, Washington, DC: George Washington University Law School.

Clarke, D.C. (2007), 'Legislating for a Market Economy in China, *China Quarterly*, Vol. 191, pp. 567–85.

Cnn.com (2010), Mobile Phones Used to Get Past China's Internet Censors, 15 June, http://edition.cnn.com/2010/TECH/mobile/06/17/china.mobile.phone.web.

Coble, P.M (1980), *The Shanghai Capitalists and the Nationalist Government, 1927–1937*, Cambridge, MA: Harvard University Press.

Collier, D. and Levitsky, S. (1997), 'Democracy with Adjectives: Conceptual Innovation in Comparative Research', *World Politics*, Vol. 49, No 3, pp. 430–51.

Collins, R. and Sun, X. (2010), 'China's Grey Channels as Access Points for Foreign Food Products to the Chinese Domestic Market', *China Information*, Vol. 24, No. 61, pp. 61–74.

Crow, C. (1933), *Handbook for China*, Hong Kong: Oxford University Press.

Crowe, D.M. (2009), 'War Crimes and Genocide in History, and the Evolution of Responsive International Law', *Nationalities Papers*, Vol. 37, No. 6, pp. 757–806.

Dahl, R.A. (1971), *Polyarchy: Participation and Opposition*, New Haven, CT: Yale University Press.

Datong, L. (2008), 'China and the Earthquake', *Democracy News Analysis*, www.opendemocracy.net/article/governments/china-and-the-earthquake.

Davis, E.V.W. (2009), 'Governance in China in 2010', *Asian Affairs: an American Review*, Vol. 35, No. 4, pp. 195–212.

deLisle, J. (2004), Democratization in Greater China: Introduction, *Orbis*, Vol. 48, No. 2, pp. 193–203.

Dewan, P. and Srivastava, S. (2009), *Tibet: Fifty Years After*, Gurgaon, India: Shubhi.

Diamant, N.J., Lubman, S.B. and O'Brien, K.B. (eds) (2005), *Engaging the Law in China: State, Society, and Possibilities for Justice*, Stanford, CA: Stanford University Press.

Diamond, L. (2003), 'The Rule of Law as Transition to Democracy in China', *Journal of Contemporary China*, Vol. 12, No. 35, pp. 319–31.

Dickson, B.J. (1997), *Democratization in China and Taiwan: The Adaptability of Leninist Parties*, Oxford: Oxford University Press.

Dickson, B.J. (2005), 'Populist Authoritarianism: The Future of the Chinese Communist Party', paper presented at the Conference on 'Chinese Leadership, Politics, and Policy', Carnegie Endowment for International Peace, 2 November.

Dickson, B.J. (2008), *Wealth into Power: The Communist Party's Embrace of China's Private Sector*, Cambridge: Cambridge University Press.

Dover, J.W. (1986), *War Without Mercy: Race and Power in the Pacific War*, New York, NY: Pantheon Books.

Dryer, T (2010), *China's Political System: Modernization and Tradition*, 7th edn, New York NY: Longman.

Economist, The (London) (2008), 'Why Grandpa Wen Has to Care: Populist Politics in China', 14 June.

Economist, The (London) (2010), 'Pilgrims and Progress: It Is Still Repression, Not Development, That Keeps Tibet Stable', 4 February.

Economist, The (London) (2010), 'Shell Game: Beijing Signals a Crackdown on Borrowing by Local Governments', 11 March.

Economist, The (London) (2011) 'China's Crackdown', 14 April.

Economy, E. and Lieberthal, K. (2007), 'Scorched Earth: Will Environmental Risks in China Overwhelm Its Opportunities?', *Harvard Business Review*, Vol. 85, No. 6, pp. 88–96.

Edin, M. (2003), 'Remaking the Communist Party-State: The Cadre Responsibility System at the Local Level in China', *China: an International Journal*, Vol. 1, No. 1, pp. 1–15.

Esherick, J. (1987), *The Origins of the Boxer Uprising*, Berkeley, CA: University of California Press.

Fairbank, J.K. and Goldman, M. (2006), *China: A New History*, Cambridge, MA: Belknap.

Farmer, E.L. (1995), *Zhu Yuanzhang and Early Ming Legislation: The Reordering of Chinese Society*, Leiden: Brill Academic Publishers.

Fenby, J. (2009a), *The Penguin History of Modern China: The Fall and Rise of a Great Power, 1850–2009*, London: Penguin.

Fenby, J. (2009b), 'China's Empire Must End Reliance on One Man', *Financial Times* (London), 12 July.

Ferguson, N. (2010), 'Complexity and Collapse: Empires on the Edge of Chaos', *Foreign Affairs*, Vol. 89, No. 2, pp. 18–32.

Fewsmith, J. (2008), *China since Tiananmen*, New York, NY: Cambridge University Press.

Financial Times (London) (2010), 'China: to the Money Born', 15 March.

Financial Times (London) (2010), 'China Will Pay for Its Arbitrary Rule', 23 March.

Forbes Magazine (2009), 'The Seven Most Powerful People in their Fields', 30 November.

Foster, P. (2009), 'Epic Film "The Foundation of a Republic" Marks 60 Years of Chinese Communism', *Daily Telegraph* (London), 17 September.

Freedom House (2009), *Undermining Democracy: Strategies and*

Methods of 21st Century Authoritarians, Washington, DC: Freedom House.

Freedom House (2010), *Freedom of the Press 2010*, Washington, DC: Freedom House.

Freeman, C. (2010), *China's Trade and Industrial Policies*, Washington, DC, testimony before the US Congress House Ways & Means Committee Hearing on China's Trade Practices, 16 June.

French, H. (2008), 'Despite Flaws, Rights in China Have Expanded', *New York Times*, 3 August.

Friedman, E. (2008), 'Raising Sheep on Wolf Milk: The Politics and Dangers of Misremembering the Past in China', *Totalitarian Movements and Political Religions*, Vol. 9, No. 2–3, pp. 389–409.

Fu, Z. (1996), *China's Legalists: The Earliest Totalitarians and Their Art of Ruling*, London: M.E. Sharpe.

Fukuyama, F. (1992), *The End of History and the Last Man*, Harmondsworth: Penguin.

Gabriel, S. (2006), *Chinese Capitalism and the Modernist Vision*, Abingdon: Routledge.

Gelber, H.G. (2008), *The Dragon and the Foreign Devils: China and the World, 1100 BC to the Present*, London: Bloomsbury.

Gertz, B. (2000) *The China Threat: How the People's Republic Targets America*, Washington, DC: Regnery.

Gewirtz, P. (2003), 'The US-China Rule of Law Initiative', *William & Mary Bill of Rights Journal*, Vol. 11, pp. 603–21.

Gill, B., Morrison, J.S and Lu, X. (2007), *China's Civil Society Organisations: What Future in the Health Sector?*, Washington, DC: Center for Strategic and International Studies.

Gittings, J. (2005), *The Changing Face of China: From Mao to Market*, Oxford: Oxford University Press.

Gladney, D. (1996), *Ethnic Conflict Prevention in the Xinjiang Uyghur Autonomous Region: New Models for China's New Region*, Derry: INCORE, University of Ulster.

Gladney, D. (2009), 'China's Ethnic Tinderbox', *BBC News*, 9 July, http://news.bbc.co.uk/2/hi/asia-pacific/8141867.stm.

Goetzmann, W. and Ukhov, A. (2001), *China and the World Financial Markets 1870–1930: Modern Lessons From Historical Globalization*, Philadelphia, PA: Wharton Financial Institutions Working Paper.

Goldstein, L. (2001), 'Return to Zhenbao Island: Who Started Shooting and Why It Matters', *China Quarterly*, No. 168, pp. 985–97.

Gottwald, J. and Duggan, N. (2008), 'China's Economic Development and the Beijing Olympics', *International Journal of the History of Sport*, Vol. 25, No. 3, pp. 339–54.

Gottwald, J., Sandschneider, E. and Zhang, J. (2008), 'Parteien', in B. Staiger, S. Freidrich and H. Schütte (eds), *Das Gross China lexicon*, Berlin: Primus Verlag.

Green, M.J. (2007), 'Future Visions of Asian Security: the Five Rings', in 'Pursuing Security in a Dynamic Northeast Asia', roundtable discussion in *Asian Policy*, No. 3, pp. 19–24.

Gruhl, W. (2007), *Imperial Japan's World War Two: 1931–1945*, New Brunswick, NJ: Transaction Publishers.

Guo, G. (2009), 'China's Local Political Budget Cycles', *American Journal of Political Science*, Vol. 53, No. 3, pp. 621–32.

Guo, S. and Zhang, J. (2010), 'Language, Work, and Learning: Exploring the Urban Experience of Ethnic Migrant Workers in China', *Diaspora, Indigenous, and Minority Education*, Vol. 44, No. 1, pp. 47–63.

Hannum, E. and Park, A. (eds) (2009), *Education and Reform in China*, Abingdon: Routledge.

Harding, H. (1987), *China's Second Revolution: Reform after Mao*, Washington, DC: Brookings Institution.

Harmel, R. and Tan, A. (2011), 'One-party Rule or Multiparty Competition? Chinese Attitudes to Party System Alternatives', *Party Politics*, Vol. 17, No. 2, pp. 1–10.

Hassid, J. and Stern, R. (2010), 'Amplifying Silence: Uncertainty and Control Parables in Contemporary China', APSA 2010 Annual Meeting Paper.

He, L. (2008), 'Has Fiscal Federalism Worked for Macroeconomic Purposes? The Chinese Experience 1994–2003', *China & World Economy*, Vol. 16, No. 1, pp. 17–33.

He, X. (2007), 'Why Did They Not Take on the Disputes? Law, Power and Politics in the Decision-making of Chinese Courts', *International Journal of Law in Context*, Vol. 3, No. 3, pp. 203–25.

Heilmann, S. (2008), 'From Local Experiments to National Policy: The Origins of China's Distinctive Policy Process', *China Journal*, No. 59, pp. 1–30.

Heuser, R. (2003), *Sozialistischer Rechsstaat und Verwaltungsrecht in der VR China (1982–2002)*, Hamburg: Institut für Asienkunde.

Hille, K. (2010), 'China Tries to Lift Uighur Language Barrier', *Financial Times* (London), 4 July.

Holbig, H. (2007), 'Democracy, Chinese Style: The 17th Party Congress of the Chinese Communist Party', *China aktuell - Journal of Current Chinese Affairs*, Vol. 6, pp. 32–55.

Holbig, H. and Gilley, B. (2010), *In Search of Legitimacy in Post-revolutionary China*, Hamburg: German Institute of Global and Area Studies.

Hu, J. (2007), Speech to the 17th CPC National Congress, *Shanghai Daily Online*, 15 October, www.shanghaidaily.com/coverage /content.asp?id=117&s=1.

Huang, Y. (1996), *Inflation and Investment Controls in China: The Political Economy of Central-Local Relations during the Reform Era*, New York, NY: Cambridge University Press.

Human Rights In China (HRIC) (2009), 'Two-year Sentence for Property Rights Advocate 70, Accused of Possessing State Secrets', press release 6 November.

Human Rights Watch (HRW) (2005), *Devastating Blows: Religious Repression of Uyghurs in Xinjiang*, New York, NY: HRW.

Human Rights Watch (HRW) (2009), *China: Government Rebuffs UN Human Rights Council*, Geneva: HRW.

Hurst, W., Liu, M. and Tao, R. (2009), 'Reassessing Collective Petitioning in Rural China: Civic Engagement, Extra-State Violence and Regional Variation', paper presented at the Annual Meeting of the American Political Science Association, Toronto, 3–6 September.

Ikenberry, J. (2008), 'The Rise of China and the Future of the West: Can the Liberal System Survive?', *Foreign Affairs*, Vol. 87, No. 1, pp. 23–37.

Information Office of the State Council of the People's Republic of China (IOSCPRC) (2008), *China's Efforts and Achievements in Promoting the Rule of Law*, Beijing: IOSCPRC (White Paper).

Information Office of the State Council of the People's Republic of China (IOSCPRC) (2009), *Fifty Years of Democratic Reform in Tibet*, Beijing: IOSCPRC (White Paper).

Information Office of the State Council of the People's Republic of China (IOSCPRC) (2011), *Sixty Years Since Peaceful Liberation of Tibet*, Beijing: IOSCPRC (White Paper).

Jacques, M. (2009), *When China Rules the World: The End of the Western World and the Birth of a New Global Order*, New York, NY: Penguin.

Jiang, S., Lambert, E. and Wang, J. (2007), 'Correlates of Formal and Informal Social/Crime Control in China: an Exploratory Study', *Journal of Criminal Justice*, Vol. 35, No. 3, pp. 261–71.

Jianrong, Y. (2008), 'Emerging Trends in Violent Riots', *China Security*, Vol. 4, No. 3, pp. 75–81.

Jinsheng, Z. (2006), 'The Vogue for 'Medicine as Food' in the Song Period (960–1279)', *Asian Medicine*, Vol. 2, No. 1, pp. 38–58.

Joffe, J. (2009), 'The Default Power: The False Prophecy of America's Decline', *Foreign Affairs*, Vol. 88, No. 5, pp. 21–35.

Kacowicz, A., Bar-Siman-Tov, Y, Elgström, O, and Jerneck, M. (eds)

(2000), *Stable Peace among Nations*, Lanham, MD: Rowman & Littlefield.

Kahn, J. (2006), 'Where's Mao? Chinese Revise History Books', *New York Times*, 1 September.

Kaibin, Z. (2007), 'Crisis Management in China', *China Security*, Winter, pp. 90–109.

Kaplan, R. (2009), 'Center Stage for the Twenty-first Century: Power Plays in the Indian Ocean', *Foreign Affairs*, Vol. 88, No. 2, pp. 16–32.

Katzenstein, P.J. (ed.) (1996), *The Culture of National Security: Norms and Identity in World Politics*, New York, NY: Columbia University Press.

Kaup, K.P. (2002), 'Regionalism versus Ethnicnationalism in the People's Republic of China', *China Quarterly*, Vol. 172, December, pp. 863–84.

Kavalski, E. (2009), *China and the Global Politics of Regionalization*, Farnham: Ashgate.

Keith, R. and Lin, Z. (2007), 'SARS in Chinese Politics and Law', *China Information*, Vol. 21, No. 3, pp. 403–24.

King, R.L. (2008), 'Olympics and Opium Wars', *Chinese American Forum*, Vol. 24, No. 2, pp. 17–18.

Kiser, E. and Cai, Y. (2003), 'War and Bureaucratization in Qin China: Exploring an Anomalous Case', *American Sociological Review*, Vol. 68, No. 4, pp. 511–39.

Kosuth, D. (2009), 'Tiananmen Square: Storming the Gates of Heavenly Peace', *International Socialist Review*, Vol. 66, July–August, online.

Krauss, C, (2010) 'In Global Energy Forecasts, China Looms Large as Energy User and Maker of Green Power', *New York Times*, 9 November.

Kutolowski, M. (2007), 'Reclaiming Chinese Culture', *Columbia Spectator*, 15 February.

Kynge, J. (2007), *China Shakes the World: The Rise of a Hungry Nation*, London: Phoenix.

Lai, H. (2006), 'Religious Policies in Post-Totalitarian China: Maintaining Political Monopoly over a Reviving Society', *Journal of Chinese Political Science*, Vol. 11, No. 1, pp. 55–77.

Lampton, D.M. (2008), *The Three Faces of Chinese Power: Might, Money, and Minds*, Berkeley, CA: University of California Press.

Lee, B. (1999), *The Security Implications of the New Taiwan*, Oxford: Oxford University Press.

Leibold, J. (2010a), 'The Beijing Olympics and China's Conflicted National Form', *China Journal*, No. 63, January, pp. 1–24.

Leibold, J. (2010b), 'More Than a Category: Han Racial Nationalism on the Chinese Internet', *China Quarterly*, Vol. 203, September, pp. 539–59.

Leonard, M. (2008), 'China's New Intelligentsia', *Prospect Magazine*, No. 144, 28 March.

Lewis, O.A. and Teets, J.C. (2009), *A China Model? Understanding the Evolution of a Socialist Market Economy*, Stockholm: Glasshouse Forum.

Li, C. (2005), 'One Party, Two Factions: Chinese Bipartisanship in the Making?', paper presented at the Conference on 'Chinese Leadership, Politics, and Policy', Carnegie Endowment for International Peace, 2 November.

Li, C. (2008b), 'Ethnic Minority Elites in China's Party-State Leadership: An Empirical Assessment', *China Leadership Monitor*, No. 25, pp. 1–13.

Li, C. (2008c), 'China's Fifth Generation: Is Diversity a Source of Strength or Weakness?', *Asia Policy*, No. 6, July, pp. 53–93.

Li, C. (ed.) (2008a), *China's Changing Political Landscape Prospects for Democracy*, Washington, DC: Brookings Institution Press.

Li, C. (2009), 'The Chinese Communist Party: Recruiting and Controlling the New Elites', *Journal of Current Chinese Affairs*, Vol. 38, No. 3, pp. 13–33.

Li, D. (2008), 'The Central Kingdom and the Realm under Heaven' Coming to Mean the Same: The Process of the Formation of Territory in Ancient China', *Frontiers of History in China*, Vol. 3, No. 3, pp. 323–52.

Li, H. and Zhou, L.A. (2005), 'Political Turnover and Economic Performance: the Incentive Role of Personnel Control in China', *Journal of Public Economics*, Vol. 89, No. 9–10, pp. 1743–62.

Li, L. (2004), 'Political Trust in Rural China', *Modern China*, Vol. 30, No. 2, pp. 228–58.

Liang, B. (2005), 'Severe Strike Campaign in Transitional China', *Journal of Criminal Justice*, Vol. 33, No. 4, pp. 387–99.

Liao, X. (2006), *Chinese Foreign Policy Think Tanks and China's Policy Towards Japan*, Hong Kong: Chinese University Press.

Lieberthal, K. (2004), 'China's Domestic Scene', paper presented at the Conference on 'China, Northeast Asia and the Next American Administration', Hong Kong, 2 December.

Lieberthal, K. and Lampton, D.M. (eds) (1992), *Bureaucracy, Politics, and Decision Making in Post-Mao China*, Berkeley, CA: University of California Press.

Lieberthal, K. and Oksenberg, M. (1988), *Making in China: Leaders, Structures, and Processes*, Princeton, NJ: Princeton University Press.

Lim, R. (2003), *The Geopolitics of East Asia: The Search for Equilibrium*, London: Routledge.

Lin, G. (2004), 'Leadership Transition, Intra-party Democracy, and Institution Building in China', *Asian Survey*, Vol. 43, No. 5, pp. 255–75.

Lin, H. (2007), *Tibet and Nationalist China's Frontier: Intrigues and Ethnopolitics, 1928–49*, Vancouver, BC: UBC Press.

Liu, G. (2008), 'Domestic Sources of China's Emerging Grand Strategy', *Journal of Asian and African Studies*, Vol. 43, No. 5, pp. 543–61.

Liu, Y. (2009), 'China's Warriors Are Handicapped', in 'Andrew C. Mertha's China's Water Warriors: Citizen Action and Policy Change', book review roundtable, *Asia Policy*, No. 8, pp. 137–41.

Lo, C.W.-H., Lo, J.M.K. and Cheung, K.C. (2001), 'Reform in Environmental Governance System of the People's Republic of China: Service Organizations as an Alternative for Administrative Enhancement', *Review of Policy Research*, Vol. 18, No. 1, pp. 36–57.

Lo, C.W.-H. and Frywell, G (2005), 'Governmental and Societal Support for Environmental Enforcement in China: an Empirical Study in Guangzhou', *Journal of Development Studies*, Vol. 41, No. 4, pp. 558–88.

Lorentzen, P.L. (2004), 'Regularized Rioting: Managing Discontent in Authoritarian States', paper presented at the annual meeting of the Midwest Political Science Association, Palmer House Hilton, Chicago, 15 April.

Lorentzen, P.L. (2008), *Regularized Rioting: The Strategic Toleration of Public Protest in China*, Working Paper, Berkeley, CA: Department of Political Science, University of California.

Lu, H. and Zhang, L. (2005), 'Death Penalty in China: The Law and the Practice', *Journal of Criminal Justice*, Vol. 33, No. 4, pp. 367–76.

Lubman, S.B. (2000), *Bird in a Cage: Legal Reform in China after Mao*, Stanford, CA: Stanford University Press.

Lum, T. (2006), *Social Unrest in China*, CRS Report for Congress, Washington, DC: Congressional Research Service.

Lynch, M. (2005), *Mao*, New York, NY: Routledge.

Macartney, J. (2010), 'China Tries to Sterilise 10,000 Parents Over One-child Rule', *The Times* (London), 17 April.

McGregor, R. (2009), 'China's Banks Lend with Communist Zeal', *Financial Times* (London), 8 July.

Mahoney, J.G. (2009), in a review of Ralph A. Thaxton, Jr., *Catastrophe and Contention in Rural China: Mao's Great Leap Forward, Famine and the Origins of Righteous Resistance in Da Fo Village*, Cambridge:

Cambridge University Press, in *Journal of Chinese Political Science*, Vol. 14, No. 3, pp. 319–20.

Malone, D.M. and Mukherjee, R. (2010), 'India and China: Conflict and Cooperation', *Survival*, Vol. 52, No. 1, pp. 137–58.

Manion, M. (2008), 'When Communist Party Candidates Can Lose, Who Wins? Assessing the Role of Local People's Congresses in the Selection of Leaders in China', *China Quarterly*, Vol. 195, pp. 607–30.

Manzenreiter, W. (2010), 'The Beijing Games in the Western Imagination of China: The Weak Power of Soft Power', *Journal of Sport and Social Issues*, Vol. 34, No. 1, pp. 29–48.

Martinsen (2009), 'Exposing the Wildcat Mines of Hengshan County, Shaanxi', *Danwei.org*, 20th July.

Mertha, A.C. (2008), *China's Water Warriors: Citizen Action and Policy Change*, Ithaca, NY: Cornell University Press.

Miles, J. (2011) 'Rising Power, Anxious State: Special Report on China', *The Economist* (London), 25 June.

Miller, A.L. (2008a), 'Institutionalization and the Changing Dynamics of Chinese Leadership Politics', in C. Li (ed.), *China's Changing Political Landscape Prospects for Democracy*, Washington, DC: Brookings Institution Press, pp. 61–80.

Miller A.L. (2011), 'Splits in the Politburo Leadership?', *China Leadership Monitor*, No. 34, Stanford, CA: Hoover Institution, Stanford University.

Miller, A.L. (2008b), 'Xi Jinping and the Party Apparatus', *China Leadership Monitor*, No. 25, Stanford, CA: Hoover Institution, Stanford University.

Mitchell, T. (2010), 'News Black-out of Strike Pays Off for Honda', *Financial Times* (London), 15 June.

Mitter, R. (2000), '*The Manchurian Myth: Nationalism, Resistance, and Collaboration in Modern China*', Berkeley, CA: University of California Press.

Mitter, R. (2004), *A Bitter Revolution: China's Struggle with the Modern World*, Oxford: Oxford University Press.

Mote, F. (1999), *Imperial China, 900–1800*, Cambridge, MA: Harvard University Press.

Murphy, M. (2008), *Decoding Chinese Politics: Intellectual Debates and Why They Matter*, Washington, DC: Center for Strategic and International Studies.

Nau, H. 2010, 'Obama's Foreign Policy: The Swing Away from Bush', *Policy Review*, No. 160, April–May, pp. 17–47.

Naughton, B.J. (1996), *Growing Out of the Plan: Chinese Economic*

Reform, 1978–1993, Cambridge: Cambridge University Press.

Naughton, B.J. and Yang, D.L (eds) (2004), *Holding China Together: Diversity and National Integration in the Post-Deng Era,* Cambridge: Cambridge University Press.

New York Times (2009), 'China Warms to New Credo: Business First', 14 August.

News.bbc.co.uk (2007), 'Text Protest Blocks China Plants', 30 May, http://news.bbc.co.uk/2/hi/asia-pacific/6704359.stm.

News.xinhuanet.com (2009), 30 June, http://news.xinhuanet.com /politics/2009–06/30/content_11626985.htm.

Norbu, D. (1997), 'Tibet in Sino-Indian Relations: The Centrality of Marginality', *Asian Survey,* Vol. 37, No. 11, pp. 1078–95.

Nylan, M. (1996), 'Confucian Piety and Individualism in Han China', *Journal of the American Oriental Society,* Vol. 116, No. 1, pp. 1–27.

O'Brien, K.J. (2009), 'Local People's Congresses and Governing China', *China Journal,* Vol. 18, No. 61, pp. 131–41.

O'Brien, K.J. and Li, L. (2000), 'Accommodating "Democracy" in a One-Party State: Introducing Village Elections in China', *China Quarterly,* Vol. 162, pp. 465–89.

O'Brien, K.J. and Li, L. (2005), 'Suing the Local State: Administrative Litigation in Rural China', in N.J. Diamant, S.B. Lubman and K.J. O'Brien (eds), *Engaging the Law in China: State, Society, and Possibilities for Justice,* Stanford CA: Stanford University Press.

O'Brien, K.J. and Rongbin, H. (2009), 'Path to Democracy? Assessing Village Elections in China', *Journal of Contemporary China,* Vol. 18, No. 60, pp. 359–78.

Ogden, C (2010), *India-China Relations and the Future of Af-Pak,* FPC Briefing, London: Foreign Policy Centre.

Patterson, G.N. (1961), 'The Situation in Tibet', *China Quarterly,* Vol. 6, June, pp. 81–6.

Peerenboom, P. (2002), *China's Long March toward Rule of Law,* Cambridge: Cambridge University Press.

Peerenboom, P. (2007), *China Modernizes: Threat to the West or Model for the Rest?,* Oxford: Oxford University Press.

Pei, M. (2006), *China's Trapped Transition: The Limits of Developmental Autocracy,* London: Harvard University Press.

Pei, M. (2009), 'Will the Chinese Communist Party Survive the Crisis? How Beijing's Shrinking Economy May Threaten One-Party Rule', *Foreign Affairs,* 12 March, online.

People's Daily (Beijing) (2008), 'Mobile Phones Make Politics More Accessible for Ordinary Chinese', 13 March.

People's Daily On line (2006), 'Top CPC Leader Pledges Greater Focus on Fighting Corruption', 17 June, http://english.cpc.people.com.cn /66097/66188/4485839.html.

People's Daily Online (2009), 'Rape Suspect Turns Himself In', 13 August, http://english.people.com.cn/90001/90776/6726643.html.

People's Daily Online (2009), 'Adhere to Chinese Socialism: President', 29 September, http://english.people.com.cn/90001/90776/90785 /6763026.html.

Perry, E.J. (1993), *Shanghai on Strike: The Politics of Chinese Labour*, Stanford, CA: Stanford University Press.

Perry, E.J. (2001), 'Challenging the Mandate of Heaven: Popular Protest in Modern China', *Critical Asian Studies*, Vol. 33, No. 2, pp. 163–80.

Perry, E.J. (2005), 'Studying Chinese Politics: Farewell to Revolution?', paper prepared for the Conference to Celebrate the Fiftieth Anniversary of the Fairbank Center for East Asian Research, Harvard University, 9–10 December.

Perry, E.J. and Selden, M. (2003), *Chinese Society Change, Conflict and Resistance*, 2nd edn, London: Routledge.

Pew Global Project Attitudes (PGPA) (2008), *The 2008 Pew Global Attitudes Survey in China*, Washington, DC: Pew Research Center.

Phillips, R.T. (1996), *China since 1911*, Basingstoke: Macmillan.

Pingfang, X. (2001), 'The Archaeology of the Great Wall of the Qin and Han Dynasties', *Journal of East Asian Archaeology*, Vol. 3, No. 1/2, pp. 259–81.

Plattner, M.F. (2010), 'Populism, Pluralism, and Liberal Democracy', *Journal of Democracy*, Vol. 21, No. 1, pp. 81–92.

Pomfret, J. (2010), 'Beijing Claims "indisputable sovereignty" over South China Sea', *Washington Post*, 31 July.

Postiglione, G.A. (ed.) (2006), *Education and Social Change in China: Inequality in a Market Economy*, Armonk, NY: M.E. Sharpe.

Powell, B. (2009), 'Can China Save the World?', *Time Magazine*, 10 August.

Preston, D. (2000a), *A Brief History of the Boxer Rebellion: China's War on Foreigner, 1900*, London: Constable and Robinson.

Preston, D. (2000b), 'The Boxer Rising', *Asian Affairs*, Vol. 31, No.1, pp. 26–36.

Puddington, A. (2009), 'Civil Society under Threat: Bureaucratic Strategies of the New Authoritarians', *Harvard International Review*, Vol. 31, No. 1, pp. 70–4.

Qi, Y., Ma, L., Zhang, H. and Li, H. (2008), 'Translating a Global Issue Into Local Priority: China's Local Government Response to Climate Change', *Journal of Environment & Development*, Vol. 17, No. 4, pp. 379–400.

Qiao, T. (2010), 'Closing the East-West Gap', *China Today*, 16 March.

Qingjun, W. (2010), 'Establishing Trade Unions within Foreign Companies in China' *Employee Relations*, Vol. 32, No. 4, pp. 349–63.

Rankin, M.B, Fairbank, J.K. and Feuerwerker, A. (1986), 'Introduction: Perspectives on Modern China's History', in J.K. Fairbank and A. Feuerwerker (eds) *Republican China 1912–1949, Part 2*, Cambridge: Cambridge University Press, pp. 1–49.

Reilly, J. (2009), 'The Rebirth of the Propaganda State: Promoting Japan in China', paper presented at the 2009 American Political Science Association Annual Meeting, Toronto, 3–6 September.

Reuters (2010), 'China Internet Population Hits 384 Million', 15 January, www.reuters.com/article/idUSTOE60E06S20100115.

Roy, D. (1998), *China's Foreign Relations*, London: Macmillan.

Roy, D. (2005), 'The Sources and Limits of Sino-Japanese Tensions', *Survival*, Vol. 47, No. 2, pp. 191–214.

Rudelson, J. (1997), *Oasis Identities: Uyghur Nationalism along China's Silk Road*, New York, NY: Columbia University Press.

Saich, T. (2002), 'The Blind Man and the Elephant: Analysing the Local State in China', in L. Tomba (ed.), *On the Roots of Growth and Crisis: Capitalism, State and Society in East Asia*, Milan: Annale Feltinelli, pp. 75–99.

Saich, T. and Kaufman, J. (2005), 'Financial Reform, Poverty, and the Impact on Reproductive Health Provision: Evidence from Three Rural Townships', in Y. Huang, T. Saich, and E. Steinfeld (eds). *Financial Sector Reform in China*, Cambridge, MA: Harvard University Asia Center Publications, pp. 187–212.

Scalapino, R.A. (2007), 'The State of International Relations in Northeast Asia', in 'Pursuing Security in a Dynamic Northeast Asia', roundtable discussion in *Asian Policy*, No. 3, pp. 25–8.

Schedler, A. (2009), 'The New Institutionalism in the Study of Authoritarian Regimes', paper prepared for delivery at the panel 'Authoritarian Regime Consolidation', Annual Meeting of the American Political Science Association, Toronto, 3–6 September.

Schrag, D. (2009), '"Flagging the Nation" in International Sport: a Chinese Olympics and a German World Cup', *International Journal of the History of Sport*, Vol. 26, No. 8, pp. 1084–104.

Shambaugh, D. (2007), 'China's 17th Party Congress: Maintaining Delicate Balances', Washington, DC: Brookings Institution.

Shambaugh D. (2008), *China's Communist Party: Atrophy and Adaptation*, Washington, DC: Woodrow Wilson Center.

Shanghai Daily (2010), 'Let's Be Civil', 23 March.

Sheldon, M. (1971), *The Yenan Way in Revolutionary China*, London:

Harvard University Press

Shen, Z. (2000), 'Sino-Soviet Relations and the Origins of the Korean War: Stalin's Strategic Goals in the Far East', *Journal of Cold War Studies*, Vol. 2, No. 2, pp. 44–68.

Shih, C. (2002). *Negotiating Ethnicity in China: Citizenship as a Response to the State*. London: Routledge.

Shijei ribao (2006), 'Survey of the Central Party School: About 30 per cent of Officials Are Not Enthusiastic about Political Reforms', 25 December. Reprinted from *Beijing ribao* (*Beijing Daily*), 18 December 2006.

Shirk, S.L. (1982), *Competitive Comrades*, Berkeley, CA: University of California Press.

Shirk, S.L. (1993), *The Political Logic of Economic Reform in China*, Berkeley, CA: University of California Press.

Shuyun, S. (2007), *The Long March: The True History of Communist China's Founding Myth*, New York, NY: Doubleday.

Simon, K. (2011), 'The Regulation of Civil Society Organizations in China', *International Journal of Civil Society Law*, Vol. 9, No. I, pp. 55–84.

Siu, A. and Fishkin, J. (2009), 'Deliberative Democracy in China: Connecting a Deliberative Poll with the Local People's Congress', paper presented at the 2009 American Political Science Association Annual Meeting, Toronto, 3–6 September.

Smith, A.D. (1993), *National Identity*, Harmondsworth: Penguin.

Smyth, R. and Qian, J.X. (2009), 'Corruption and Left-wing Beliefs in a Post-socialist Transition Economy: Evidence from China's "harmonious society"', *Economics Letters*, Vol. 102, No. 1, pp. 42–4.

Solomon, J. (2010), 'US Takes on Maritime Spats', *Wall Street Journal*, 24 July.

Spiegel Online International (2010), 'Dalai Lama "Deceived his Motherland"', 16 August.

Straussman, J.D. and Zhang, M. (2001), 'Chinese Administrative Reforms in International Perspective', *International Journal of Public Sector Management*, Vol. 14, No. 4–5, pp. 411–22.

Strawbridge, D. (2008), 'The Challenges of Bilingual Education in the Xinjiang Uyghur Autonomous Region People's Republic of China', paper presented at the Second Conference on Language Development, Revitalization and Multilingual Education in Ethnolinguistic Communities, Bangkok, 1–3 July.

Su, Y. (2009) in a book review of K. O'Brien (ed.), 'Popular Protest in China', *China Quarterly*, Vol.198, pp. 465–7.

Sugihara, K. (1997), 'Economic Motivations behind Japanese

Aggression in the Late 1930s: Perspectives of Freda Utley and Nawa Toichl', *Journal of Contemporary History*, Vol. 32, No. 2, pp. 259–80.

Sun, J. (2009), 'Resisting Marginalization in Late Qing China: Local Dynamics in Jining's Initial Modern Transformation, 1881–1911', *East Asia*, Vol. 26, pp. 191–212.

Tang, W. (2005), *Public Opinion and Political Change in China*, Stanford, CA: Stanford University Press.

Tanner, M.S. and Green, E. (2007), 'Principals and Secret Agents: Central versus Local Control Over Policing and Obstacles to "Rule of Law" in China', *China Quarterly*, Vol. 191, pp. 644–70.

Teets, J.C., Rosen, S. and Gries, P.H. (2010), 'Political Change, Contestation, and Pluralisation in China Today', in P. Gries and S. Rosen (eds), *Chinese Politics: State, Society and the Market*, New York NY: Routledge.

Thøgersen, S. (2008), 'Frontline Soldiers of the CCP: The Selection of China's Township Leaders', *China Quarterly*, Vol. 194, pp. 414–23.

Thornton, P.M. (2007), *Disciplining the State: Virtue, Violence, and State-making in Modern China*, Cambridge, MA: Harvard University Press.

Tsai, K.S. (2004), 'Off Balance: the Unintended Consequences of Fiscal Federalism', *Journal of Chinese Political Science*, Vol. 9, No. 2, pp. 7–26.

Tsai, L.L. (2007), 'Solidary Groups, Informal Accountability and Local Public Goods Provision in Rural China', *American Political Science Review*, Vol. 101, No. 2, pp. 355–72.

Tsao, K.K. and Worthley, J.A. (2009), 'Civil Service Development in China and America: A Comparative Perspective', *Public Administration Review*, Vol. 69, No. 6, pp. 588–94.

Tseng, W. and Zebregs, H. (2002), *Foreign Direct Investment in China: Some Lessons for Other Countries*, Washington, DC: International Monetary Fund.

Tsui, K.Y. and Wang, Y. (2004), 'Between Separate Stoves and a Single Menu: Fiscal Decentralization in China', *China Quarterly*, Vol. 177, pp. 71–90.

Tu, W. (1991), 'The Living Tree: The Changing Meaning of Being Chinese Today', *Daedalus*, Vol. 120, No. 2, pp. 1–32.

Twitchett, D. and Loewe, M. (ed.) (1986), *The Cambridge History of China*, Cambridge: Cambridge University Press.

UK Reuters (2008), Girl's Death Sparks Rioting in China, 28 June, sourced at http://uk.reuters.com/article/idUKPEK27256220080628?sp=true.

UPI Asia.com (2010), 'Tibet Gets a "Strong Willed" Governor', 18 January, www.upiasia.com/Top_News/Special/2010/01/18/Tibet-gets-a-strong-willed-governor/UPI-22131263832511/.

US Congressional-Executive Commission on China (2006), *Development of the Rule of Law and Institutions of Democratic Governance*, Annual Report, Washington, DC: US Government Printing Office.

US Congressional-Executive Commission on China (2008), Annual Report, Washington, DC: US Government Printing Office.

Van de Ven H.J. (2003), *War and Nationalism in China 1925–1945*, New York, NY: Routledge.

Waldron, A. (1990), *The Great Wall of China: From History to Myth*, Cambridge: Cambridge University Press.

Walt, S. (1987), *The Origins of Alliances*, Ithaca, NY: Cornell University Press.

Waltz, K.N. (1979), *Theory of International Politics*, New York, NY: McGraw Hill.

Wang, D. (2008), *The Quarrelling Brothers: New Chinese Archives and a Reappraisal of the Sino-Soviet Split, 1959–62*, Washington, DC: Woodrow Wilson International Center.

Wang, G. (1993), 'To Reform a Revolution: Under the Righteous Mandate', *Daedalus*, Vol. 122, No. 2, pp. 73.

Wang, L. (2008), 'The Marginality of Migrant Children in the Urban Chinese Educational System', *British Journal of Sociology of Education*, Vol. 29, No. 6, pp. 691–703.

Wang, S. (2004), 'The People's Republic of China's Policy on Minorities and International Approaches to Ethnic Groups: A Comparative Study', *International Journal on Minority and Group Rights*, Vol. 11, No. 1–2, pp. 159–85.

Watkins, J. (2009), 'Beijing's Path Forward', *New York Times*, 11 November.

Weale, A. (2007), *Democracy*, Basingstoke: Palgrave Macmillan.

Weifang, H. (2007), 'The Police and the Rule of Law: Commentary on "Principals and Secret Agents', *China Quarterly*, Vol. 191, pp. 671–4.

Wessel, M. (2005), 'Opening Statement' to *Hearing on China's Growing Global Influence: Objectives and Strategies*, Washington, DC: US-China Economic and Security Review Commission.

Whiting, S.H. (2000), *Power and Wealth in Rural China: The Political Economy of Institutional Change*, Cambridge: Cambridge University Press.

Whiting, S.H. (2007), *Central–Local Fiscal Relations in China*, New York, NY: National Committee on US-China Relations, China Policy Series, No. 22, April.

Winston, K (2005), 'The Internal Morality of Chinese Legalism', *Singapore Journal of Legal Studies*, December, pp. 313–47.

Winston, K. (2009), 'Chinese Legalism', in M. Bevir (ed.) *Encyclopaedia of Political Theory*, London: Sage, pp. 313–47.

Wong, C. (2007), *Fiscal Management for a Harmonious Society: Assessing the Central Government's Capacity to Implement*, Oxford: British Inter-University China Centre (BICC) Working Paper, No. 4.

Wong, C. (2009), 'Rebuilding Government for the 21st Century: Can China Incrementally Reform the Public Sector?', *China Quarterly*, Vol. 200, December, pp. 929–52.

Wong, C.L. (2006), 'Corporatism and Agricultural Reform in China: A Comparison with Hong Kong', *China: an International Journal*, Vol. 4, No. 1, pp. 151–64.

Wong, E. (2008), 'China Presses Grieving Parents to Take Hush Money', *New York Times*, 24 July.

Wong, G. (2009), 'China Orders Local Gov'ns to Listen to Petitioners', *Associated Press*, 14 April.

Worden, R.L., Savada, A.L. and Dolan, R.E. (eds) (1988), *China: A Country Study*, Washington, DC: Federal Research Division, Library of Congress.

World Bank (2008), *Quarterly Update*, Beijing Office.

Wright, Q. (1942), *A Study of War*, Chicago, IL: University of Chicago Press.

Wu, X. (2010), 'A Revolutionary Technology for an Evolutionary Cause', *Asia Policy*, No. 10, pp. 167–71.

Xiang, L. (1995), *Recasting the imperial Far East: Britain and America in China, 1945–1950*, New York, NY: M.E. Sharpe.

Xiao, F. (2005), 'Constructivism and Chinese Foreign Policy', paper presented at the annual meeting of the International Studies Association, Honolulu, Hawaii.

Xinhua Economic News Service (2008), 'China's Communist Party Sets up Branches under Quake Zone Tents', 28 May.

Xinhua News (2009), 'Communist Party of China Chief Stresses Inner-Party Democracy', 30 June.

Yadav, V. (2008), 'Business Lobbies and Policymaking in Developing Countries Today', *Journal of Public Affairs*, Vol. 8, pp. 67–82.

Yan, X. (2006), 'The Rise of China and Its Power Status', *Chinese Journal of International Politics*, Vol. 1, No. 1, pp. 5–33.

Yang, D.L. (1996), *Calamity and Reform in China: State, Rural Society, and Institutional Change since the Great Leap Famine*, Palo Alto, CA: Stanford University Press.

Yang, D.L. (2001), 'Can China Overcome Legal Balkanization?', 5 November, http://home.uchicago.edu/~daliyang/new_page_2.htm.

Yang, D.L. (2006), 'Economic Transformation and Its Political

Discontents in China: Authoritarianism, Unequal Growth, and the Dilemmas of Political Development', *Annual Review of Political Science*, Vol. 9, No. 1, pp. 143–64.

Yang, D.L. and Clarke, P. (2005), 'Globalisation and Intellectual Property in China', *Technovation*, Vol. 25, No, 5, pp. 545–55.

Yang, G. (2009), *The Power of the Internet in China: Citizen Activism Online*, New York, NY: Columbia University Press.

Yang, L. and Lahr, M.L. (2008), *Interregional Decomposition of Labor Productivity Differences In China, 1987–1997*, Munich: MPRA Paper, No. 8313.

Yardley, J. (2005), 'Desperate Search for Justice: One Man vs. China', *New York Times*, 12 November.

Yardley, J. (2008), 'China's Leaders Are Resilient in Face of Change', *New York Times*, 7 August.

Yeo, Y. (2009), 'Remaking the Chinese State and the Nature of Economic Governance? The *Early* Appraisal of the 2008 'Superministry' Reform', *Journal of Contemporary China*, Vol. 18, No. 62, pp. 729–43 (emphasis original).

Yi, L. (2007), 'Ethnicization through Schooling: the Mainstream Discursive Repertoires of Ethnic Minorities', *China Quarterly*, Vol. 192, pp. 933–48.

Yue, J. (1998), 'The Formulation Process of the Labour Law of the People's Republic of China: A Garbage Can Model Analysis', Thesis (Ph.D.), City University of Hong Kong.

Zang, X. (2001), 'University Education, Party Seniority, and Elite Recruitment in China', *Social Science Research*, Vol. 30, No. 1, pp. 62–75.

Zang, X. (2008), 'Market Reforms and Han–Muslim Variation in Employment in the Chinese State Sector in a Chinese City', *World Development*, Vol. 36, No. 11, pp. 2341–52.

Zaret, D. (1996), 'Petitions and the 'Invention' of Public Opinion in the English Revolution', *American Journal of Sociology*, Vol. 101, No. 6, pp. 1497–555.

Zhan, J.V. (2009), 'Decentralizing China: Analysis of Central Strategies in China's Fiscal Reforms', *Journal of Contemporary China*, Vol. 18, No. 60, pp. 445–62.

Zhang, B. (2010) 'Chinese Foreign Policy in Transition: Trends and Implications', *Journal of Current Chinese Affairs*, Vol. 39, No. 2, pp. 39–68.

Zhang, J. (2002), 'A Critical Review of the Development of Chinese e-Government', *Perspectives*, Vol. 3, No. 7, pp. 163–84.

Zhang, X. (2007), *Ethnicity and Urban Life in China: A Comparative*

Study of Hui Muslims and Han Chinese, London: Routledge.

Zhang, Y. (2003), 'Public Opinion without Public? State Democracy, Middle-class Consumerism, and Opinion Surveys in Post-Mao China', paper presented at the annual meeting of the International Communication Association, San Diego, CA, 27 May.

Zhang, Z. (2010), 'Cixi and Modernization of China', *Asian Social Science*, Vol. 6, No. 4, pp. 154–9.

Zhao, S. (1998), A State-led Nationalism: The Patriotic Education Campaign in Post-Tiananmen China, *Communist and Post-Communist Studies*, Vol. 31, No. 3, pp. 287–302.

Zheng, B. (2005), 'China's Peaceful Rise to Great Power Status', *Foreign Affairs*, Vol. 84, No. 5, pp. 18–24.

Zheng, H., De Jong, M. and Koppenjan, J. (2010), 'Applying Policy Network Theory to Policy-making In China: The Case of Urban Health Insurance Reform', *Public Administration,* Vol. 88, No. 2, pp. 398–417.

Zheng, S. (2003), 'Leadership Change, Legitimacy, and Party Transition in China', *Journal of Chinese Political Science,* Vol. 8, No. 1–2, pp. 47–63.

Zheng, Y. (2008), 'Globalization, Openness and Transformation in China', paper presented at the 58th Political Studies Association Conference, Swansea University, 1–3 April.

Zheng, Y. (2009), 'Can the Communist Party Sustain its Rule in China?', in K. Lee, Kim J. and Woo W. (2008), *Power and Sustainability of the Chinese State*, London: Routledge, pp. 186–210.

Zhu, X. (2008), 'Strategy of Chinese Policy Entrepreneurs in the Third Sector: Challenges of "Technical Infeasibility"', *Policy Sciences*, Vol. 41, No. 4, pp. 315–34.

Zhu, Y. and Blachford, D. (2005), 'Ethnic Minority Issues in China's Foreign Policy: Perspectives and Implications', *Pacific Review*, Vol. 18, No. 2, pp. 243–64.

Zhu Z. (2010), 'China's election won't be Western-style', *China Daily*, 20 March, www.chinadaily.com.cn/china/2010-03/20/contents _9616962.htm, accessed 10 January 2012.

Index

EU authorised representative for GPSR:
Easy Access System Europe, Mustamäe tee 50,
10621 Tallinn, Estonia
gpsr.requests@easproject.com

9 780719 084287